GREAT WAR LITERATURE

NOTES

Written by W Lawrance

on

SCARS UPON MY HEART

AN ANTHOLOGY, EDITED BY CATHERINE REILLY

Great War Literature Notes on Scars Upon My Heart, an anthology edited by Catherine Reilly.
Written by W Lawrance

Published by:
Great War Literature Publishing LLP
Forum House, Stirling Road, Chichester PO19 7DN
Web site: www.greatwarliterature.co.uk
E-Mail: enquiries@greatwarliterature.co.uk

Produced in Great Britain

ISBN 978-1905378999 (1905378998) Paperback Edition

10 9 8 7 6 5 4 3 2 1

Design and production by Great War Literature Publishing LLP
Typeset in Neue Helvetica, ITC Berkeley Old Style and Trajan Pro

Great War Literature Notes on

Scars Upon My Heart

CONTENTS

INTRODUCTION

Scars Upon My Heart was first published in 1981 and is the first - and to a certain extent only - anthology dedicated solely to the poetry of women during the First World War. Other anthologies have appeared since, in similar veins, but none really have the reputation given to Catherine Reilly's collection.

The anthology provides an insight into the perspective of women during the conflict and represents many viewpoints, from the rallying patriotism of Sybil Bristowe's *Over the Top*, to the solemn, mournful tones of Marjorie Wilson's *To Tony (Aged 3)*. The women come from different areas, both geographically and socially. Their outlooks vary greatly, depending upon their own personal experiences of the conflict, and their age at the time of writing.

Whether or not this is a 'good' anthology is a matter of personal opinion, although few could deny that for every gem, there is at least one poem which could, at best, be described as second-rate. The messages contained in the poems are also somewhat monotonous, focusing mainly on emotions such as grief, gratitude and anger and there is not enough on 'calls to arms' poetry, which was significantly more popular at the time. This imbalance leads the reader to wonder whether Catherine Reilly's intention was mainly to show the female poets in the best possible light and, thereby, to denounce their male critics.

In this study guide, we have given biographies of the poets, where possible. On some occasions, we have been unable to ascertain any relevant information regarding the poet and, in these circumstances, the biography is absent. However, where we have been able to discover verifiable details, these have been included, no matter how brief. These biographies are followed by analysis of the poems themselves. Again, the length of the analysis varies greatly, depending on many factors, including the quality and length of the poem concerned and its overall relevance to the anthology.

Being as students are often asked to look at the anthologies on a thematic basis we have, at the end of this guide, re-arranged the anthology using eight basic themes, placing each poem within the one which is most appropriate.

Students must bear in mind that any critical assessments given are based entirely upon the opinion of the author of this guide.

Scars Upon My Heart

an Anthology Edited by Catherine Reilly

Marian Allen

BIOGRAPHICAL DETAILS

Eleanor Marian Dundas Allen was born on January 18th 1892, one of the six children of George and Isabella Allen. Although she was born in Sydney, Australia, Marian - as she came to be known - grew up in Oxford, where the family moved during her childhood. One of Marian's brothers was studying law at New College, Oxford and introduced his sister to a fellow student, Arthur Tylston Greg during 1913. The young couple fell in love and planned to marry, although their plans were interrupted by the outbreak of the First World War in August 1914. Arthur enlisted, together with Marian's brother and fought on the Western Front. He was wounded in May 1915, but returned to fight, joining the Royal Flying Corps. He was granted leave in spring 1917 and spent this time with happily with Marian, before they said goodbye at Charing Cross Station on 4th April. Arthur was shot down and killed on the 23rd of that month, although it took about one week for this news to reach Marian. She threw herself into writing poetry as a means of dealing with her grief and continued to write for the rest of her life, as well as illustrating several children's books. She never married and died on September 12th 1953 in Oxford.

THE RAIDERS

This is a poem about flight - specifically about flying over the battlefields of the First World War. Marian Allen's fiancé, Captain Arthur Greg served with the Royal Flying Corps and one can imagine that either in his letters, or in person, he might well have explained to her exactly how it felt to fly. Allen creates a mysterious atmosphere at the beginning of her poem, as the planes take off into the night. Her description of the stars as 'eyes' is, in this way, made somewhat sinister. However, when focusing on the flight itself, Allen's tone changes as she now talks of 'thrilled' expectancy and 'adventures'. This contrast in language makes one wonder whether Captain Greg had spoken to her of the thrill of flying, but she, nonetheless, remained fearful of his involvement. In addition, her descriptions of the battlefields beneath the airborne planes was probably given to her by Greg, who had initially served with the infantry. Here Allen's tone is depressing and constricting when compared to her accounts of the freedom afforded by flight. When Marian Allen wrote this poem on April 29th 1917, Greg was already dead, although at the time she was unaware of this fact. Her lack of knowledge as to his demise, seems quite surprising, given that her descriptions of flight could be said to apply to the freedom which most war poets only normally associated with death.

THE WIND ON THE DOWNS

This poem was written after the death of Marian Allen's fiancé, Captain Arthur Greg, on 23rd April 1917 and was published in a volume of poetry of the same name in 1918. The poem opens with Allen recalling her fiancé's appearance and demeanour. She remembers him laughing in his uniform and this may well be a recollection of their final days together in early April 1917, when Arthur was home on leave. He served with the Royal Flying Corps and, although Marian Allen describes him as wearing a 'Khaki tunic' and 'Sam Brown' belt, which one would more readily associate with the infantry, this might well be accurate as Arthur Greg had originally served in the trenches and then transferred to the RFC. Many of the men who did this chose to retain the uniform of their old regiment, but wear the badges and insignia of the RFC.

It would seem in this poem that Allen is finding it difficult to accept Greg's death, as she goes on to say that she prefers to think of him as still seeking 'adventure'. Again, she recalls his laughter, suggesting that they must have been a very happy and relaxed couple. She also seems to believe that he is watching over her, which again reinforces her refusal to believe that he can really be dead. In the second verse, she remembers more details of the time which they spent together, clearly enjoying life and never really believing that Greg might not live. Instead of walking with him and thinking of their plans for a shared future, she now walks alone and simply thinks about him. She seems haunted by him, imagining his presence still beside her and, although she obviously realises that she is really alone, his spirit remains.

This poem could be compared with *Perhaps* by Vera Brittain or *Lamplight* by May Wedderburn Cannan, both of which deal with the subject of the loss of a loved-one. Vera Brittain, like Marian Allen, was writing from first-hand experience, while May Cannan was not, but there are actually greater similarities between her and Allen's poems than Vera Brittain's. All three have, however, stuck to fairly traditional and simple rhymes, forms and language, suggesting that their message and, therefore, their grief did not require the use of any 'clever' or complicated techniques to achieve their purpose.

Lilian M. Anderson

BIOGRAPHICAL DETAILS

Lilian May Anderson was born in 1890 in Mattishall, Norfolk, the second child of Arthur and Helena Anderson. Arthur was a Church of England priest, and while Lilian was still an infant the family, including her older sister, Kathleen, moved to Camberwell in London, taking their two servants with them. Lilian's mother came from Cornwall and soon the family moved back to that county, settling in Launceston, where another daughter, Dorothy was born in 1894. From there, the family moved once again, to Plymouth in Devon. Lilian was educated at St Mary's Priory in Torquay. As an adult, Lilian remained in Devon, where she later married.

LEAVE IN 1917

Although it is not clear, one way or the other, this poem may have been written from personal experience. Lilian Anderson did marry and live in Devon, in common with the characters in her poem, which opens with a description of a pilot flying home on leave. He no longer thinks of his home country in the same way as he did before: gone are his thoughts of a peaceful countryside, replaced instead with images of a land threatened by war. This is, presumably, a reference not only to the notion of people being threatened by the loss of a loved-one, but also to the Zeppelin raids which cost many lives at home. It is quite easy to imagine a pilot seeing himself as the protector of his home land, when put into that perspective.

The pilot flies on and Anderson describes the various towns and landscapes over which he passes, until he finally lands at Coventry, leaving his plane in one of the sheds. He has two days of leave and, wanting to make the most of every hour, he boards a train, bound for Devon - his home. Initially he still cannot reconcile the sights before him which remind him of war, with his image of England, but as he nears his home, he is able to forget the conflict and focus instead on the beauty of spring. It would seem that he has not seen his home - or his wife - since the winter, when they had married, and Anderson remarks on the changes in the scenery, between one season and the next. Eventually husband and wife are reunited, but even this joyous moment is tinged with sadness, presumably because they have so little time together, but also because they would have been unsure as to 'Sheringham's' chances of survival, thus making their reunion bittersweet. These feelings are epitomised near the end of the poem as Anderson contrasts the 'sunshine-golden honey' and the 'barren winter'. Finally, 'Sheringham' tries to gather together all of these sights and thoughts so that he might be able to remember them when he is back fighting the war.

Whether or not this poem was written from personal experience is really irrelevant as Lilian Anderson has captured, to perfection, the hopeless expectancy of love during the First World War. She portrays a young, newly married couple for whom, in peacetime, the future would have been full of optimism. They are clearly very much in love and have a 'little house' in which to build their dreams. However, their plans for the future cannot yet be fulfilled and all that they can do at present is make the most of the 'precious' hours which they may spend together.

Pauline Barrington

BIOGRAPHICAL DETAILS

Born in Philadelphia in 1876, Pauline was employed as a secretary, although she also contributed poems and stories to various magazines. She married Charles Barrington in 1901.

EDUCATION

This poem, by Pauline Barrington, appears to be an indictment of the women, presumably mothers, who sit at home sewing and dreaming, while young men are dying. In a repetitive fashion, the poet persists in a depressing view of the impact of the war, while portraying the woman's role as pointless and ineffectual - some might even say culpable - in the situation in which she and her children have found themselves. One could argue that this is not a mother of a man in the trenches, as her sons are young enough to be play-fighting, so perhaps it is her husband for whom she sews and dreams. Alternatively, her dreams may be memories of when her sons were children. Throughout the poem, Barrington has adopted a preaching and superior tone, implying that all this woman does is sew, rather than discouraging her sons from following in their father's footsteps, or realising the link between a 'toy gun' and the real thing [Krupp was a German arms manufacturer]. Although one can appreciate and even sympathise with the message in this poem, unfortunately it is lost, due to the fact that the style and tone of the piece are not sufficiently engaging.

MADELINE IDA BEDFORD

BIOGRAPHICAL DETAILS

Madeline Ida Bedford was born in 1884 in Kent, where her father, Edward was a civil engineer. He and Madeline's mother, Sarah, had four children: Ellen was the oldest, born in 1878; Alice was two years older than Madeline and finally Edward, who was eleven years younger. Madeline appears to have remained in the Greater London area, at least until her marriage in the spring of 1919.

MUNITION WAGES

This is Madeline Bedford's most well-known war poem and here she seems to be extolling the virtues of being able to earn a high wage for working in a munitions factory. She says that, rather than saving any of her wages, she spends it all on clothing and going out. She lists the many items which she is now able to afford and compares this to the relative poverty of her pre-war lifestyle. Her fortune comes at a high price, however, as her work is dangerous and accidents in a munitions factory would normally be fatal. There is an element of seizing the day in this poem, since it would seem that there may not necessarily be a tomorrow. She does not seem to feel guilty about her wealth, and right up until the last verse, one could believe that she feels completely justified. At the end, however, there is an implication that her death would be the only way in which she could repay her 'wages'. This might imply that she doesn't really believe her wages to be reasonable after all, or that she feels guilty that the arms which she is helping to manufacture will be used to kill young men and that the only thing which could justify that situation would be her own death. Whether or not this poem has its foundation in reality is not known, but either way, Madeline Bedford seems to be satirising the role of women and their high wages, with an air of distaste.

THE PARSON'S JOB

In this poem, Madeline Bedford relates how a woman might react to a visit from a 'parson' following the death in action of her husband. In this instance, the woman's response is not favourable. She is angry that the parson makes moral platitudes about her loss. It would seem that the parson persists and the woman, although still angry, begins to talk to him. She is outraged that her husband, Jim, who was a 'good 'un' has been taken, while other men, such as a 'forger' and a 'criminal' have been allowed to survive. Her anger, although persistent, is dissipating as she reveals that she is pregnant with their first child. In the final verse, she changes her mind completely and states that she wants to do what is 'right', before asking the parson to show her how 'to pray'. This alteration seems to have come about as a result of her realising that through their child, a part of 'Jim' would still be alive. Madeline Bedford has used colloquial language throughout this poem to reinforce the notion of the war's impact on ordinary people. However, this is also distracting as is the irregular rhythm of the piece. It is quite difficult to believe in a poem, where the subject claims to 'hate' religion in one breath, yet asks for lessons in prayer in the next. Everything in this poem is too forceful: there is too much anger, which makes the contrition at the end seem false; there is too much colloquialism, which makes the whole piece difficult to follow and interrupts its flow.

MAUD ANNA BELL

BIOGRAPHICAL DETAILS

Little is known about this poet, except that she was born in 1869 in London, the fourth child of barrister, George Bell and his wife, Jessie.

FROM A TRENCH

This poem is written from the perspective of a man serving in the front line trenches. It opens with a Shakespearian reference to 'the dogs of war', taken from *Julius Caesar*. When read in more detail, this quotation seems quite appropriate

'And Caesar's spirit, ranging for revenge,
With Ate by his side, come hot from hell,
Shall in these confines, with a monarch's voice
Cry havoc and let slip the dogs of war,
That this foul deed shall smell above the earth
With carrion men, groaning for burial.'

In Shakespearian terms, the 'dogs of war' were the soldiers, so according to Maud Bell, it would seem that the only thing which can contain or control the men, is death. She goes on to describe how many have died, suggesting that they have, effectively, consumed the living fields. This image is then contrasted with the thought that the landscape at home is unchanged. The poem's style then becomes more jaunty, as Maud Bell recites a supposed ditty about the flowers - specifically 'crocuses', which are still growing in Nottingham - presumably a town chosen either because of some link with the poet, or simply because it fitted in with the metre of the poem.

Then, although the cheerful rhyme and rhythm continue, each line is now alternated with a taste of reality, culminating in the suggestion that some people at home are 'silly fools' who continue to believe that the war is 'fun'. In the fourth verse, one begins to see a glimpse of a possible secondary meaning: it may still be a reference to the flowers 'at Nottingham', but it might also refer to young people (girls or boys), whom 'the Hun' has not yet been able to touch, but who may not always be so safe.

As the poem continues, Maud Bell gives a brief, harsh, but quite realistic portrayal of the grim reality of war - especially in her description of the fields as 'purple slime' which, while nauseating, also provides a good connection with the colourful crocuses. Finally, at the end of the poem, we discover the poet's real message: gratitude. She reveals that the 'crocuses', whether real or imagined, are only allowed to flourish because there are men who are prepared to live and die in 'Hell' for the sole purpose of their preservation.

Like a great many of the female war poets, Maud Bell is using this poem to show her indebtedness, but also to make others appreciate the sacrifices which are being made on their behalf, so that life might still carry on as before. The fact that she has written this poem from the perspective of a soldier, rather than a woman on the home front, makes it more effective still.

NORA BOMFORD

BIOGRAPHICAL DETAILS

Nora Bomford was born in India on 24th March 1894. She was the third child of Sir Gerald Bomford and his wife Mary. Sir Gerald Bomford was Surgeon-General of the Indian Medical Service. Her younger brother, Guy (later a Brigadier) served in the First World War, as a Captain in the Royal Engineers. The family home in England was in Dover, Kent. Nora married Major-General Claude le Bas Goldney MC in June 1938. Claude was of Irish descent and had served in the First World War with the Army Service Corps, leaving with the British Expeditionary Force in August 1914. Nora Bomford died on 12th May 1968.

DRAFTS

This poem opens with the poet waking up to realise that the approaching sounds which she can hear are of soldiers marching away to war. She says that this idea 'sickens' her heart as she listens to them sing their marching songs, while she is safely tucked up in bed. In the second verse, we learn the real message behind this poem, which is that Nora Bomford resents that, as a woman, she is not permitted to fight alongside the men. In her view, this is simply a matter of having been born the wrong sex and the, in her opinion, outdated custom that fighting in wars is the role of men alone. Nora Bomford also resents the fact that men are denied the opportunity to enjoy life in the same way that women can. In fact, she sees it as pure chance that a person is born male or female, when they might just as easily have been born as a seagull.

SYBIL BRISTOWE

BIOGRAPHICAL DETAILS

Born in London in 1870, Sybil was eighth of the ten children of John and Miriam. John Bristowe was a physician and the family lived in the city, together with their servants. Her younger brother Vivian served in the South African Medical Corps during the First World War and died in April 1917 at the age of 42. He is buried at Morogoro Cemetery in Tanzania. Sybil Bristowe died in 1954, aged 84.

OVER THE TOP

Presumably this poem was written early in the First World War and certainly before the death of the poet's brother in early 1917. Here Sybil Bristowe carries out a countdown to going 'over the top' into an attack. We start with ten minutes to go and it would seem that some men are reading their Bibles, while others enjoy their 'tot' of rum.

Time ticks on and soon there are only nine minutes left. Bristowe asserts that the soldier is not afraid, although in the second verse, she goes on to describe the feelings which are afflicting his stomach. Some of the men begin to play a game to pass the time. As the moment approaches, the narrator/soldier finds himself recalling things which he has said in the past. By the fourth verse, he has begun to reflect on the notion that the stars which he had been looking at up in the sky during the previous evening's bombardment, had also been looked at by people at home, which provides a link with 'Blighty' - army slang for Britain, or home. In the final verse, Bristowe states that the soldier would pray, although once again this is not through fear and then, finally the waiting is finished and they go 'over the top'.

There are elements here which are reminiscent of Jessie Pope's poetry, in the naive lack of understanding about how a soldier might really feel as he waited to go over the top. She repeatedly asserts that they are not afraid and that even if they die, they would not be unhappy as they would be going up God's 'golden stairs'. One could argue that Bristowe is being ironic here, but this is not convincing as even at the very end, she continues to paint a glorious picture of death in battle. Whilst this is not exactly a warmongering 'call to arms', the colloquial language implies that this poem is meant to represent the ranking soldiers, rather than the officers, in a manner which implies that they should not be afraid of facing their own deaths.

VERA BRITTAIN

BIOGRAPHICAL DETAILS

Vera Mary Brittain was born on December 29th 1893 in Newcastle-under-Lyme, Staffordshire. She was the oldest child of Arthur Brittain, a paper manufacturer, and his wife Edith. Within two years, Vera's beloved brother, Edward was born and they quickly became very close. In 1905, the family moved to Buxton in Derbyshire. Vera and Edward were initially educated at home, but then Vera was sent away to St Monica's School in Kingswood, Surrey, while Edward attended Uppingham.

In 1914, Vera gained entrance to Somerville College, Oxford, although she only remained there for one year, before becoming a VAD nurse in June 1915. In the meantime, she had become romantically involved with Roland Leighton, a friend of her brother's, and they became engaged in August. Roland and Edward had both enlisted, along with Victor Richardson, another friend from Uppingham School. Victor, Edward and Vera were all devastated when Roland was killed on December 23rd 1915.

Vera applied for overseas service and left for Malta in September 1916, from where she regularly corresponded with Edward, Victor and Geoffrey Thurlow, who was serving in the same regiment as Edward. Thurlow was killed on 23rd April 1917 and Victor was wounded and died on 10th June. By this time, Vera had returned home, but after these two deaths, she decided to apply for another overseas posting - this time in France. By March 1918, she was back in England, having been summoned home by her father, in order to nurse her mother, who had become unwell. On June 22nd, she and her father received a telegram informing them that Edward had been killed in action one week earlier.

After the war, Vera returned to Oxford, where she completed her degree. While there, she made friends with another aspiring author, Winifred Holtby and once they had graduated, they moved to London and rented a flat together. In 1925, Vera married George Catlin, a Liverpool-born professor, who was teaching in America. They spent most of their married lives apart and Vera's main companion remained Winifred.

Vera and George had two children: John was born in 1927 and Shirley in 1930, by which time Vera had begun writing her autobiographical account of the war and its aftermath, *Testament of Youth*, which was published in 1933. 1935 saw two great tragedies for Vera as firstly her father committed suicide and then Winifred Holtby died.

Vera recovered from these setbacks and in 1937 she joined the Peace Pledge Union and supported attempts to appease Hitler. When the Second World War began, she continued to campaign for a negotiated peace, but also dispatched John and Shirley to America for their own safety. As the war progressed, her popularity waned, mainly due to her outspoken criticisms of the war.

John and Shirley returned to England in 1943 and after the war, in 1948, Vera became Chairman of the Peace Pledge Union. John always had a troubled relationship with his mother, which continued to deteriorate, but Shirley made Vera especially proud when she became a Labour MP in 1964. Two years later, Vera's health began to suffer and she died on March 29th 1970. George was knighted later that year and remarried in 1971.

THE LAMENT OF THE DEMOBILISED

Written after the war and published in the 1920 edition of *Oxford Poetry*, of which Vera Brittain was co-editor, this is an angry poem, which derides the women who had chosen to remain at home and further their careers, while others did war work. In the autumn of 1919, many young women took up their places at Somerville College, Oxford. Some, like Vera Brittain, had postponed their studies in favour of war work, but the majority were girls who had been too young to participate in the conflict. In the first week of that term, there was a debate in which Vera participated, at which she proposed that the experiences she had gained during the war were more significant and valuable than anything which the University might have to offer. Unfortunately, her tone was rather arrogant and superior and she ended up losing the debate and feeling somewhat angry and humiliated. In addition, Vera felt outraged that one of the college lecturers (Maude Clarke) was the same age as her, but because she had chosen to continue with her studies during the war, she was academically streets ahead of Vera. It was in this frame of mind that, a few days after the debate, Vera wrote *The Lament of the Demobilised*. Interestingly, however, it was not Maude Clarke, or anyone like her, who opposed Vera in the debate, but Winifred Holtby, with whom Vera would later become very good friends. Holtby, like Vera had done war work, but had regarded her service, nursing in France with the WAACs, as a privilege. The knowledge of the background behind this poem, sheds a different light on its meaning and significance.

One can see Vera Brittain's anger and resentment right from the beginning of the poem, as it opens in a supercilious, conversational tone, with someone - presumably an older person - suggesting that those women who served in the war should not 'lament' their situation, as they have been able to gain 'experience' and they are still 'young'. These seems like quite a reasonable statement, but it is loaded with irony and, therefore, becomes a criticism of this opinion. Vera Brittain goes on to show her disagreement with this insinuation, recalling how others have been able to pursue their normal lives and ambitions, even implying that they have been able to achieve more because they have faced less competition.

She goes on to show her resentment of the fact that these other women are now admired for their achievements, while her war service is forgotten. Next she suggests that these 'others' mock her too, for her sacrifices, suggesting that she was a 'fool' to throw away 'four years' of her life. Finally, and ironically, she asserts that the 'others' might well be right.

Taken at face value, this poem might easily have been written by anyone who served in the war - male or female. Many who returned found that their position in society, and society itself, had changed beyond recognition and for some it would be years, or even decades, before they could once again settle into civilian life. Others never achieved this and remained 'damaged' by their experiences for the rest of their lives. Some of the war poets, after the conflict, tended to focus on their memories and experiences, while others tried to forget the war altogether and wrote about something completely different. Vera Brittain was, however, someone obsessed with her own sacrifices and believed that no-one else could really understand her, or what she had experienced, because their suffering had not been as severe as hers. It was, in fact, this arrogance and superiority which occasionally made others single her out for criticism.

Simply by reading through the poems in *Scars Upon My Heart* and other anthologies, as well as the memoirs and historical or military books about the aftermath of the conflict, one can see that there was understanding and gratitude, sorrow and remembrance, but that this was coupled with a natural desire to move on and leave the past alone. The sacrifices were not forgotten, although perhaps they were not always given the attention which many felt they deserved, but Vera Brittain's anger, rings a little hollow, when taken in the full context of her attitude towards her own experiences.

PERHAPS

NOTE: This poem has the subtitle (To R.A.L. Died of wounds in France, December 23rd 1915). R.A.L. refers to Roland Aubrey Leighton - also a poet - who was Vera Brittain's fiancé. He had been due to return to England on leave on 24th December and was expecting to be reunited with Vera on Boxing Day. However, that morning, rather than the anticipated news of his impending arrival, Vera received a telephone call informing her of Roland's death. From that moment, she always wrote of Him with a capital letter and this can be seen throughout this poem as Roland is addressed as You with a capital 'Y'.

The first verse of this poem introduces its central theme: that the poet doubts that her life can ever be the same again, because she has lost Roland. The following three verses are more specific, in that they each describe a particular time of year. The language of verses two and three is cheerful and even optimistic as the poet relates all of the sights she hopes to be able to enjoy at some time in the future, although Roland will not be with her. This comparison between her hopes for the future and her current sadness is made more acute by the use of this positive vocabulary. So flowers are sweet, the woods glisten in the sunshine and the red roses are beautiful despite her great loss.

Then, in the fourth verse, her tone changes slightly as she wonders whether she will ever be able to celebrate Christmas and New Year again. This is hardly surprising, given the date of Roland's death and the fact that Vera heard of it on Boxing Day.

The final verse of this poem is possibly the most ambiguous. Initially, Vera asserts that, with the passage of time, her life may, once again be happy. She then goes on to say that her most significant delight will never come again. Exactly what she meant by this is unclear, but it would seem that she believed she would never love again. She may, however, be referring to her own great longing for Roland's physical presence and she might be implying that any love she feels in the future will not have the same intensity. In the final line, she states that her heart was broken, when she lost him 'long ago'. This is the most difficult aspect of the poem to comprehend since, when it was written, Roland had only been dead a matter of weeks. There are two possible explanations for this. Following Roland's final return to France, in late August 1915, there was a marked change in the tone and frequency of his letters to Vera. Rather than writing letters full of love on an almost daily basis, by October, he sometimes went for weeks without writing at all and then he merely described his actions and surroundings. He seems to have been aware and was occasionally apologetic for the content of his correspondence and it may be that Vera sensed this change in him and believed that she had already lost him to the horrors of the war even before it claimed his life. Alternatively, it may be that, although only a few weeks had passed since Roland's death, it seemed much longer to her. This latter explanation is, to a certain extent, reinforced in the rest of the poem, where it would seem that she has ceased to enjoy life without him.

This poem makes great use of repetition. Although the poet uses a different phrase, at the end of the first four verses, she reiterates the fact that Roland is dead. To the reader, this serves as a reminder that, no matter what she is doing, she can never escape from her grief. Despite the changing seasons, her life has already reached its culmination as she realises that nothing which she experiences in the future will have the same meaning because she cannot share it with him. For this reason the title and continuous use of the word 'perhaps' reinforces the idea that she herself doubts what she is saying.

Vera Brittain wrote this poem while working as a VAD at the First London General Hospital in February 1916. Following Roland's death, she had returned to her nursing duties on January 3rd 1916, but felt as though she were doing everything automatically, rather than knowingly. Mid-February saw the departure of her beloved brother, Edward, for the front line, so it is hardly surprising that her state of mind was somewhat desperate when she wrote this piece. She continued to correspond with her brother (who had known Roland from school days) and two of his other friends - Victor Richardson and Geoffrey Thurlow. One by one, however, these three also died, leaving Vera to believe that the sacrifices which had been demanded of her generation had been too great.

This poem has a great deal in common with other home-front pieces - especially *Lamplight* by May Wedderburn Cannan and *Reported Missing* by Anna Gordon Keown. Both of these poems refer to the loss of a specific loved-one. Vera

Brittain's losses became well known and well documented through the publication of her letters, her diary and her memoirs.

TO MY BROTHER

This poem was written in June 1918, one week before Edward Brittain was killed in action, and commemorates his participation in the first day of the Battle of the Somme. At that time, Edward had been wounded, but had also been awarded a Military Cross for gallantry, for his actions on 1st July 1916.

This poem has a surprisingly patriotic and fervent tone, considering that by this stage of the war, Vera Brittain had already lost her fiancé, Roland Leighton and two close friends, Victor Richardson and Geoffrey Thurlow. Therefore, her language, such as 'grand... 'show", 'courage glow' and 'flying foe' seems somewhat out of place. The fact that these lines rhyme also adds to their significance.

The opening line of the poem has been used by Catherine Reilly to form the title of her anthology, *Scars Upon My Heart*, and shows how connected Vera Brittain felt to her brother. She goes on to recall the Military Cross which he had been awarded and, in the third verse, she subconsciously links this 'silver... cross' with the metal 'shrapnel' which Edward would now be witnessing. Finally, she voices her hope that he will survive, although again, the tone used here is surprising as she seems to hope that he will live long enough to lead his men into the final battle and chase away the enemy, rather than expressing her hopes that he will return home.

Given Vera Brittain's later pacifist beliefs, this poem has a strangely glorifying undertone, and this, when coupled with her strong feelings for her brother, makes this poem seem rather out of place. One wonders, therefore, whether it was Edward's death, rather than all the others, which really affected her outlook on war, or whether it was actually her feelings about her own experiences and lost opportunities. There would only have been a few months between the composition of this piece and *The Lament of the Demobilised*, and thus, the latter suggestion might account for her change of heart.

May Wedderburn Cannan

BIOGRAPHICAL DETAILS

May Wedderburn Cannan was born on 14th October 1893, together with her twin sister Frances, in Oxford, although Frances died at the age of just two months. May was the middle of the three daughters of Charles and Mary Cannan and her father was a tutor in Classics. The family lived at Magdalen College, Oxford and May was educated initially at home, then at Wychwood School and finally at Downe House in Kent. In May's final year at Downe House, however, she became seriously ill, firstly with measles and then pneumonia, which resulted in her returning to Wychwood School to complete her education. It was at this stage that May first became acquainted with a young man named Bevil Quiller-Couch, whose father was a friend of the family.

When she turned 18 in October 1911, May took the examinations to join the Voluntary Aid Detachment, of which her mother was the local Commandant and, in addition, she helped out at her father's business - the Oxford University Press. As war approached, May's life became a strange combination of VAD work - organising a new hospital for 60 patients - and the usual summer social activities of dancing, tennis and picnics. When war was declared, however, everything changed. Her hospital was organised and ready for its first patients within 2 days. However, she was soon notified that the authorities had changed their minds and no longer required the use of such establishments. In addition, Bevil - an army reservist - was mobilised and sailed for France on August 17th. He wrote to May very often but was disappointed that the proposal of marriage which he had intended making before his departure, would now have to wait.

With her nursing skills seemingly not required at present, May decided to stay on at the Oxford University Press to help her father, since most of the male workers had gone off to enlist. She was joined there by both of her sisters and their father always ensured that the families of his former workers, who had gone to fight, were well cared for. In April 1915, May and a friend, Lucie Raleigh, went to Rouen in France, to work in a canteen. Initially the girls could only stay for four weeks, but May was keen to remain, although she also knew that her father needed her at The Press, so she reluctantly returned home.

The summer of 1915 was very different from its predecessor: many of May's friends had been wounded, some killed; there were no lavish parties; and what little spare time she had, she filled with war work. As the war progressed, May and Bevil continued to correspond and she also wrote poetry, publishing a volume entitled *In War Time* in 1917. Both of May's sisters were married in 1918, leaving May alone at The Press, contemplating an uncertain future. That summer, however, her life changed once again, when she was offered a job in a War Office department in Paris. She knew almost nothing about her new job, other than the fact that it was 'in intelligence' and only when she arrived in Paris did she discover that she would be working for MI5 in the Espionage department. She enjoyed her work, especially when she was promoted to the position of Acting Head of the Women's Espionage Unit. Then, on the morning of the 11th November 1918, May was summoned to the office of the Colonel in charge of her unit, where she was instructed to take down a dictation of the Terms of the Armistice. She then returned to her office and typed out four copies of the document, before bursting into tears - the war was finally over.

A few days later, quite unexpectedly, Bevil arrived at her office - he had five days leave and they spent it together. Before returning to his unit, he proposed to May and she accepted. By early December she was back in England, anxiously awaiting Bevil's return. Their wedding date was fixed for 3rd June 1919. At the beginning of February, May received word that Bevil was seriously ill with influenza and before she could travel to him, he died. May felt that her life - forever changed by the war - was now over. In the immediate aftermath, loneliness engulfed her - along with anger and frustration. By November, however, all had changed again: her father died following a stroke and her mother decided she and May should move to London. She eventually found work at the Athenaeum Club, as assistant Librarian: she was the first woman they had ever employed. She continued to write poetry and joined a writer's club.

In 1924 she received an unsolicited, but intriguing letter, signed simply P.J.S. The writer said that he was a great admirer of her poetry and wondered if they could meet. May decided to accept this invitation - which was actually from a former infantry officer - Captain P. J. Slater. Before the year was out, May and P. J. Slater were married. Little is known of what happened to May in the following years. She died in 1973, leaving behind an unpublished manuscript which detailed her experiences of the First World War: her lost dreams and hopes; her anger and ultimate acceptance of her fate and, above all, the thoughts of a generation, whose lives would forever be different.

LAMPLIGHT

This poem tells of dreams and plans, built up by two young lovers, and the shattering of those hopes by war and death.

The first verse almost mocks the wisdom of youth, as there is a touch of irony in the first two lines. This couple made great plans, and being young and believing themselves invincible, they could see no obstacle to prevent their dreams from coming true. However, their wisdom has proved unfounded. The poem speaks of this couple, through their own hard work, building their own Empire. They do not seek for fame, but they want to serve their country.

All of this is reiterated in the second verse, where we now learn that while the man's desire was to see active military service for his country, the poet's choice is to become a nurse. In both of these verses, it is made clear that the poet is now alone, although she still believes she can see and hear her beloved, as she remembers their plans.

In the final verse, comes the revelation that none of their dreams will come true. They had never discussed him not coming back from the war, but this is the reality with which the poet is now faced. She only has her memories now and the crossed swords which denoted his active service have been replaced in her mind's eye, by a torn wooden cross which marks his grave.

This poem was written in December 1916, by which time many of May's friends had experienced the death of a loved-one. Although her closest friend, Bevil Quiller-Couch (to whom she would later become engaged) was safe, it would not have taken a great leap of the imagination to write this poem.

May felt, very strongly, right from the beginning of the war, that her generation would be changed beyond recognition by events over which they had no control. In the final few years before the war, which many have since described as 'golden', May's life had been quite pleasurable. There was, generally, a sense that youth gave one a certain invulnerability and that young people would in fact create a new and more exciting world, as they stepped out of the Victorian era into which they had been born. The war ended such hopes and this poem demonstrates the sense of anguish which affected many people at the time. The personal sacrifices made by so many reflect the overall loss suffered by an entire generation, who felt that they no longer had a future.

This would have been especially true at the end of 1916; a year which saw so many casualties in ultimately futile battles. The winter of 1916-17 was particularly long and harsh, which must have made the poet's outlook even more bleak.

Lamplight is similar in tone to *Perhaps* by Vera Brittain, which was addressed to her late fiancé Roland Leighton who died in December 1915. This poem lists the experiences which the poet believes she will either miss out on altogether, or which she will never enjoy again, because her beloved is dead.

Many of Vera Brittain's poems have this theme, such as May Morning (which was published in the *Oxford Magazine*), in which she wonders whether the survivors of the war will ever be able to recapture that carefree spirit which they used to have.

Lamplight beautifully evokes a sense of shattered youth and broken dreams, ended by a war in which many of its young participants had been keen to be involved. That blind enthusiasm made the end of their world all the harder to contemplate. The contrast, demonstrated in this poem, between the heady days of youth, and the cold bleak future, must have been almost unbearable.

ROUEN (26th April - 25th May 1915)

This poem offers a very evocative description of May's time at Rouen, working in a Canteen at the Rail Head. In it, she conveys the atmosphere both in and around her workplace; sights, sounds and smells are brought to life.

May wrote this poem in the form of questions about remembrances of a time which, for her, was very happy and fulfilling. For her this was a great adventure, as she had longed to be in France and taste the reality of war first hand.

Throughout the poem she describes various aspects of daily life in the canteen, from the sunrises she witnessed at the end of her shift (May worked mainly during the night), to the strange voices of the Indian soldiers who served during the war. One phrase which often provokes questions in this poem relates to tatties and why they would make a clicking sound. A tattie is the name given, in India, to a screen of grass fibres which was hung at a door or window opening. In India, this screen would have been kept wet to moisten and cool the air. We may, therefore, suppose that screens similar to these were used in the canteens. Either they would be caught in the wind, or as people passed through them, they would bang on the door frame, thus making the clicking sound referred to. May might have heard the Indian soldiers refer to the screens as tatties, or she might have already known about them, since she had some old Oxford friends who had gone out to India with the regular army before the First World War, and she may have picked up the word from them.

She describes the contrast between the still sleeping town, and the hoards of hungry soldiers, laughing over their coffee and sandwiches before going on towards the front. When the soldiers finish and their trains are ready to depart, they are called to attention and sing God Save the King.

Suddenly the canteen is quiet again, all the men have left, and although dawn approaches promising a new beginning, she perceives that the men are travelling to and from darkness. However, everything carries on: there is another shift of workers to hand over to; another train full of soldiers in need of refreshment and a smile. Having completed her own shift, May is now free to enjoy the cool calmness of the morning and to sleep.

In the final two verses, the tone of the poem changes, May is no longer asking whether others share her remembrances - she is telling us that she does remember. She is looking back to her time in Rouen and her adventures there, with an almost romantic air. Her pride in the soldiers is there in the final verse, in that her most abiding memory is of the trains carrying them towards the war. May perceived that the men were fighting gallantly for a worthy cause, and held the soldiers in high esteem.

The fondness of May's memories of that time is apparent in this poem. When she returned to Oxford after her month in Rouen, she felt that she would give almost anything to be able to return to France. She had a profound sense of belonging there: that she was, even only in a small way, doing 'her bit' for the war effort, and in doing so, she felt fulfilled.

SINCE THEY HAVE DIED

This short poem, written in February 1916, has a more optimistic tone than *Lamplight*. It is more a celebration of those who have died, and an urging to their survivors to remember the dead, not with sorrow, but with smiles.

The poet implies that the survivors owe their happiness to those who have died and that the best way to repay this gift is to perpetuate this emotion. By doing so, the dead will, themselves, find contentment.

This rose-coloured vision of the dead was commonly portrayed, especially in the first two years of the war, when many preferred to believe that their loved ones had died in a just cause and would rest in peace knowing that their survivors lived on in happiness. This made the whole idea of the gallant sacrifice seem more worthy.

Other poets who wrote in this tone included Rupert Brooke and John McCrae, who, in particular spoke of the dead in similar terms, as witnesses to the behaviour of their survivors. In *The Anxious Dead*, McCrae echoes the sentiments of *Since They Have Died*, in that his dead may finally turned contentedly to sleep, in the knowledge that they have not died in vain.

Later in the war, many poets would change their tone, allowing for the fact that slaughter on such as scale should not be seen as glorious at all. However, in the early days of the war, particularly before the Somme had claimed so many lives, May's opinion, demonstrated here, was no unusual.

One notable exception was Charles Hamilton Sorley, who in 1915 wrote *When You See Millions of the Mouthless Dead*. In this poem, the dead he describes are not laughing or contented. In fact they are unable to respond to the surviving mourners in any way for the simple reason that they are dead. This is a much harsher, and to those on the home-front, less palatable vision of death.

LOVE, 1916

This poem, written in August 1916, is essentially about how the emotion of love has changed and been transformed by the war. The date of the poem is worth noting, as by this stage, the full horror of the casualties from the beginning of the Battle of the Somme would have been realised.

In the poem, love is equated with other emotions, such as joy, the pursuit of power and fame, or the desire for peace. All of these are feelings which various people would have experienced. For example, before the war, May, as a young innocent girl, would have looked upon love as a joyous emotion - at once exciting and fulfilling and bringing happiness. On the other hand, many, including those who had sought war had a passion for power as intense as any conventional love affair. Equal to this was the deep desire which everyone felt for peace.

The poet asserts that, upon summoning love, in any of these forms, she has discovered that it bears another name: sacrifice. The demands which have been placed on all of her generation far outweigh their previously powerful emotions. Joy, power, fame and the hope for peace have all been erased and replaced by the sacrifice of love and youth.

She could also have been implying here that to sacrifice a loved-one demonstrates the ultimate love of someone who will relinquish their own happiness for the sake of others. Either way, her previously held convictions on that emotion have been altered beyond recognition.

This is a sad poem which evokes a feeling of loneliness: she is looking for love, calling out for it even, only to discover that it no longer exists in any form known to her, or her generation. It signifies the fact that everything has changed - nothing is as it used to be.

ISABEL C. CLARKE

BIOGRAPHICAL DETAILS

Isabel Constance Clarke was born in 1869 at Plympton, near Plymouth in Devon. Her father, Francis, who was born in Brussels, was a Colonel in the Royal Artillery and her mother, Elizabeth Stainton, came from Kent. Isabel was the third of six children. Her oldest brother, also called Francis, was born in 1867, but died at the age of twenty-five. Alice was just one year older than Isabel, while Eveline was four years younger. Then came two more brothers - Robert in 1879 and Mordaunt in 1885. The family moved about quite a lot, living in Somerset, Surrey and London, but when Isabel's father died in 1893, they settled in Brighton on the South Coast. Isabel's youngest brother, Mordaunt, served as a Lieutenant in the 3rd Battalion of the Worcester Regiment and was killed in action at Caudry in France on 26th August 1914. Isabel continued to write novels and biographies, especially about other authors, including the Brontë sisters and Elizabeth Barrett Browning. She died in Jamaica in 1951.

ANNIVERSARY OF THE GREAT RETREAT

Although this is a poem which seeks to glorify death in battle, it is also immeasurably sad, as in this instance the death concerned had been that of the poet's youngest brother, Mordaunt. His regiment was involved in the fighting around a French village called Caudry and, during the 26th August 1914, they held off superior numbers of German forces, allowing other troops to withdraw, as part of the Retreat from Mons. This allowed British soldiers to regroup at Le Cateau and cause further, costly casualties to the enemy. Mordaunt's regiment were among the last to retreat and it was during this action that he died.

Isabel Clarke wrote this poem on the first anniversary of the Retreat from Mons, which became known as The Great Retreat for the simple reason that, although it could have been seen as a defeat, it did in fact allow the British Army to pull back to the Marne, where they defended Paris from the advancing German army and forced them not only to retreat themselves, but also to abandon the Schlieffen Plan and thus change the course of the war. It would have been within this atmosphere of having snatched a victory - of sorts - out of almost certain defeat, that Isabel Clarke would have written this poem and although we might now look at her words, almost disbelieving that she could be talking of 'victory' in the late summer of 1915, it is only the benefit of hindsight which affords us that perspective.

She writes of the 1914 battleground names being etched into her heart, together with the image of the graves of those who died and the flowers which, she hopes, now cover them. She recalls the men as young and cheerful and urges England to remember them as victorious in death. Her reference to these soldiers as 'Contemptible' is not meant as an insult, but alludes instead to the nickname adopted by the Regular Army of the 'old contemptibles', which reputedly stems from a remark made by Kaiser Wilhelm II in the early days of the war. Finally, Isabel Clarke asserts that the survivors should always revere the men who died, since they earned this early victory. Throughout the poem, Isabel Clarke is at pains to remember that it is not only her brother who died, and not only her family who have lost someone. She is careful to say 'they' rather than 'he' and 'we' rather than 'I', showing that her sympathies and understanding lay outside of her own sorrow.

MARGARET POSTGATE COLE

BIOGRAPHICAL DETAILS

Born in Cambridge on May 6th 1893, Margaret Isabel Postgate was the daughter of John Percival Postgate and Edith Allen. She was the eldest of three children. Raymond and Percival, her brothers, were three and six years younger than her, respectively. The family lived in a house called Sunnyside in Church Road, Stapleford, in Cambridgeshire. Her father had been Professor of Latin at the University of Liverpool. Margaret was educated at Roedean School, overlooking the Sussex Downs. She then returned to Cambridge and attended Girton College.

Although she had been raised in the Anglican faith, while Margaret was at University, she began questioning her religious beliefs. She became a socialist, a feminist and a pacifist and upon the outbreak of the First World War she became actively involved in the peace movement. She and her brother, Raymond, campaigned against conscription and Raymond was imprisoned as a conscientious objector.

Margaret met George Douglas Cole, another conscientious objector, and the two were married in 1918, working together at the Fabian Research Department. After the war, the couple moved to Oxford where Margaret taught evening classes. Between 1923 and 1946, Margaret and George wrote many crime novels featuring Superintendent Henry Wilson of Scotland Yard.

During the 1930s, following the destruction of the Socialist movement in Germany, Margaret lost her belief in pacifism and supported Britain's role in the Second World War. She died in 1980.

THE FALLING LEAVES

This short poem compares the falling leaves of autumn with the fallen soldiers in Flanders.

A picture is conjured of a young woman riding down a lane on a late autumn day, witnessing the falling of leaves, despite there being no wind. She compares this scene with the silence of a heavy snowfall, rather than the noise and bluster usually associated with a windy autumn day. This makes the rider think of the brave young men who are dying at the Front, not through old-age or illness, but because of war. Like the leaves, their dying youth and beauty reminds her of snowflakes which must by now be falling at the Front.

This poem is beautiful and yet without hope. The use of autumn leaves and snowflakes are symbolic of death. When the leaves reach the ground, they are dead because they are starved of nutrients; the snowflakes must also eventually "die" because they melt. This represents the dying men at the Front and it could be interpreted that the soldiers die because they too are starved. In their case, however, they are deprived of hope, of a future, of the warmth and love of home and family. One feels that their lives are wasted, just like the leaves. The dead soldiers will also eventually "melt" into the soil, and disappear just as the snowflakes do.

The author perceives the soldiers as brave and comments on the vast number of men who will perish, which again relates back to the leaves and the snowflakes. This ability to recognise that the quantity of dead will be multitudinous, demonstrates great foresight on the part of the writer, bearing in mind that this poem was written fairly early in the War.

There is no sense of glory or patriotism here, merely sadness at the passing of so many, for so little. These men have not been allowed to grow old, or even become ill, but have been struck down in their prime, at their most beautiful, their deaths being as inevitable as the falling of the leaves.

AFTERWARDS

This poem opens with Margaret Postgate Cole dreamily reminiscing about the days before the war, when she and her 'beloved' would plan their future together. She creates a wonderfully joyous impression of that time, simply by the repetition of the words 'O cakes', which immediately gives this section of the poem a warm and homely atmosphere. This is enhanced even further by the smaller details, such as the fact that these cakes come 'from Fuller's', which makes this whole memory seem so much more realistic. In the second verse, however, she begins to shatter this happy scene as, although peace has now come, the 'larches' under which she had lain are all dead. They have been cut down and used to make pit-props for the mines. This thought makes her sad, as she realises that the trees won't come back: a dead tree cannot just be replanted and brought back to life. This, however, is also a metaphor for the dead soldiers, who also won't come back and carry on their lives as before. The final verse is the most depressing of all, as she brings all of these earlier thoughts and memories together. She links the dead men, buried underground, with the pit-props which once were just as alive as the soldiers. Finally, a the very end of the poem, however, there is a twist as the poet wonders 'what use' it would be for her 'beloved' to be buried in 'Sheer', as opposed to somewhere else. Presumably, her point here is that, once dead - whether a larch or a man - it does not really matter where the body is, because it cannot be brought back to life.

PRAEMATURI

This poem contrasts the feelings of old people, whose friends die, with those of the young, who must face a long future alone.

In the first verse the poet describes her imagined sense of how an older person might feel upon the death of a contemporary. Although they might feel sad, they have many years of memories, and, being old, will, in theory not have too long to dwell on the prospect of being alone.

The second stanza deals with the effects of the death of young people on the young. These people who have had precious little time to experience the joys of life, are now torn apart, with no hope for the future, but many years to rue their youth.

This is a sad poem which reflects on the feelings of those who have lost someone in the war: not the mother losing a son, but the girl losing a friend or lover. The contrast is drawn between old and young: the old have lived their lives, had their opportunities, and now have happy memories upon which to reflect.

The young, on the other hand, have had no chance to even create happy memories and must spend many years considering what might have been. Youth is portrayed as a curse, since the old people are shown as contentedly looking forward to rejoining their departed friends. The young people wish to be dead, and join those they have lost, but are doomed to live for many years, an empty and unfulfilling life.

This poem paints a fairly depressing picture of a generation torn apart, whose capacity to enjoy life to the full has been snatched away by the war and the deaths of so many young men. These deaths have come suddenly, not as the result of old-age or illness, not naturally with the passing of time, but through violence.

Despite the fact that she is female, and one assumes she is writing from a woman's perspective, the author compares the survivors to old men, making use of irony. This could be because she feels that when she becomes old, there will be no old men, because they have all been killed in their youth and none will, therefore, survive to old age.

In the hopeless world created by this poem, such an attitude is quite easy to understand: as the casualty lists grew longer, it must have seemed that all hope for the future was dying too.

THE VETERAN

This poem relates an episode in which a group of (presumably) young ladies, come upon a blinded soldier sitting in the sunshine. They are joined by some young soldiers, fresh from the pub, who ask the blind man's advice. He tells them his stories, which seem to fall on deaf ears. After the soldiers have gone, the blind man becomes aware that someone else is still present and openly pities the young soldiers' inexperience. He sits, his eyes turning towards where he believes his companions have gone, until one of the young ladies asks him how old he is and he reveals that he is just nineteen years of age.

The irony in the title of this poem should not go unnoticed. This man is considered a veteran when, having only just turned nineteen, he was not old enough to have been serving in the first place. (The age for going overseas on active service during the First World War was nineteen, although many young men lied about their age, particularly in the early years of the war, fearing that if they waited they would "miss out"). One should also notice the date within the title. This places the poem almost immediately before the Battle of the Somme, which means that although this "veteran", at the age of nineteen, has already served his country and paid his price, much worse is to follow. Within weeks, thousands of other young men would have been killed or wounded, and more of

Margaret's generation would be destroyed.Possibly the young men who ask the veteran's advice will be among those who do not return.

For the first two verses, the reader is unaware of the man's age, and one assumes that he is older, in view of the fact that the other soldiers are referred to as being young and are asking advice from this more experienced man. These young soldiers are complacent and pay little heed to what the blind man tells them. He does not berate them, but pities their innocence which he knows will soon be lost. It is also easier for the reader to make the assumption that the man must be older: after all who wants to believe that someone so young could have lost his sight? This lulls the reader into a false sense of security.

The blind man is portrayed as lonely, while the others are all in groups, which is reminiscent of Wilfred Owen's poem *Disabled*, in which a maimed soldier sits alone, abandoned by his friends who fear the sight of him, and rejected by women, in favour of the men who are "whole". In *The Veteran*, the young soldiers, although keen for the blind man's advice, do not remain long, possibly because his plight reminds them of what might await them in France.

The young ladies remain a little longer, and eventually one of them asks how old the blind man is - this shows that his extreme youth is not obvious and maybe, like Owen's maimed soldier in *Disabled*, he has grown old before his time.

This poem does not glorify war, nor is there a hint of patriotism. Like much of Margaret Postgate Cole's poetry one is left with an acute feeling of sadness: youth is being wasted and the expectations of a nation, which are being placed on these young men, are too great for their generation to bear.

MARY GABRIELLE COLLINS

BIOGRAPHICAL DETAILS

Mary Gabrielle Collins was born in 1875 in Penderyn, Breconshire. She was the oldest of the eight children of Henry and Mary Collins. Henry was a banker from Bristol, while Mary, whose maiden name was Ackerman, came from Bridgwater in Somerset. The children - four girls and four boys - were educated at home by a French governess, and they grew up in Cardiff. After her father's death in 1899, the family moved to London, where Mary became an author and journalist.

WOMEN AT MUNITION MAKING

This poem demonstrates the poet's belief that, in the First World War, women have been drawn away from their natural role as creators and carers, towards a more destructive position in society. She opens with the reminder that a woman's place is traditionally in the home, nurturing children, before contrasting this with the war-time notion of women as the manufacturers of the implements of death. Collins goes on to assert that war is normally the creation of men, but that by involving women, the very balance of nature is threatened. She does not seem to have an issue with the war itself, but more with the position which women have adopted within the war effort. There were those who felt enthusiastic that women had the opportunity to 'do their bit'; there were even those who would have like to do more, but found that the very fact of their womanhood prevented this. Mary Collins, on the other hand, seems to have been most concerned, at least within this poem, that the war would eventually bring about the destruction of the female role and, presumably, femininity itself.

ALICE CORBIN

BIOGRAPHICAL DETAILS

Alice Corbin was born in April 16th 1881 in St Louis, Missouri to Fillmore Mallory Corbin and his wife, Lula Hebe Carradine. When Alice was three years old, her mother died and the child was sent to live with her father's cousin, Alice Mallory Richardson in Chicago. This arrangement lasted for seven years, until Fillmore remarried and Alice joined her father and his new wife in Kansas. However, she only remained there for three years, returning to Chicago in 1894. When she had graduated from high school, Alice attended the University of Chicago, publishing her first volume of poetry, The Linnet Songs, in 1898. While at university, Alice lived with Harriet C. Brainard, who had been her English teacher in high school and who clearly influenced Alice's educational direction. Following her graduation from the University of Chicago, Alice moved to a studio at the Academy of Fine Arts and began writing reviews for local newspapers. In 1904, she met the painter, William Penhallow Henderson, a teacher at the Academy, and the two were married in October of the following year.

Their only child, a daughter, also named Alice, was born in January 1907, although this new arrival did not prevent her mother and father from collaborating on a children's book entitled Andersen's Best Fairy Tales, using Alice's translations from the original texts and William's illustrations to accompany them. Further editions of poetry followed as well as a spell as associate editor at *Poetry* magazine with Harriet Monroe, until in 1916, Alice Snr., was diagnosed with tuberculosis, necessitating a move to a warmer climate.

The family settled in Santa Fe, New Mexico, which had a great impact on both Alice's health and the couple's work, as they both became interested in the plight of Native Americans, which is reflected in William's art and Alice's writing from then on. William also became an architect and furniture designer, setting up a business with his first son-in-law, John Evans, whom Alice Jnr., married shortly before her sixteenth birthday, in December 1922. The couple had three children before they divorced in 1933, leaving them temporarily in the care of Alice and William, until Alice Jnr., remarried in 1938. This unexpected addition to the family, together with the necessary disintegration of the business caused a great deal of financial hardship for Alice and William, who died of a heart attack in 1943. Following this, Alice, whose health had never been sound, became even more unwell, and died in July 1949.

FALLEN

It is believed that this poem was written in 1918, by which time American soldiers were beginning to become involved with the fighting on the Western Front, so it is possible that this poem actually relates to a specific death, perhaps of someone that the poet knew. Alternatively, she may simply have read about, or heard of, the deaths of soldiers, and decided to write something on this subject.

The poem opens at the moment of wounding, although we are given no details as to the nature of the wound or the method employed to injure this man. So we do not know whether he has received a gun shot wound, or fallen victim to a shell-blast, in which case, his injuries would probably be much more severe. It would seem, however, that he has fallen in the midst of a battle, as he is surrounded by 'hoarse shouting' which even suggests an element of panic. 'The tide', which passes over the soldier in 'waves' may refer to pain or death, which could appear to wash over him as he drifts in and out of consciousness.

Next comes the first of many interminglings of reality and imagination, as the man hears a 'cock crow' in the distance, but then imagines that he hears 'children laughing' and running around in an early morning orchard, where the petals of the apple blossom have recently fallen to the ground. This must be imagined rather than real, as children would not be allowed so close to the front lines. However, this might be a childhood memory, or perhaps something more recent, from time spent behind the lines, observing local children. Either way, in turning, he faces another fantasy from his imagination, which is either the 'breast' of a lover, or alternatively, this might be a reference to his mother, which would tie in with his childhood remembrance. This memory seems to leave him with a feeling of confusion, possibly because he cannot reconcile his pain and impending death, with recollections from his childhood, although he now appears to be sinking further into unconsciousness.

As he drifts away, the memories, imagination and reality become even more intertwined than before. Voices from the trenches sound like ghosts from the past and then, as though he is floating above both scenes, the 'wreckage' of No Man's Land becomes 'mingled with the storm of petals' in the apple orchard. 'Suddenly' he is dead. The woman - whether she is a lover, or his mother - is beside him and the burden of life has been lifted from him.

Alice Corbin has offered us a somewhat rose-tinted and sanitised perspective of death in battle. As previously stated, we know nothing of the man's wounds or how he came by them; we are not told how long it takes him to die, and rather than being wracked with pain, this man's experience of death seems to be quite pleasant! She is, perhaps, showing us how she would like to believe death was, rather than portraying anything remotely realistic. The idea that life has become a burden or 'weight' is also quite interesting, as it implies that death is preferable, but conveniently ignores the manner of that death.

Nancy Cunard

BIOGRAPHICAL DETAILS

Nancy Cunard was born on 10th March 1896 at her family's home, Nevill Holt in Leicestershire. She was the only child of Sir Bache Cunard, a Baronet and heir to the Cunard Shipping line. Although a British subject, he was born in New York in 1852. Nancy's mother, an heiress in her own right, had been born Maud Alice Burke in San Francisco in 1872. The couple married when Maud was just twenty years old and she and Sir Bache - who was twice her age - moved into the Cunard family residence.

Maud's exuberant and youthful personality ensured that Nevill Holt became a centre of social activity. Nancy's arrival cause little change, and the young child was brought up mainly by servants and governesses. When her parents were present, there were many parties, where Nancy was allowed to stay up late and mix with prominent figures from the worlds of literature, art, music and politics.

In 1910, when Nancy was fourteen, her parents separated and mother and daughter moved to London. Nancy's mother, by now better known as 'Emerald', continued to live up to her reputation of leading socialite, while Nancy was sent to private schools in London, Paris and Germany.

It was during 1914, while attending school in Paris, that Nancy became involved with a group known as the 'Corrupt Coterie' - an unconventional collection of writers and artists, including Osbert Sitwell, Ezra Pound, Augustus John and Diana Manners. This group would be found, most evenings, sitting in Parisian cafés discussing poetry and politics. Nancy's involvement was acknowledged as a rebellion against her mother - and the traditions of debutantes and marriage. Nancy and her particular friend, Iris Tree, were reputedly 'truly bad girls' - they rented a studio room, Nancy wore men's clothes and they indulged in unusually promiscuous behaviour, liberally fuelled by excessive amounts of alcohol. Other participants in the group included the younger members of many leading families of the British aristocracy, such as the Grenfells, Tennants and Asquiths - most of whom would die in the trenches of the First World War - the 'Coterie' dying with them.

Given Nancy's behaviour at this time, it came as quite a shock to both her family and friends, when in 1916, she announced her engagement to Sydney Fairbairn, an army officer of short acquaintance. Fairbairn was regarded as socially acceptable, but dull and most unlike Nancy's other male acquaintances. Nobody was particular surprised when their marriage ended in separation after only twenty months, although they did not officially divorce until 1925.

Nancy almost immediately became intimately involved with another serving army officer: Peter Broughton-Adderley. It has been claimed that she never fully recovered from his death, less than one month before Armistice Day.

Returning to Paris in 1920, Nancy became increasingly dependant on alcohol and also started to experiment with various recreational drugs. She became involved in Dadaism, Modernism and Surrealism and, although not an active member of a political organisation, she took a keen interest in Communism. She embarked on a series of affairs with, amongst others, novelist Michael Arlen, writer Aldous Huxley and historian and poet Louis Aragon. When this last relationship ended, it is alleged that Aragon attempted suicide.

In 1927, Nancy founded The Hours Press at a farmhouse in Reanville, outside Paris. Here she set about publishing works by authors who, for various reasons, had struggled to gain recognition elsewhere. These included Ezra Pound, Samuel Beckett, Robert Graves and Richard Aldington.

Always one to flout convention, Nancy's next relationship would shock many, including her mother. She had earlier met the black American jazz musician, Henry Crowder, and in 1928 he moved into the farmhouse. When 'Emerald' heard of Nancy's newest lover, she disinherited her daughter and the two women did not speak for many years.

Nancy's involvement with Crowder fuelled her interest in the Civil Rights movement in America, although her behaviour continued to cause controversy. She painted her face white, her lips dark red and generously applied rouge (many say she did this with a rabbit's foot); she wore ivory and bakelite bangles on both arms, from wrist to elbow. She and Crowder certainly made an unusually striking couple. In addition to this, theirs was a turbulent relationship

- the calm, placid Crowder often falling victim to Nancy's violent, alcohol-driven temper.

In customary style, once Nancy had tired of Crowder, she moved on - to Spain. She lived there through most of the 1930's, working as a freelance writer during the Spanish Civil War. For some of this time, she lived with the poet Pablo Neruda, whose poems she translated. She spent the Second World War in London, returning to the Reanville farmhouse upon its conclusion. Here, she discovered that most of her possessions had been destroyed or stolen - whether by the Nazi's or the locals is unclear. She never lived there again.

Over the ensuing years, she drifted around in an alcoholic haze, on at least one occasion appearing in a magistrate's court on a charge of disorderly conduct. Even here, however, her temper got the better of her and she removed her shoes and hurled them at the presiding official.

By 1960 her wild lifestyle had started to really catch up with her and she was committed to Holloway Sanitorium due to her mental instability. Her cousin Victor Cunard secured her release and took care of her until she could arrange to return to France. Once there, however, her health and mental stability continued to deteriorate; she alienated all of her friends, who had always tried to be understanding of her behaviour. On 15th March 1965, the Parisian police found her walking the streets in a confused state. They took her to the Cochin charity hospital, where she died two days later, aged sixty-nine.

One observer reportedly said that despite the outrageous behaviour, unusual clothes and make-up, if you looked into her blue eyes you would find a visible, deep sadness. This remained with her, despite all the supposed advantages of her birth, from her early wild-child days, through her hedonistic, yet unfulfilling love-affairs, to her ultimately sad and lonely death.

ZEPPELINS

This poem describes the fear, almost to the point of madness, which results from a Zeppelin raid. These raids became quite common - at a rate of roughly two per month - from early 1915. During that year, the Germans launched many successful raids on London, causing loss of life and destruction of property on a scale never witnessed before. Zeppelin raids tailed off slightly from 1916 onwards, but they had done more damage than merely the physical: the psychological effect on civilians was their greatest achievement and Nancy Cunard's poem reflects this.

Initially, she describes the people as 'climbing' to escape from the approaching Zeppelin. This could be because they are, literally, running uphill; alternatively this word may be used to represent a greater sense of fear and panic - it is more difficult to have to climb up away from something than merely to run.

It would seem that the people have gone mad with fear, yet they have also gained a certain strength and through this, a wish to avenge the deaths of so many in the trenches. Therefore, they initially manage to overcome their fear with thoughts of vengeance and killing. Death, in the form of the Zeppelin, pursues them, appearing almost stately, as it hovers above them, waiting to unleash its bombs. The explosions caused sound like this giant representative of death is stamping its feet.

The fires which follow destroy the rows of houses. 'Serried' means closed ranks and while here it refers to the houses, it is more usually used in reference to troops. This provides an interesting metaphor between the home of these frightened civilians and the soldiers serving in the trenches. The area most affected is the poorer district, which is also referred to as sad. This may be a reference to the fact that Cunard might have automatically assumed that poor people would be sad, it could also mean that the people in poorer areas seemed to suffer more than most - especially at that time. Although many upper and middle class families had relatives serving at the front, sheer numbers alone dictated that most of the losses would occur in the working class areas. So, in addition to their usual fears and worries, they are now faced with the additional threat of the loss of a loved-one, and now their own destruction.

Both death and the people are portrayed as mad. However, death is perceived as superior because its stamping feet - the bombs - are 'proud'. This makes death more powerful and controlling than the panicking crowds, many of whom die or hide away in their fear. The blackness of the night would have been enhanced by the blackout which the authorities had put into operation in an attempt to thwart the Zeppelin raids. One side-effect of this, however, was that the bombings became more indiscriminate - so the night may well have appeared 'frenzied', since the people would not know when or where the bombs would fall - and to a certain extent, neither would the bombers themselves - it has been estimated that only about 10% of the bombs dropped by the Zeppelins actually hit their intended target.

Despite their attempts to hide, or run away, death continues to pursue the people. However, Cunard now gives death an ecclesiastical - almost innocent - air, in that the Zeppelin's covering, rather than being the ragged fabric of the first verse, is now a gown, like those worn by choirboys. It seems to be streaked, like the people's faces - the shadows on both creating an almost mirrored expression - one fearsome, one frightened.

Finally, however, daylight returns and fear abates. There is a contrast here between light and dark, the mad fear of death and the mocking arrogance of having escaped and survived.

This poem illustrates the power of death and how the fear of it can easily control ones actions. Although the symbol of death in this poem is the Zeppelin, this could be seen as representative of all the death and destruction surrounding everyone at that time, from which there was no escape. This is particularly so, given Cunard's reference to the destroyed houses appearing to be like rows of soldiers. There is an element of relentless fear in this poem, which over the course of time has led to madness. Again, this could be an allusion to the soldiers who, having eventually become exhausted by the constant fear, noise and destruction of the trenches, exhibited outward signs of terror, almost like madness - better known eventually as shellshock. The overpowering dread of the people is contrasted with the calm, controlling Zeppelin which wreaks havoc on so many, just like the war has done.

Other poets described Zeppelin raids, using them to represent the feelings of those on the home-front. For example, Laurence Binyon's *The Zeppelin* which describes the initial fear of the civilians, turning into a sense of pride and thanksgiving that they are able to share in the danger being experienced by those at the front, and by doing so, they gain a greater understanding of the war.

Cunard's poem has a different focus - concentrating more on fear, tinged with an element of madness. This is partly because she is trying to point out that death comes unseen, in whatever form it strikes - as a bomb from a Zeppelin, or a telegram delivered to the door. It also has something to do with the underlying message of her poem: that any group of people who live in constant fear of anything, will eventually start to lose their sense of proportion and control over their own lives and that while daylight may bring relief from these terrors, that is only temporary: the darkness of one's fear and the unknown is blacker than ever.

ELIZABETH DARYUSH

BIOGRAPHICAL DETAILS

Elizabeth Daryush (née Bridges) was born on 5th December 1887, in London. Her father, Robert Bridges had been a physician, but was also a poet and was made Poet Laureate from 1913 to 1930. Elizabeth's mother was Monica Waterhouse, whose father Alfred had been a famous architect - his best known design probably being the Natural History Museum in London. Elizabeth was the oldest of three children, her sister Margaret was born in 1889 and brother, Edward, three years later. When Elizabeth was still an infant, the family moved out of London to Yattendon in Berkshire, where she was privately educated. By her early twenties, Elizabeth was already a published poet, producing three volumes of work between 1911 and 1921 although later, she would disown these poems, which were published under her maiden name. In 1926 Elizabeth married a Persian government official called Ali Akbar Daryush and for the first three years of their marriage, they lived in Persia. Upon their return to England, they settled at Boars Hill in Oxford and the 1930s would become her most productive period of writing with her poems often taking the form of criticisms of the upper classes. Her popularity faded in the 1940s and she died in 1977.

FLANDERS FIELDS

This short poem is, at first glance, a description of the fields of Flanders, presumably some time after the First World War. Daryush opens the poem by describing the flowers: she compares the daisies, which are after all little more than weeds, with crimson roses. In doing this, she appears to imply that even the most common and ordinary flower is as 'glorious' as the best blooms in the land. This description could be taken as a metaphor for the dead soldiers who, in her eyes, have all been made equally 'glorious' by death.

She goes on to describe the lush grass as 'unfading', which again may be symbolic of the dead soldiers, whose memories have not faded, even though they are dead. She is also suggesting in this first verse that the men live on, through the countryside over which they fought. In the final lines of this verse, she reminds us that they are, in fact dead, but even then it appears that these deaths, while regretted, are also celebrated.

In the second verse, Daryush urges those who are left behind to spare a thought for the dead; to show them a mark of respect for their sacrifices. Only at the very end of the poem does Daryush acknowledge that no quantity of flowers or 'wheat' (by which she may be suggesting food, or nourishment), can atone for the loneliness of lost love.

This poem feels a little contrived, especially in its somewhat forced rhyme scheme, which detracts from the themes of initial hope, followed by gratitude and ending with sorrow.

FOR A SURVIVOR OF THE MESOPOTAMIAN CAMPAIGN

The First World War battles on the Mesopotamian front are now all-but forgotten, as we tend to assume that most, if not all of the fighting took place in France and Flanders. At the time, the main public focus was also on the Western Front, although those with loved-ones serving in the Middle East would have been just as familiar as a 21st Century audience with the battlegrounds of Falluja, Basra and Baghdad, where much of the fighting then took place in what is now known as Iraq.

In this poem, Daryush commemorates these largely forgotten soldiers, by referring to their generation as 'wasted'. She gives a haunting description of this area, as much wracked by battle as it was by the less visible signs of death. In this area, it was as easy to die from disease as it was to be shot or blown up. She also refers to the campaign as 'folly', suggesting that she can see no reason for its occurrence, or its consequences, especially considering that so many men died from disease, which she presumably felt was unnecessary.

In the second verse, Daryush goes on to criticise those who have sought war and found only a desert - both metaphorical and literal in meaning. She ends with the declaration that those who have witnessed such death and destruction can never enjoy the simple pleasures of life again.

In this poem, Daryush seems to be both critical and pitying of those who have survived this campaign, making this an ambiguous and somewhat confusing poem, where really each reader must decide for themselves what they feel is the real meaning.

SUBALTERNS

A subaltern is an officer in the British Army, below the rank of Captain. This is usually the title given to the most junior of officers, such as Second Lieutenants, reflecting their lower status among the officer ranks. Nonetheless, the subaltern would be responsible for a Platoon of men and would also have to assist the more senior officers in running the Company. Due to their junior rank, many subalterns were quite often younger than the men they were leading, and some of them would have entered the war straight from school in their late teens.

This poem was written after the war as a conversation between a woman who seeks to glorify the role of men in battle and former soldiers who reveal their realities. In the opening verse, the woman makes a somewhat gushing statement, that the thought of men fighting in battle makes her heart thrill. This seems like a rather careless and immature statement, leading one to believe that it was probably made by a young women, innocent in the ways of the world. The subaltern in question then response that his thoughts of war are not warm and glowing and she supposes, but are cold recollections of an initially optimistic time, made barren by experience. It is interesting to note that he regards his happier moments as having been "bought" with, presumably other mens' lives, or his experiences of horror.

The second verse continues with the woman now suggesting to a subaltern that he must feel relieved to be free of fighting, since the war is over and peace has returned. His response is to doubt her implication before going on to remark that at least the war had given him something worthwhile to do, whereas now everything seems rather dull and boring.

It is not completely clear whether there is more than one subaltern involved here, although the title of the poem being plural would seem to indicate this. If this is the case, it certainly makes sense of the fact that the two male responses are somewhat contradictory, since the first recalls "icy memories", while the second seems to have more fond recollections, resenting the peace, rather than the war.

The format of this poem, with a question and answer, allows Daryush to create an automatic contrast within the piece as the man contradicts the woman's statements each time.

Daryush doesn't paint a very positive portrait of her own sex here, portraying the female character as insensitive and innocent to the ways of war, even at its end. It is possible to compare this piece with *Glory of Women* by Siegfried Sassoon, in which he initially and ironically portrays women in a similar, harsh light, decrying them for their delight in war and their wilful misunderstanding of reality. Only at the end of the poem does Sassoon allow for any other type of woman: the lonely mother who continues to knit socks for her dead son. In Kipling's *Epitaphs* the poet also makes several references to women and their role in the war, such as in *An Only Son, Shock, VAD (Mediterranean), Unknown Female Corpse*, and *Raped and Revenged*, although many of these are written from the perspective of a mother's relationship with her son, making them different to *Subalterns*.

UNKNOWN WARRIOR

An obscure poem, which might be open to more than one interpretation, but in which Elizabeth Daryush seems to be pouring praise on those who have died quietly, or almost unnoticed, with no grave to mark the place of their falling - thus making them 'unknown'. These men, it would seem, do not receive the 'earthly' recognition of having their names carved in remembrance, but remain anonymous victims - or heroes. Daryush appears to imply that their is somehow a greater sacrifice, because they leave nothing of themselves behind. She goes on to suggest that she would surrender everything which she values to make up for the loss of such men. Daryush seems to believe that by giving so much, in such a noble way, these men have gained their 'immortality'.

One might presume that this poem was written after the burial of the Unknown Warrior at Westminster Abbey on 11th November 1920. In this tomb are buried the remains of a British soldier who died on active duty. His name and rank are unknown, but it was decided that regardless of these, he should be buried alongside the Kings in Westminster Abbey, as a fitting resting place to represent all those who had given so much in the service of their country.

Helen Dircks

BIOGRAPHICAL DETAILS

Although little is known of the childhood of Helen Dircks, it would seem from a volume of poetry, entitled *Finding*, which she published in 1918, that she had a lover or fiancé who served during the First World War. The poems contained in this volume are full of sorrow and regret, but are coupled with hope for the future, and are some of the simplest and yet most poignant and beautiful within this genre. After the war, in October 1920, Helen Dircks married Frank Arthur Swinnerton, a writer and publisher. This marriage, however, did not last more than a couple of years, as Swinnerton remarried in 1924. Helen Dircks was also married again, to English scholar and teacher James Runcieman Sutherland, in 1931. They remained married until Helen's death in 1975.

AFTER BOURLON WOOD

Bourlon Wood - or to be more precise, the capture of it - became a strategic element in the Battle of Cambrai, which began on November 20th 1917 and continued until the end of the year, with a cost to both sides of almost 100,000 men.

In this poem, which is set after the capture of Bourlon Wood, at the end of November 1917, Helen Dircks describes a scene at a London club, where young people have met up with the intention of momentarily forgetting the war, rationing and all their other hardships. Throughout this poem, she creates an atmosphere of eager enthusiasm for the war, but this is a satirical piece, so her meaning is, in fact, quite the opposite.

In the poem, she and a young Major, who has just returned from the fighting, strike up a conversation in which he seems almost ludicrously ardent for war. She, on the other hand, describes her own life as a WAAC - the Women's Army Auxiliary Corps, which was established in January 1917. Her life is not so exciting as the Major's and, in fact, it is only when the Major is home on leave that her existence brightens up. He wishes that they could do something to cheer themselves up and she suggests Saturday afternoon as an appropriate time. The Major, however, will not be available as he is going to be presented with his Military Cross by the King.

This humorous poem, which appeared in Helen Dircks's volume entitled *Passenger*, published in 1920, disguises the poet's feelings that the lives of her generation are being wasted. This applies to both the men and women, as they cannot seem to even find time to enjoy themselves without the war interfering with their plans.

LONDON IN WAR

In this poem, which was published in the poet's 1920 volume entitled *Passenger*, Helen Dircks paints a hopeless picture of wartime life in London, filled with sorrow and despair. She uses metaphors throughout to create the impression that the war has come to dominate everything, even on the home front.

The faces of the people, she asserts, have begun to resemble 'helpless petals', which suggests that they have no control and are merely drifting 'on the stream' which their lives have become. The sunshine does not cheer; instead it 'burns' and despite its 'brightness', the heat only serves to remind her of death. This verse suggests that there is no joy left in life; only the constant reminders of death which seem to consume every thought and heartbeat.

In the third verse, everything is muddled: 'tears' and 'laughter'; 'God' and 'war'; 'joy' and 'agony' have all been merged together. This, therefore, suggests that traditional thoughts and emotions have become blurred and confused, although the cause of this, according to Helen Dircks, seems to be that God has forsaken all the 'gallant spirits' - by which we may assume that she is referring to the dead soldiers.

Finally, at night time, she almost believes that the 'olden touch' has returned, as presumably the night hides the realities and sorrows of the day. But then, she re-asserts that hopelessness abounds, as even in sleep the war and death cannot be forgotten. The stars, which might normally signify hopes and dreams, are now reminiscent of 'wounded birds' and she implies that, as long as there are stars in the sky, the sorrow will go on.

This is an immeasurably sad poem, demonstrating the small but significant changes in civilian life - especially amongst young women - over the course of the war, which accumulated until everything was different and affected by one's personal experiences. Above all, the feeling here seems to be one of helplessness: as though these events are happening and there is nothing that can be done to stop them, or to regain that which has been lost.

Eva Dobell

BIOGRAPHICAL DETAILS

Eveline Jessie Dobell was born in Charlton Kings, near Cheltenham in Gloucestershire in the spring of 1876. She was the youngest of the three children of Clarence Dobell and his wife Emily. Their first child, also named Clarence, was born in 1870, followed by Walter in 1872. Clarence Snr., was a wine merchant, employing over forty people and the family kept several servants. Like many fairly well-to-do young ladies, Eva, as she became known, volunteered as a Voluntary Aid Detachment nurse during the First World War. As the conflict progressed, she became increasingly affected by the effects of the war on the men she was treating and her poems on the subject are some of the very finest and most thought-provoking. After the war, she campaigned for the protection of the countryside and its wildlife. Eva Dobell died in 1963.

PLUCK

This poem describes a fairly typical hospital scene, but this is done in a way which only one who had witnessed such horrors could really achieve. Eva Dobell opens with the information that the young man in question is both 'crippled' and just 'seventeen' years old. This not only sets the scene very succinctly, but also prepares the reader for the fact that what is to follow is going to be worthy of our pity. The man seems to wonder why his life has been thus affected, which also shows his innocence: an older man would probably realise that there does not always have to be a reason for such events as this. Eva Dobell then voices the question which many might fear to ask in these circumstances: namely, would it not have been better for this young man to have died, than to live on in this 'crippled' state.

In the second verse, she introduces a contrast between the 'wasted' and 'white' man lying in the bed, and the 'child' who had lied about his age in order to get into the army. A note of cynicism creeps in at the end of this verse, as Eva Dobell suggests that her readers might like to assume that this 'lie' shows how brave the young man was and yet there is an unspoken implication that she would not necessarily agree with that interpretation, which may be inferred by her use of the possessive adjective 'your', rather than 'our'.

The third verse is probably the most disturbing in its accuracy and atmosphere, as here Eva Dobell describes, with searing realism, the young man's reaction to the nurse who is about to change the dressings on his wounds. He shakes with fear and pulls the bed clothes around his head, so that no-one will be able to see his face. Despite this, his cries of panic may still be heard by everyone else.

However, when the nurse actually begins to perform her task, he can no longer hide and, instead, shows only courage as his wounds are revealed. There is only one tell-tale sign of his earlier fright: his eye lashes are still wet from crying.

Eva Dobell's comparative maturity shows through here. Although many of her fellow nurses and VADs were probably in their late teens or early twenties, she would have been around forty years of age. Therefore, she looks upon the scene she is describing, with an older and possibly more maternal perspective. There is no glorifying of death or war here and, although she mentions his courage or 'pluck', this is done with an air of simple respect, rather than gushing awe.

There are many prose descriptions of scenes such as this amongst the novels and memoirs of the war. However, this is a setting less frequently portrayed in poetry. Siegfried Sassoon and Wilfred Owen wrote poems based in hospitals, such as *The Death Bed*, *Died of Wounds* or *Conscious*, but none of these, despite their many assets, really capture that element of fear and panic in the same way as Eva Dobell has achieved here. She does not need to describe the man's wounds in any detail, because it is enough to inform us of his reaction to them. All the while, she also reminds us of his youth, especially in the contrasts which she makes with his 'adult' behaviour, such as smoking a cigarette, while his eyes are still wet with tears.

This poem stands unique amongst its type as a truthful and realistic portrayal of a heart-rending scene, into which the poet has poured little or no sentimentality, but still retained a sense of sympathy for the young man.

GRAMOPHONE TUNES

The first three verses of this poem offer a description of a hospital ward during the First World War. Eva Dobell begins by describing the gramophone records which are playing in the ward, and the male patients who sit on their beds listening, relaxing and smoking. These are, presumably, men who have been wounded some time ago, as they seem relatively active. The patients are personalised, either by the recognition of their wounds, their nationalities or their names. Their injuries are varied, but we are not given any graphic details, as the point here is really the atmosphere which the gramophone creates in the ward. It is only in the final verse that a more sombre mood begins to pervade. Here, Eva Dobell points out that to her, these songs will never hold the same meaning again. This is not, however, because they make her sad, but because they remind her of the courage of the young soldiers. In common with many other poems within this genre, the central theme here is Eva Dobell's admiration for the bravery of the patients in her care.

NIGHT DUTY

This poem opens with a simple description of a hospital ward at night, before Eva Dobell moves on to wonder what the sleeping men might be dreaming about. One of the men seems to be having a nightmare and she is curious as the cause of this. Another man seems more cheerful, causing Dobell to suppose that he is recalling his athletic past. This thought rouses her pity for the man, whose injuries have ensured that his sporting prowess is a thing of the past. Others mutter the names of loved-ones and one man, who seems perhaps a little older and more experienced than the rest, lies quite still, although Eva Dobell still imagines that his mind is cast back to his service further afield, presumably before the war. In the final verse, she asserts that these wounded men are only really present in body; their souls, or minds are as far away as the stars in the sky.

HELEN PARRY EDEN

BIOGRAPHICAL DETAILS

Helen Parry was born in 1885, the daughter of His Honour, Judge Sir Edward Parry. She was educated at Roedean School, where she gained a History Scholarship to attend Manchester University in 1902. She won the Vice-Chancellor's Prize for English Verse the following year. Then she studied painting under Byam Shaw at King's College between 1903-05.

In 1906, Helen Parry married the artist Denis Eden and they had three children: one son and two daughters. Throughout her marriage, Helen wrote poetry, short stories and literary criticisms. Denis Eden died in 1949, and Helen in December 1960.

A VOLUNTEER

Here, the poet is describing (it could be argued from a very sentimental perspective), the reason why a normally peace-loving man might choose to go to war. The subject of this poem, it would seem, has never desired to fight and does not really believe in the politics and purposes of war, which seem to hold some mystery. However, at this point in his life, he also has no other claims upon him, by which we may assume that he is probably single and childless. The description of his reaction to war suggests an element of acceptance and resignation towards the situation. In addition though, the poet implies that part of the responsibility for war lies in England's 'greed', which would be a reference to the country's pre-war Empire building strategies.

The man supposes that he wouldn't personally be any less cheerful, if the Germans dropped bombs on London, suggesting that the war should really make no difference to him. In fact, he even seems to find a positive aspect to this, in that the conflict, by not discriminating between the 'poor' of Rotherhithe, and the 'rich' of Mayfair, seems to be eradicating the class system.

The poet then asks a direct question, as to why the man enlisted, before revealing that his reason is to avoid having to explain to young children, at some point in the future, why he had failed to protect them.

This could be seen as an overly sentimental poem, because it rather romanticises the reasons behind enlistment. For some men, especially at the beginning of the war, their motives might have had more to do with a craving for adventure, to escape either from a meaningless existence, or poverty. For others the reason was a patriotic desire to protect their country and preserve their way of life. Helen Parry Eden, however, dismisses these reasons, although her solution is open to interpretation. She is either implying that he really wants to protect young children from the doom of war; or that he has enlisted because he would be ashamed not to. The first suggestion paints the man as a hero; the second is much less favourable, but judging from the general tone of the poem, this is the more likely.

Gabrielle Elliot

BIOGRAPHICAL DETAILS

An American poet, little is known of Gabrielle Elliot, although she wrote poetry for US War organisations, such as the American Fund for French Wounded and the Nursing Committee of the Council of National Defence.

PIERROT GOES TO WAR

[Pierrot is a character from the 16th Century Italian improvised theatre, Commedia dell'Arte. His personality is that of a sad clown, while his female counterpart is Pierrette. The characters became popular both before and during the First World War and were often used in fancy dress and entertainments both on the home front and for the troops.]

In this poem, Gabrielle Elliot opens with a description of two lovers parting. Her male character, whom she likens to Pierrot, goes away to fight in the war, leaving his lover Pierrette behind. The second verse essentially deals with the call to arms, suggesting that Pierrot has gone to seek glory. In the third verse, the scene changes to the trenches, while the final stanza is really about the consequences of his departure and, presumably, death.

As such, the story and message of this poem are quite straightforward: namely, the departure of a lover and what happens afterwards, both to him and to his beloved. The interesting point here is that, despite only briefly mentioning Pierrette in the first verse, the reader remains acutely aware of her throughout the whole piece, even though she is not named again until the very last word.

There is a repetitive structure to the poem, which belies the contrasts which the poet is subliminally making between the war scenes and those that come before.

Repetition is normally used to reiterate a point, not to make a contrast, but here it is used for that purpose very effectively. In verse one, the garden scene is heady with romance; the 'shadows' suggest a passionate interlude, enhanced by the moonlight and 'swaying fragrance' from the flowers. Verse three mirrors this, but now the scene has changed. The romantic garden has been replaced by 'muddy trenches' and now the 'shadows' signify dark corners, where young men, now soldiers instead of lovers, lie dead. The same effect is achieved in verses two and four. In the second stanza, the scene is almost redolent of a medieval joust, as the poet suggests that, although Pierrot has been forced to leave his Pierrette, he has effectively turned towards the light, rather than away from it. By the fourth verse, however, the 'bugles' are no longer glorious, but 'ghostly'; the 'dreams' of the past are now only 'shadows' of what they once were and we are left unsure as what has happened to Pierrette.

This final implication is that, as a lover, rather than a wife or mother, Pierrette's loss might almost go unnoticed. No-one knows what becomes of her, but by asking this in the form of a question, the poet also suggests that no-one really cares either. This was a fairly common attitude during the war: wives and mothers who lost husbands and sons found sympathy and assistance, while girlfriends, lovers and fiancées were often overlooked.

Eleanor Farjeon

BIOGRAPHICAL DETAILS

Eleanor Farjeon was born in London on 13th February 1881. Her father, Benjamin, was a writer and her mother, Margaret was the daughter of American actor, Joseph Jefferson. Eleanor, or Nellie, as the family called her, had two older brothers: Harry who was born in 1878 and Charles who was almost exactly one year older than Eleanor. Unfortunately, Charles was a sickly child and he died not long after Eleanor's birth. Joe was born in 1883 and Herbert in 1887, but it was Harry and Eleanor who became inseparable as children.

They had an exceptionally happy childhood and, although all three boys attended day schools, Eleanor was educated at home, where she quickly developed a passion for books. In 1903, Benjamin Farjeon died and the family was forced to move to a smaller house, while the three young brothers all sought work to support them. Throughout this time, Eleanor wrote poems and collaborated with Herbert in the creation of a light opera.

In 1912, Eleanor met fellow-poet, Edward Thomas and, while Eleanor's feelings for him soon matured into love, he remained devoted to his wife. Eleanor became a regular visitor at the Thomas's and, when Edward was killed in April 1917, it was Eleanor to whom his widow, Helen, turned for comfort.

After the war, Eleanor became involved with George Earl, a married English teacher. Even after his divorce, they never married, but their relationship lasted until his death in 1949. Herbert Farjeon died in 1945, followed in 1948 by Eleanor's beloved Harry. In 1950, Eleanor began a relationship with an actor named Denys Blakelock, which would last until her death on 5th June 1965.

EASTER MONDAY (IN MEMORIAM E.T.)

This poem is dedicated to Edward Thomas who died on Easter Monday, 9th April 1917. In it, Eleanor Farjeon remembers a letter which she has received from Thomas which had thanked her for a small silver egg which she had sent him as an Easter present. She had obviously sent him a box of apples to remind him of his beloved home, and had concealed the egg amongst them. This simple gift and the thought behind it must have touched Edward Thomas and moved him to write a letter of thanks to Eleanor.

She recalls that on that occasion, Easter Monday had been a seemingly glorious spring day during which she had spent some time in the garden (presumably at the family home in Fellows Road). She remarks on the outward signs of the coming of spring. Edward's letter had been written on the eve of a battle, and this sense of impending doom is reiterated in the second verse as Eleanor realises that after this day, her life will be changed for ever - it was the following evening that she learned of Edward's death. She remembers the letters she has written to him which he will never receive.

This poem was written after its given date of 9th April 1917, but it is about that day, and shows the impact of the death of Edward Thomas on Eleanor Farjeon. She saw him not only as the great unrequited love of her life, but also as a soulmate: someone with whom she had so much to share - their love of poetry, the countryside and nature.

The tone of *Easter Monday* is similar to that employed by many other home-front poets, such as Vera Brittain and Edith Nesbit. There is an element of regret for what has been lost and Eleanor Farjeon mingles this sadness with fond memories of the person who has died. Like Edith Nesbit in *The Fields of Flanders*, Eleanor also mentions the joy and hope that come with the arrival of each new spring before reminding us of the sorrow that would come to dominate the lives of those left behind.

PEACE

In this poem, Eleanor Farjeon begins by describing the various attributes of peace, which, it would seem, she does not view as an entirely positive or permanent state. She compares peace with war, describing both in similar terms. Peace, she implies, is merely one of the inevitable consequences of war. In peacetime memories of war are like an ugly scar which serves only to remind the survivors of the madness that has gone before. Her description of the war as glamourous is interesting as many young men (and women) had thought of the war in those terms, particularly in the early days. Yet once the fighting dies down, battles can be viewed more realistically and war does not seem glamourous any more. It becomes clear that Eleanor regards peace as a mere interlude between wars. This, she says, should be a time for reflection and for counting the cost. Peace should provide an opportunity for men to re-evaluate their position and take stock - to look back on what has happened with a more critical eye - as historians will do in years to come.

Eleanor asserts that all nations are to blame - they are greedy for growth and victory and they do not care how many generations of men must be sacrificed in the process of achieving their aims. She believes that peace shines a revealing light on the ambitions of the warmongers, which should enable them to see the consequences of their actions. However, she appears to believe that these nations behave more like predators than the conventional doves of peace: preferring to pursue a course of hatred than one of love and friendship.

Next, Eleanor paints an even more negative picture of peace. War, she says, is a crime - and the only righteous quality of peace is to put an end to this senseless activity. In peacetime, the fear of death and war is finished, but again she implies that this relaxation is a temporary state and that peace can bring even more uncertainty than war. Although in times of war the people must learn to cope with their anxieties, at least they know what it is that they are afraid of. Peace brings a different type of apprehension - one which, if allowed to develop, can paralyse the nation in fear, just as if it had looked upon the face of Medusa and turned to stone. (Medusa was a character, known as a Gorgon, in Greek mythology who had snakes for hair and eyes that turned the beholder to stone). Eleanor seems to imply that the warmongers believe the only way avert this stagnation is war and the nationalist fervour which war promotes.

Peace gives men more freedom and allows individual countries to prove themselves as worthy, or otherwise, by their actions and reactions. Finally Eleanor challenges the war-loving nations to put an end to talk of hatred and speak instead of love. However, she puts her final point in the form of a question, which remains unanswered. This suggests that she does not hold out much hope that her request will be heard or adhered to.

This thought-provoking poem is a harsh indictment on those responsible for the war. Eleanor Farjeon does not seem to blame any one particular country or group of countries, but she asserts that all nations involved should share an equal burden of responsibility. Somewhat prophetically, she sees such periods of peace as a mere pause in the fighting which she thinks will inevitably continue until such time as one nation has the courage to put aside their fears and hatred and build a future based on love and hope.

'NOW THAT YOU TOO'

This poem is addressed to a soldier who is about to embark for the front. The soldier in question may have been Edward Thomas, although there is no evidence for this, or the poem may have been directed more generally, to the many men who went away to war, and the women they left behind.

The second and third lines of the first verse are particularly interesting: Eleanor Farjeon describes the war-years in terms of bloodshed and weariness; she implies that the number of dead is so vast that it cannot even be counted and that every day brings news of another hoard who have vanished and will never return. She re-asserts this by suggesting that the world will never know this number of young men again. In this she seems to be implying that the war will have far-reaching and costly consequences for generations to come.

Then, in the desperate tones of a young lover, she reminds us of the sorrow of parting - the effort required not to spoil a final meeting by dwelling too much on what might happen, but struggling to enjoy a last farewell, while holding on to happy memories. She remembers that, while both parties are mortal, their love for each other is not and this will live on in the future, whatever that may bring.

Even if this poem is not addressed to one particular soldier, the description of a final farewell is very poignantly written. The hopeless anguish of saying goodbye to a loved-one for the last time comes through especially well in this poem because at the beginning, we are told that there is no hope - so many have gone this way before. The description of seeing, hearing and feeling everything for the last time, implies that if he dies, her life will also end and yet she is resigned to this because their fate lies elsewhere. Thus, although this is a sad and reflective poem, which begins with talk of death, fear and loss, it ends on a more positive note - of love.

S. GERTRUDE FORD

BIOGRAPHICAL DETAILS

This American poet was a tireless campaigner for women's rights - a subject on which she wrote often. She submitted her poetry to many periodicals, as well as publishing volumes of her own work and editing for other writers and authors.

A FIGHT TO THE FINISH

This poem, in the form of five rhyming couplets, makes a series of statements, which are followed by questions or arguments which challenge those views. Each couplet begins with a rather gung-ho or jingoistic declaration, always in support of the war and ends with a mocking statement. However, the tone of this poem rather spoils its message, as it is overtly sentimental, creating an emotive atmosphere. This poem appeared in a volume of the same title, published in 1917 and throughout this, Ford's feminism and outrage are the most obvious convictions, which are also echoed in this piece.

NATURE IN WAR-TIME

In this poem, written before or during 1917, Ford depicts a fairly common theme amongst First World War poets: namely, the effects which the battles have on their natural surroundings. She describes the birds as 'homeless', because there are no longer any trees in which they can nest. The meadows are 'scarred', there are no grass or flowers and the streams are no longer 'clear', but 'fouled'. All of this, in the first two verses, is written with an underlying question as to whether or not this really matters. The birds are, after all, just sharing man's fate, as the local people would have evacuated and left their homes too. Ford wonders whether the trees and fields will 'mourn' and 'grieve' for their losses, which also reminds us of these human traits. In the final verse, she makes a more direct comparison, by explaining that the daffodils which once grew in the area have been replaced only by the wind and guns. Therefore, Ford's message here could be said to be a realisation that nature and man are more closely linked than one might like to suppose and that both will take many years to recover from the damage wrought by war.

THE TENTH ARMISTICE DAY

This poem, which we must assume was written in 1928, provides a perspective of the war and its aftermath, from ten years later. It opens with the recollection of the first Armistice day, when war ended and people rejoiced. Then Ford goes on to wonder whether people have actually forgotten what the war was really like and the one man who, according to her, was responsible for bringing peace to the world. She asserts that Woodrow's words of wisdom and hope should mingle with those of the dead soldiers, whom she presumes do not crave flowers or remembrance, but want people to rebuild their lives and ensure that the poor do not go hungry. However, in the second part of the poem, Ford concedes that on Armistice Day, at least, people should remember the fallen. She advocates that they ought to take flowers to the Cenotaph to commemorate the dead and goes on to name those flowers: the rose, which traditionally represents England; 'amaranth' which is a mystical flower which never dies and poppies which had, by 1928 become established as the flower most representative of the war dead. Ford then asserts that the dead are entitled to ask for one more thing: namely lasting peace, which she believes can only be achieved through the auspices of the League of Nations.

Like many of S Gertrude Ford's poems, this one contains a political and moral message: that there is little point in dwelling on the past, when men should really be building a future. Unfortunately, the future to which she aspired would falter, when the League of Nations floundered, due in no small part to America's failure to join the organisation.

ELIZABETH CHANDLER FORMAN

BIOGRAPHICAL DETAILS

Although little is known of Elizabeth Chandler Forman, it is believed that she was born in 1883 and lived in London.

THE THREE LADS

This simple poem basically offers three very similar portrayals of men, one German, one Russian and one English, who are all riding off to war for, essentially, the same reason. Each one believes that he has God, freedom and truth on his side; that his own ruler is supreme and that he is doing his duty, by protecting those whom he loves. Each verse gives a slightly different description of the physical countryside through which each 'lad' is riding, which serves to highlight the similarities in their reasons for going.

It could be said that this poem provides a fairly elementary explanation as to why men go to war. Alternatively, this could be seen as a more ironic suggestion that, if they are all going to fight for the same reason, is there really any need for a war in the first place.

Lillian Gard

BIOGRAPHICAL DETAILS

Another poet of whom little is known, other than the fact that she received the dubious accolade of having Dylan Thomas try to pass off one of her poems as his own!

HER 'ALLOWANCE'!

Poems like this are written in a conversational and colloquial tone, for a reason, which is normally to make them seem more down-to-earth and representative of the working classes. However, when read today, they can sometimes be quite difficult to understand. The easiest solution is, while bearing in mind the style in which the poem was written, to re-write it in more conventional language and, therefore, be more readily able to understand its meaning.

In this case, the poet's message is the struggle faced by those who are left at home. The narrator believes that those around her are judging her, based on their reactions to the appearance of herself and her children. She defends herself vehemently, before going on to pray for her husband, who is away fighting.

MURIEL ELSIE GRAHAM

BIOGRAPHICAL DETAILS

There are no verifiable biographical details available for Muriel Elsie Graham.

THE LARK ABOVE THE TRENCHES

As an introduction to this poem, there is a short excerpt which explains that some entrenched French soldiers had been filled with hope by the sound of a lark singing. The setting for this scene and the poem which follows is also given as February 1915, which immediately conjures up an image in the reader's mind, of extreme cold.

The first verse opens by recreating this scene of a frozen land, being wasted by gunfire, but ends with the introduction of the birdsong, referred to earlier. In the second verse, the poem basically repeats herself, although the scene here is on a larger scale, so she is not describing a single set of men in a trench, but a whole landscape which has been ruined. Again, the lark and its song are introduced at the end of the verse, contrasting with the earlier barren imagery.

The final verse describes the men's reactions to the birdsong. They are cheered and given hope, not only by the sound itself, but also by the promise of spring which accompanies the returning birds.

This poem features two fairly common themes: that with each new spring comes hope and that the war is inflicting terrible damage upon the countryside. The former of these two subjects tended to die out as the war progressed, but was quite popular in the spring of 1915.

THE BATTLE OF THE SWAMPS

This poem, we might assume, is probably set in 1917, during the Third Battle of Ypres, also known as Passchendaele, when prolonged and heavy rain resulted in the whole area becoming flooded, turning the mud into a quagmire, in which it was not unheard of for men and horses to drown. Here, we are offered a description of these scenes in the first two verses. In the third, however, the poet turns her attention to the home-front and the reactions of those left behind, to the pouring rain. The poet makes good use of metaphors throughout, which helps the reader to identify with the scene which she is creating.

Nora Griffiths

BIOGRAPHICAL DETAILS

There are no verifiable biographical details available for Nora Griffiths.

THE WYKHAMIST

'Wykhamist' is a term describing a student or graduate of Winchester College, which was founded in the 14th Century by William of Wykeham, the Bishop of Winchester.

In this poem, Nora Griffiths describes the scene in the Hampshire town where the boys and young men of Winchester College, used to dwell. She recounts a dusky setting, where many of the sights and sounds seem to have taken on a ghostly aspect, which is further enhanced by her use of words such as 'wake', 'pallid' and 'mystery', which all suggest death.

In the second half of the poem, although the same atmosphere pervades, Nora Griffiths changes the aim of the piece slightly and addresses herself more directly to 'The Wykhamist', reminding him of his experiences while at the College. Finally, we learn that the young man in question has 'died of wounds', although even here, the poet seems to harbour some doubt, since she only knows this because someone else has 'told her'. She also believes that she can still hear his footsteps, along with many others, on the streets around the College.

Schools such as Winchester lost a great many of their young men during the war and this poem provides us with a home-front, female perspective of such losses.

Diana Gurney

BIOGRAPHICAL DETAILS

There are no verifiable biographical details available for Diana Gurney.

THE FALLEN

The Fallen is, ostensibly a poem about those who have died during the First World War and who are remembered by those left behind. However, in the final line, it also becomes clear that there is a secondary group of people who have also 'fallen' - namely those who grieve.

The setting for this poem is Christmas and it would seem to be after the end of the war, so possibly 1918 or 1919. The poem opens with a question, which suggests some doubt over whether mourners should lay a 'holly wreath' at the base of a memorial. Diana Gurney justifies this by her hope that in doing so, the dead will, somehow become aware that they are not forgotten. She then goes on to paint a somewhat rose-tinted view of death, describing the men as 'sleeping' and 'quiet', before adding that, while they have given up happiness, they need no longer feel sad either. Finally, she explains her perspective by pointing out that the real 'sorrow' and 'loss' belong to those who mourn the dead.

This is just the type of poem which one could easily imagine angering someone like Siegfried Sassoon, who was known for his dislike of women who tried to claim sympathy for themselves, while underplaying the sacrifices made by the men involved. Diana Gurney's perspective of a soldier's death and a seemingly glorious and happy afterlife are completely unrealistic and, when taken in conjunction with the emphasis which she places on her own 'sorrow' and 'loss', in which she seems to belittle the dead, this piece is, indeed rather distasteful.

CICELY HAMILTON

BIOGRAPHICAL DETAILS

Cicely Mary Hammill was born on 15th June 1872 in Paddington, London. Her father Danzil Hammill was an officer in the Gordon Highlanders and he and Cicely's mother, Maude, were frequently away from home. When Cicely was ten years old, her mother was committed to an asylum, so Cicely and her three siblings were cared for by foster parents and family members. Following her education at boarding school, Cicely briefly became a school teacher, but soon tired of this and went on to be an actress, at which point, she changed her name to Hamilton. When her acting career faltered, she turned her hand to writing plays, some of which were quite successful. She also became involved in the Womens Suffrage movement, writing both books and plays on the subject. During the First World War, Hamilton worked in a hospital in France and then in 1917, she formed a repertory company to entertain the troops. After the war, she became a journalist and also continued to write books until her death in 1952.

NON-COMBATANT

This poem is really about the female role and feminism during the First World War. Cicely Hamilton was a firm supporter of the Women's Suffrage movement and here, she is explaining her feelings, and those of women who shared her viewpoint.

In the first verse, she explains that before the war even started, she - or to be more precise, women in general - had been wounded by the system. Her reference to 'War-Lords' is a direct allusion to the politicians of the day, whom she not only accuses of creating the war, but also of waging war on women. The second verse makes reference to the supposed perception that women, and especially feminists, served no useful purpose, other than to orate. Hamilton describes herself, both here and at the beginning of the third verse, as ready and willing to 'give', but also affirms that there is no-one who actually needs her.

The fourth verse really just describes Hamilton's feelings of uselessness and a longing to be acknowledged as having something worth offering to society. Finally, at the end of the poem, we learn of her solution. She will suffer quietly and patiently all of the indignities of wounded 'pride' because she knows that her sacrifice is small when compared to those who 'give a life'.

This is a rather thought-provoking poem, in that it explains quite well the frustrations of the feminists who found that their message was no longer relevant, or attracted sympathy, but also that their role had changed anyway. Despite the increased power and position afforded to women during the war, which gave them more freedom than they'd had before, most realised that the leaders of the day - all of them men - were only tolerating the involvement of women in the conflict because they had no alternative.

Helen Hamilton

BIOGRAPHICAL DETAILS

Very little is known about Helen Hamilton, other than the fact that she was a school teacher. In 1922, she published a book entitled *Mountain Madness* in which she recounted her experiences of rock climbing in the Alps.

THE GHOULS

Here, we can see a fairly unusual female poet, in that Helen Hamilton is not seeking self-glorification, or gratitude for the role of her own sex, and is in fact being rather critical of those who, in her view, seem to take some satisfaction in the conflict. This poem's subjects are the older women, who seem to rather enjoy reading the casualty lists, searching for a familiar name, through which they may be able to draw attention to themselves. Helen Hamilton paints a very unfavourable picture of these women who, with no useful purpose left in their own lives, now 'gloat' upon the misfortunes of others. Although this is quite an unusual poem, this subject has been touched upon elsewhere in First World War literature. In Helen Zenna Smith's novel *Not So Quiet...*, Mrs Smith delights in keeping score with her friends as to which of them has sacrificed the most by 'giving' their offspring to the cause.

THE JINGO-WOMAN

This is probably one of the most well-known poems by a lesser-known female poet. Here, as in the *The Ghouls*, Helen Hamilton targets her own sex, although now her subjects are not the old women, but the younger ones, who dish out white feathers to men whom they decide should be fighting. Helen Hamilton's judgement of these women, whose viewpoint she clearly does not share, is uncompromising. She defends the non-combatant men, pointing out that they are not all shirkers and that many have tried, and failed, to enlist, thus making them 'twice-insulted'. Indeed, Hamilton goes on to praise these men for their 'forbearance' in dealing with such women.

It is in the final part of this poem that Hamilton's message really comes into its own, as she suggests that, when all the men have been killed, women will be called upon to fight. She sarcastically wonders whether they will be so keen to 'do their bit' as they are to ensure that others do it for them. The final sentence is both pertinent and perfectly put, since it quite simply is not 'decent' to expect someone else to do something which you are not prepared to do yourself.

While it must be said that there were a great many women who did not go around handing out white feathers to men whom they deemed too cowardly to fight, those that did were generally rather superior and arrogant about their self-appointed role and were, hopefully, suitably shamed by Hamilton's fitting riposte.

THE ROMANCING POET

In this poem, Helen Hamilton turns her attention to other poets, who romanticise about the war, although again her subject is the attitude of her fellow women. She opens this poem with the suggestion that while others might write better poetry than her own, she would prefer it if they did not try to glorify the war, or their own role. She also calls for a degree of accuracy and realism in these poems, claiming that to write in such a lyrical fashion is really an 'insult to the men'.

This poem suffers, unfortunately, from a rather ineffective ending, which is a shame as Hamilton's message is quite valid. Many, including Hamilton herself, have accused her of writing bad poetry, which may or may not be the case and is surely a matter of personal preference. What is beyond doubt, however, is her unfailing ability to capture a scene and a mood, which must have reflected the views of many.

ADA M. HARRISON

BIOGRAPHICAL DETAILS

Very little is known about Ada Harrison, other than the fact that, during the war, she was studying at Newnham College, Cambridge.

NEW YEAR 1916

The opening line of this poem seems to be a reference to Psalm 115, verse 17, which says 'The dead praise not the Lord, neither any that go down into silence' and provides an introduction to the remainder of the poem. The first verse initially contradicts this statement, by pointing out that the men have not died or 'gone down' in silence, presumably because there has been a great deal of noise associated with death in battle. Ordinarily, of course, silence might well attend death, but not in this case, and neither are there any 'tears' or 'Grief' present at their passing. In fact, it appears that, according to this poet at least, the dead soldiers have gained nothing - not even recognition of their years of life and service.

In the second verse, we learn that nothing has changed; the war continues and people live their lives just as they did before. At the very end of the poem, however, Ada Harrison seems to contradict herself by saying that even the 'dust' is full of admiration for the dead soldiers, by which she probably means that their sacrifices have not really gone as unnoticed as it might seem. Like many female poets and non-combatants, the central theme in Ada Harrison's poem is gratitude, which is accompanied in this case by an air of shame that, in her view, not enough is done to recognise the efforts of the soldiers.

Mary H. J. Henderson

BIOGRAPHICAL DETAILS

Very little is known about Mary Henderson, other than the details that she was a native of Durham in the north-east of England; she served as a nurse during the First World War and in 1918, she published a volume of poetry entitled *In War and Peace*.

AN INCIDENT

In this poem, Mary Henderson makes many comparisons between the plight of wounded or dying soldiers, and the crucifixion of Christ. In addition, the role of women during the war is likened to that of Mary, the mother of Jesus.

The poem opens with the description of a scene in which the poet, in her capacity of nurse, attends the bedside of a young soldier, while a doctor changes the dressings on his wounded hands. Henderson describes these wounds as being more distressing than those which, according to religious texts, were inflicted on Jesus Christ, when he was nailed through his hands, to a cross and crucified. In the second verse, the poet relates how, due to his wounded hands, she had to help the young man to eat and drink, just as though he had been a child and she his mother.

At the end of this verse, Henderson makes a direct comparison between the mother of Jesus and 'all women' who, in her view have followed in the same footsteps of raising their sons and then seeing them sacrificed. The third verse of this poem shows a change of scene, as the poet suggests that each death on the battlefield is comparable to the death of Christ. She asserts that every man is as worthy as Christ himself, and not only to his own mother, but to the country for which he is giving his life.

This poem is one of many which draws on religion and religious imagery and makes either a contrast or a comparison with a biblical scene, character or story. These include *The Parable of the Old Man and the Young* by Wilfred Owen, *Christ and the Soldier* by Siegfried Sassoon and *Goliath and David* by Robert Graves.

Agnes Grozier Herbertson

BIOGRAPHICAL DETAILS

Agnes Grozier Herbertson was born in Oslo, Norway in 1875. Her parents, James and Jessie had moved to Norway three years earlier, when James was appointed as local representative for shipping agents, Henderson Brothers. In 1873, their first daughter, Annie was born, followed by Agnes two years later. By 1876 the family had moved to Paris and it was here that their first son, Thomas was born. A third daughter, Jessie was born in 1878 and Isabel followed in 1881. By this time the family were back in James Herbertson's native Scotland, although their final child, another son, named James, was born in Liverpool. Initially, all of the children were educated at home, but before long, Agnes was sent to a boarding school called Cumberland Lodge in Croydon, Surrey. By the time that Agnes had completed her education, the family had moved to St Albans in Hertfordshire and james Herbertson had become a Quantity Surveyor, enabling them to have a more settled life. By the time Agnes reached the age of 26, she had already become a published author. In March 1901, tragedy struck the family when Agnes's youngest sister, Isabel died, followed shortly afterwards by the death of her mother. Over the years, although Agnes was a poet and journalist, she became best known for her children's stories, which are mainly fantasies or legends, such as tales of knights and dragons.

AIRMAN, RFC

This poem gives the impression of having been written during the Second World War, when Agnes Grozier Herbertson would have been in her mid-sixties. She tells the story here of a former pilot, who served with the Royal Flying Corps during the First World War and who, in the more recent conflict, compares his own service with that of Royal Air Force pilots in the Second World War.

Set at night, the poem opens with the older pilot listening to the sounds of aircraft overhead. He reflects upon their mission and remembers back to his own days as a pilot, contemplating the sights and sounds to which he had been a witness. In the second verse, this pilot begins to make comparisons between the pilots of the modern war and himself, and especially notes the cavalier attitude for which both the RFC and the RAF pilots have become renowned.

Finally, he offers up a prayer that the young pilots will survive unharmed and hopes that, after the war, their world will be a better place than his had been for him. This closing statement offers an insight into the perspective of many of lived through both conflicts. During the First World War, people believed that their sacrifices would be leading to a better world and many were disappointed by the reality which greeted them at the end of the conflict, especially when, after a gap of merely twenty-one years, the world was, once again, in the throes of a world war. This poem brings to life that sense of disillusion and sorrow, together with the notion of a shared understanding between the older and younger generations of fighters.

THE SEED MERCHANT'S SON

The opening couplet of this poem immediately reveals the fact that the seed-merchant's son has died and that he was an only and much-beloved boy. The second verse discloses the boy's youth: the narrator remembers the young man as a child, although this may also refer to the fact that the boy had seemed much older than his years when he left for the war, in his uniform, when in reality he was still so young. There could also be an inference here that the boy was underage. This is reiterated in the following lines, where the emphasis is clearly on the young man's youthful appearance and boyish qualities. The image of the merchant's son running across the fields also brings to mind a picture of the boy crossing No-Man's Land, full of innocence and enthusiasm. This takes us into the next verse, where we are given a description of the young man. Again, the reference to his long legs and fair hair serve to remind us that his fitness and good-looks are irrelevant now: the magnificence of his youth has been lost. Also, this description makes the young man's plight more personal to the reader as one can now picture a tall, fair-haired youth, so he has lost his anonymity. Then, we are reminded of the effect of his death on others, as the narrator recalls that just seeing the young man could make people feel young again, which demonstrates the boy's popularity, in that he must have attracted attention.

In the next verse, the boy's youth is once again, reinforced as we are told that he had barely left school. This strengthens the suggestion that he had not in fact been old enough to enlist in the first place. It would also seem that the boy may have been keen to follow in his father's footsteps, as he had put away his books, in favour of an outdoor life. Next, there follows the first mention of the war and this contrasts with the previous verses, which concentrate on the young man himself, rather than the manner of his death. It would seem that the narrator assumes that death would have come as a surprise to this young man, again suggesting that he has led a happy and innocent life. There could also be a hint here of the invulnerability of youth: the assumption, that the very young tend to make, that they are somehow immune from danger. It could also be inferred from this statement that the young man's death occurred quite early in the war, as he has not had time to become accustomed to the loss of life and also that he maybe looked upon the war, in common with many others of his generation, as a bit of an adventure.

In the next couplet, the narrator points out that life goes on; the seed-merchant must continue as before, despite his son's death. We also learn that he is a familiar figure, clearly recognisable to his neighbours. The father, it would seem, is quite old, suggesting that he may have hoped to be able to rely on his son in the near future and, possibly retire himself. However, all hopes for the time to come are gone now and the merchant seems older than ever. This echoes the notion in verse four, that the young man had been able to inspire youthful feelings in others.

The narrator now questions how others react to the seed-merchant; what is there to be said which can make up for his loss? Despite wanting to help the old man, the narrator remains merely an observer, watching how still the old man is: so still in fact that the birds are not frightened by him, but fly around his head. These two couplets tell us that the man is not working: in fact he is just standing in the field, like a statue and this makes him appear less than human. This may imply that the narrator thinks the old man's reaction is not as emotional as might be expected. We are also reminded of his age again, by the description of his grey hair.

It would seem from reading the next verse, that the man may have been standing still for some time, as the narrator comments that no-one was able to understand the man's behaviour - suggesting that the narrator may not have been the only observer. Once again, we are reminded that the man is not working, as he simply looks down at the ground and at the seeds which he is holding in his hand. Perhaps this is because the man is trying to reconcile his life with the death of his son.

These once familiar things now seem strange to him, as though he is seeing everything for the first time. This may reflect the man's feelings that the seeds bring new life - possibly even that through their new growth, his son, who clearly loved the countryside, may live on. The man then thanks God - this is the first sound or movement he has made and yet it seems incongruous that he should be grateful to God at this time. There could be more than one interpretation of this: it may be that the seed-merchant is grateful to still have something left in his life - namely his work and the countryside, through which, like the seeds in his hand, he can begin again. Alternatively, the man may be thanking God for the preservation of his way of life: that his son did not die in vain, but like so many others, for the love of his country.

The first point of interest is the title. Agnes Grozier Herbertson has chosen a seed-merchant for the subject of her poem, which could be for two reasons: the seeds represent re-birth and life continuing, while the fact that the man is a merchant shows that she wished to demonstrate the impact of the war on an ordinary man. The dead man is the merchant's son, which reflects the poet's own age and experiences. She would have been thirty-nine years old when the war started and may have found it easier to equate her own feelings with those of a parent, rather than a child, spouse or lover.

There is no mention in the poem of the seed-merchant's wife and there could be more than one explanation for this. Possibly, we are meant to infer that his wife is no longer alive, which may be why he and his son were so close. Alternatively, it may be that this has been done intentionally so that the reader focuses on the impact of the boy's death on a normally strong and well-respected man, rather than on the boy's mother - which would be a more common viewpoint. During the time of the First World War, men were expected to hide their emotions and Agnes Grozier Herbertson may want her readers to realise that the death of a beloved child could have just as much significance to a father, as a mother.

Agnes may have witnessed such parental grief at first-hand, when her youngest sister, Isabel died early in 1901. For the Herbertson family, this tragedy was compounded when Agnes's mother, Jessie also died within six months. Agnes's father, James, was a normal working man and witnessing his reaction to these losses may have inspired her to write this piece to demonstrate the male perspective of grief.

Another inference which may be drawn in this respect is that the poet wanted to show a parent's loss of control over his son's life. The merchant had come to rely on his son, but like many fathers, would have also wanted to protect his child and now he can do neither of these things, as the war has taken his son's innocence as well as his life, leaving the merchant with little more than a handful of seeds and his memories. It would seem, however, that he is grateful even for these small mercies. His gratitude to God also reflects the strength of his faith as, despite everything, he can still demonstrate his beliefs.

In many ways, this is a typical home-front poem, with its central theme of the devastating effects of the death of the merchant's son. Most poems within this genre, however, look at how this event impacts on a lover, wife or mother and it is, therefore, quite unusual to be given this male perspective of grief. Agnes Grozier Herbertson makes one realise that the man has not just lost his beloved son, but also his hopes and ambitions for the future. He will no longer be able to pass his business on to his son, so eventually that too will end and his own future is much less certain. Many female poets of the First World War wrote about how their losses affected them - as in *Perhaps* by Vera Brittain or *Praematuri* by Margaret Postgate Cole. Theirs is a personal voice, either about the loss of a specific person, or about the deaths of many friends, without whom these women's lives are shown to be forever changed. In *The Seed-Merchant's Son*, however, we are given a more general picture of someone else's grief, no less devastating, for all the merchant's restraint.

This poem has something in common with Charlotte Mew's *May 1915*. Both poets use the idea of re-birth as a means of coping with grief. Charlotte Mew asserts that, eventually, the spring will return to the wasted lands and that, despite their current miseries, those who have lost a loved-one will one day be able to experience the positive side of life again. Agnes Grozier Herbertson also reminds us of the power of nature to overcome human losses, as the seeds appear to signify a new beginning. As such, both pieces have an air of optimism: grief may seem to consume, but there is still hope.

MAY HERSCHEL-CLARKE

BIOGRAPHICAL DETAILS

Little is known about May Herschel-Clarke, although it is believed she was born in 1850 and wrote one volume of poetry in 1917.

FOR VALOUR

This poem is told from the perspective of an older woman, who has lost her son, although in dying, he had been awarded a Victoria Cross, 'for valour'. Initially, the poet describes the medal as having been created from the features and physical attributes of her son, which are, she asserts also her own characteristics, since he is her flesh and blood.

She then goes on to relate the manner of her son's death, which has been told to her in a letter, which also reveals that his last thoughts and words were of her. Finally, the poet admits to sorrow that she had been 'so far away' from her son when he died and declares that, by any standards, she has done her bit for the war effort.

This is a conversational poem, in which the poet would appear to be discussing her own situation with a third party, who does not actually take part, but whose presence may be inferred from the content of the piece. As such, the language used here is colloquial and, possibly regional, which may account for the use of the word 'jest', instead of 'just'. Alternatively, the poet may have intended this as ironic play on words, using the word 'jest' to signify a joke, thus implying that the medal and her son's death in earning it, are akin to a farce or travesty, or even that the medal is a poor substitute for her son's young life. Like many of the female poets, especially the older ones, May Hershel-Clarke's main theme here is the waste of young, brave men, but also the sacrifices of the loved-ones whom they left behind.

NOTHING TO REPORT

Despite being very brief, this poem is actually quite difficult to interpret. However, one should bear in mind initially that May Hershel-Clarke was probably quite old during the First World War (based on the tone and content of her other poems, including *For Valour* and *The Mother*). Therefore, we might assume here that the situation, and death, which she is describing does not relate directly to the war, but to the home front. She is probably, therefore, relating an account of an older couple who are, in one minute, happy and enjoying themselves and then, in the next moment, the husband dies quite suddenly. Despite this personal loss, the newspapers report that there is 'nothing' happening, because they are concerned only with the war and the men at the front, and not with the lives of those at home. There is an underlying bitterness here which suggests that May Hershel-Clarke believed that the people at home were being forgotten, because all of the country's focus was on the war.

TERESA HOOLEY

BIOGRAPHICAL DETAILS

Teresa Mary Hooley was born in 1888 at Risley in Derbyshire. She was the second of the three children, and the only daughter, of Terah and Mary Hooley. Her father was a lace manufacturer and all three children were initially educated at home before attending boarding schools. Her younger brother, Basil, served during the First World War, as a Major in the 7th Battalion of the Sherwood Foresters. He was awarded the Military Cross late in the war - his citation appearing in the London Gazette on 11th November 1918. By this time, however, Basil was already dead. Having contracted influenza, he died at home at Risley Lodge in Derbyshire on 28th October, leaving a widow. Teresa Hooley wrote of her brother's death in a poem entitled *To My Brother*. She also knew Theodore Percival Cameron Wilson, who served with her brother and who also wrote war poetry. He was killed in March 1918 and Teresa recalled his life in a poem entitled *In Memoriam*. When Teresa married, her son, who was born in 1924, was named Basil in memory of her late brother. She continued to write poetry throughout her life and died in 1973.

A WAR FILM

This poem was published in a volume of the poet's work entitled *Songs of All Seasons* in 1927 and may, therefore, have been written some time after the end of the First World War. This supposition is supported by the fact that, in this poem, Teresa Hooley mentions her infant son, who was born in 1924.

In this poem, the poet describes watching a 'war film' in which she sees the retreat from Mons, which took place in August 1914; she relates the bravery and fortitude of the 'Old Contemptibles' (the nickname given to the men of the British Regular Army, who were virtually wiped out in the first few weeks of the war).

When the film is finished, she goes outside and seems quite surprised that life is actually quite normal. She returns home and bathes her little boy, being more affectionate than normal, because of the images which she had seen in the earlier film. She imagines how she might feel if her own child were to be called upon to fight in a war. She recalls her son as being part of herself, having spent nine months (or 'moons', as she puts it) carrying him, but then realises that those soldiers' mothers must have felt exactly the same as she does. Her son, meanwhile, being only very young, has no understanding of her fears and thinks that her kisses are part of a game.

This poem explains the feelings of all mothers, who did not lose a son in the war, or whose sons were born too late to participate and it is easy to imagine their sense of gratitude that they are not being called upon to make the same sacrifices as an earlier generation of mothers. It is also interesting to note, with the benefit of hindsight, that for all her hopes and fears, Basil Butler, Teresa Hooley's son, might well have served in the Second World War.

ELINOR JENKINS

BIOGRAPHICAL DETAILS

Little is known about Elinor Jenkins, other than the fact that she published a volume of poetry in 1915, simply entitled *Poems*. The book is dedicated to 'H. S. T.', which may refer to Harry Spottiswoode Trevor, who served with the Royal Engineers and who died on 15th August 1915, aged 26. He is buried at Cabaret-Rouge British Cemetery at Souchez.

DULCE ET DECORUM?

Published in 1960, the poem's title is the Roman numeral for 1914 - the year in The title of this poem has nothing to do with Wilfred Owen's poem of similar name, but like Owen's version, refers to the Roman poet Horace's Odes and means 'sweet and meet'. The full quotation would be 'Dulce et Decorum est Pro Patria Mori', which translates as 'It is sweet and meet to die for one's country'. In this case, like Owen, Elinor Jenkins has telegraphed the irony of her title by adding a question mark, which shows that she does not take seriously Horace's suggestion, which was propounded by many at the time of the First World War.

The poem opens with a burial scene, which represents the many interments that took place during the war. To each family, their lost loved-one was their 'dearest', and many who performed the duty of burial on the field of battle, chose a landmark, such as a tree, so that in theory, the grave would be more easily found afterwards.

The second verse opens with a somewhat romanticised image of the dead: their youth, intelligence and bravery forever preserved. Then, however, Elinor Jenkins changes her tone and reminds us that the dead are just that: dead, and that once buried, all they do is provide food for worms. In the third verse, she begins to assume some of the blame for these deaths. This verse does not suggest that a soldier's loved-ones carried out the physical burials, because that would have been impossible. Instead, Jenkins asserts that they are, nonetheless, responsible for each soldier's death, presumably because they allowed them to go to war in the first place.

The fourth verse likens the bent 'hawthorn' tree to a grieving woman, as it seems to weep over the grave of the young man, covering him with a metaphorical 'shroud'. In the final verse, the tone changes yet again. All notions of sadness and regret are gone; replaced by a defiance that those who are left behind should mimic their forebears and take up arms to avenge the dead, just as they would have done in more ancient times.

The messages in this poem are somewhat mixed and confused. There is sadness, regret, guilt, blame, realism and a desire for revenge which, while complicated, may be a true reflection of the complex emotions through which many civilians went during the war.

Anna Gordon Keown

BIOGRAPHICAL DETAILS

Anna Gordon Keown was born at Edmonton, London in early 1897. She was the third child of Robert and Sarah Keown, both of whom came from Ireland. During the First World War, Anna's brother Robert White Keown served as a Second Lieutenant in the 7th Battalion of the East Kent Regiment. Over the course of the conflict, he was promoted to Captain and in 1917 was mentioned in dispatches and awarded the Military Cross. Robert survived the First World War, but served again with the East Kents, also known as The Buffs, at the rank of Brevet Major during the Second World War and was reported missing on 2nd June 1940 during the evacuation from Dunkirk. His body was never found and he is commemorated on the Dunkirk Memorial. Anna married Philip Gosse, son of the eminent author and critic, Edmund Gosse, who had been a great influence upon Siegfried Sassoon in his younger years. Although he was nearly twenty years her senior, Philip and Anna were an extremely close couple and he was devastated by her death in 1957.

REPORTED MISSING

This poem opens with the writer's assertion that she will never be able to accept the death of the person to whom this piece is addressed. His laughter still rings in her ears, despite the peace of her surroundings. It may be that everything is quiet because the people around her are in mourning, or this description may be used to contrast her current situation with the noise of war or the sounds which he made when he was alive. Her description of his features shows a profound familiarity with the subject, echoing her assertion that she can still hear his laughter. These statements reinforce the idea that he is not dead. She seems to believe that not even death can rob her of his vitality, which almost gives him an air of immortality.

The tone changes in the next line as the writer expresses her contempt for those who have accepted his death.They have tried to offer her consolation, but she regards their statements of regret as hollow and meaningless. These words, she believes, have been said too often to be of use - especially to her. In fact, rather than wallowing in self-pity, she laughs at their unnecessary sympathies, because she knows he is still alive, since if he were not, her own heart would also have stopped beating.

It seems to the writer as though the whole world is in peaceful mourning, almost as though they are sleeping, or giving in to their grief, rather than living in hope as she does. Again, there is a sense of peace and tranquillity here, as though everyone is waiting. Then she recalls the sweet-smelling flowers which are in his bedroom, again implying that they have been placed there to await his return. The fact that she tells him this detail suggests she believes that he is able to hear her and that this knowledge will make him want to return to her.

Next, the poet remarks, for the second time, that the end of the day is approaching. Here, however, she describes her surroundings with an air of melancholy. She knows, rather than sees, that the young boys are out in the fields gathering the crop of watercress. Her use of the word 'culling' is of interest as implies selective slaughter which brings us back to the subject of war. However, despite this introduction of a darker note, she is still unafraid for her own future because she is absolutely certain that he will return.

This is a very sad poem, as the writer is in denial of the death of someone she loves very deeply. In addressing the poem to the person who is missing she is reasserting her notion that he is still alive. However, the poet's optimism seems misplaced as she alone believes that he will return. This poem reflects the genuine turmoil of having a loved-one declared as 'missing'. Such a report had dreadful implications, as the exact fate of the victim may never be known and, therefore, survivors lived in a permanent state of uncertainty and, in all probability, unfulfilled hope.

The writer appears to be angry that others have assumed that 'missing' means 'dead', although her irritation may stem from a desire to convince herself that this is not the case. The fact that she loved the subject of this poem intensely is clear from her language and her certainty that if he were dead, she too would die.

As such, this poem has a great deal in common with other pieces by female writers of the First World War, such as *Perhaps* by Vera Brittain in which the poet recounts all of the many pleasures of life that she will no longer enjoy because her beloved has died. However, despite Vera Brittain's deep sadness at the loss of her fiancé, Roland Leighton, to whom this poem is addressed, she at least had the certainty of knowing how and where he died. Such information was denied to those whose loved-ones were reported as 'missing' and the vast numbers commemorated on memorials throughout Belgium and Northern France bear witness to the countless families who suffered through this uncertainty. One such person was Rudyard Kipling, whose son John was reported missing in early October 1915. There seemed little doubt that John had died on 27th September during the Battle of Loos, however, his father and mother, Carrie, spent the rest of their lives in a fruitless search to discover the truth. Such is the hopeless uncertainty of those whose desire for an answer is never fulfilled. This sentiment is very well represented in this poem, regardless of the relationship of the deceased or the conflict in which they are serving.

Again, this element of waiting hopefully and silently for dreaded news is depicted in another poem - from an unexpected source - *The Hawthorn Tree* by Siegfried Sassoon. Like Anna Gordon Keown, Sassoon captures the desperation of those left at home, wondering about the fate of their beloved. Similarly, he uses surroundings which are familiar to both the soldier and his loved-one, to remind us of their shared happier times. Yet at the end of both poems, the poets make a point of mentioning death, showing that one can never escape its certainty, no matter how much one might want to. Sassoon's poem, written in May 1917, might seem uncharacteristically sympathetic, especially to those who are more familiar with his satirical work. However, this poem goes to show that one of his many chosen topics during the conflict was the antithesis of war: love.

MARGERY LAWRENCE

BIOGRAPHICAL DETAILS

Margery Lawrence was born in 1889 in Wolverhampton. She was the oldest child of Richard Lawrence, a solicitor, and his wife, Grace. Margery and her siblings, Alan and Monica were initially educated at home by a governess. Her brother Alan may well have served in the First World War in the 7th Battalion of the South Staffordshire Regiment and, therefore, would have seen action in Gallipoli. In the summer of 1927, Margery Lawrence married Arthur E. Towle at St Pancras in London. She was mainly famous as a writer of fiction, including science fiction and detective stories and she died in 1969.

THE LOST ARMY

The version of Sir Ian Hamilton's despatch which appears at the beginning of this poem, is incomplete and, therefore, slightly misleading. The full text is extremely long and, although it dealt with the fighting which took place in Gallipoli during August 1915, it was not published in the London Gazette until January 1916. The part of Hamilton's despatch which relates to the 1st Battalion of the 5th Norfolk Regiment is as follows:

'The 1/5th Norfolks were on the right of the line, and found themselves for a moment less strongly opposed than the rest of the brigade. Against the yielding forces of the enemy, Colonel Sir H Beauchamp, a bold self-confident officer, eagerly pressed forward, followed by the best part of the battalion. The fighting grew hotter, and the ground became more wooded and broken. At this stage many men were wounded or grew exhausted with thirst. These found their way back to camp during the night. But the Colonel, with 16 officers and 250 men, still kept pushing on, driving the enemy before

him. Amongst these ardent souls was part of a fine company enlisted from the King's Sandringham estates. Nothing more was ever seen or heard of any of them. They charged into the forest, and were lost to sight or sound. Not one of them ever came back.'

Out of this account of events, a military legend was born. The 'Sandringham Company' had been recruited from the King's estate of the same name. These men were involved in an attack which took place on 12th August 1915 in Gallipoli, in which they became isolated from the rest of their battalion. A myth was founded, that the men of 'Sandringham Company' had simply disappeared into a mist. The reality of the situation remains a mystery, although there are those who propound the theory that the men were taken prisoner and then massacred by the Turks.

In her poem, *The Lost Army*, Margery Lawrence has used these events as her subject, portraying the gallant attack when these men undertook, and outlining their disappearance. She depicts their sacrifice in ringing tones, emphasising their courage and contrasting this with the 'darkness and silence' both of the woods in which they died and of death itself. This description gives the poem a mysterious quality, which suits the growing myths which quickly began to surface. The final line of the poem, however, dismisses these mysteries and, Margery Lawrence purports that all the public really need to know is that the men fought bravely and died for their country.

TRANSPORT OF WOUNDED IN MESOPOTAMIA, 1917

In this poem, Margery Lawrence demonstrates a sense of anger at the perceived treatment of troops in Mesopotamia. In that particular theatre of war, many men died of disease as well as of wounds sustained and yet their plight was all-but forgotten by those at home, who focused more avidly on the battles of the Western Front. In addition, there were many at home who believed that the Mesopotamian campaign was being seriously mis-managed by those in charge, who were then, in the eyes of the press and the public, allowed to 'get away with it'. It may be this sentiment which lies behind Margery Lawrence's poem, in which she voices the opinion of the men who have been left to die, while others 'sat safe at home'.

WINIFRED M. LETTS

BIOGRAPHICAL DETAILS

Born in 1882 in County Wexford, Ireland, Winifred Letts was educated at St Anne's Abbots in Bromley and then at Alexandra College in Dublin. Her parents lived in Blackrock, County Dublin.

During the First World War, Winifred served as a Voluntary Aid Detachment nurse in Manchester. She went on to become a masseuse, joining the Almeric Paget Military Massage Corps. Later, she married William Henry Foster Verschoyle and they lived together in Dublin and then in Faversham in Kent, where Winifred remained until her death in 1972.

William Verschoyle had been married before and had lost two sons in the First World War. Francis Stuart died, aged 19, in April 1915 and William Arthur died almost exactly two years later, at the age of 27.

Winifred was a prolific writer, her first book, The Story Spinner, being published in 1907. She wrote stories, children's books, plays and poems.

CASUALTY

This poem opens with the simple statement that a man named 'John Delaney' 'has been shot'. The use of this particular name, coupled with the fact that Winifred M Letts came from Ireland, suggests the 'rifles' to whom she refers are the Royal Irish Rifles. She goes on to wonder whether others will be affected by this man's death, being as they did not know him. The way in which she asks this question implies a hint of sarcasm, but also forces the reader to suppose that she already knows that the answer will be 'no'.

In the second verse, the poet asserts that, essentially, 'John Delaney's' death will not be marked in any way and that no-one will really remember his sacrifice. The third verse reiterates this notion, suggesting that when the war is over and the 'victorious' soldiers come back home, the dead will be forgotten amid the excitement and celebration. In the fourth verse, this message continues, except that now Winifred Letts applies it to all of the dead soldiers. At the very end of the poem, however, she starkly reminds the reader that the dead mens' sacrifices were made in the name of ordinary people just like the reader and herself.

Throughout this poem, there is an atmosphere of blame and guilt, which is not unusual in First World War poetry. It is also interesting to note, however, that Winifred Letts has no doubt that the army will be 'victorious', which may suggest that this poem was written quite early in the war, when people still refused to raise the possibility of defeat.

THE DESERTER

This poem tells the story of a young man, so overcome with fear that he runs away from the fighting and is executed for desertion.

We learn that this man has been afraid for a long time and that this fear has become overwhelming. Winifred Letts compares his fear with that of a frightened child or a hunted animal, who will do anything in his desperation to escape, regardless of the consequences. This man would have known that the penalty for desertion was execution by firing squad, but he chooses to opt for the certainty of death, rather than the uncertainty of continuing at the front, never knowing when or in what form his death will come.

The author urges us not to judge this man and then, somewhat ambiguously, speaks of the shame one feels in witnessing a man thus overcome with fear. To her the "irony of life" is not that this young man died anyway, despite his attempts to escape, or that he died at the hands of his fellow Englishmen, but that his mother believes he died a hero and remains unaware of the reality of her son's death. Winifred Letts seems to be implying that the mother is better off not knowing how her son died.

This poem judges the young soldier quite harshly - his name is unimportant and not worth mentioning, and while the author claims not to judge him, she also appears to show little sympathy for his plight, pointing out that even in death, he has chosen a blindfold (possibly seen as a cowardly option), as she says that the men cannot see his eyes. The reason for this attitude is possibly that many of those at home preferred to believe that men should fight bravely and never show fear. It is, after all, more acceptable to suppose that the soldiers were going, happily, to their deaths, than that they were terrified out of their wits. In the case of Winifred Letts, this feeling would probably have been enhanced by her work as a VAD which would have brought her into close contact with men who had been injured in the trenches. For a man to try to desert his position would have seemed shameful to her, when she was faced every day with men who had accepted their wounds with stoicism. For a woman at home during the war, even one serving as a nurse, the realities of trench life were often impossible to comprehend.

This poem bears some comparison with Siegfried Sassoon's *The Hero*, which also deals with the fate of a soldier attempting to evade the fighting. Sassoon's hero is given a name, Jack, which gives him an identity and makes him seem more human to the reader, and although he has not been executed, his death is not seen by his fellow men as one of heroism, since he had panicked and become hysterical at the explosion of a mine. Again, Jack's mother is deluded into believing that her son died a hero and this helps her to cope with her grief. Sassoon's sympathies are different from those of Winifred Letts, however, since through his use of satire and irony, he seems to be questioning the importance placed on the manner of a soldier's death, rather than the death itself.

SCREENS (IN A HOSPITAL)

Written, probably, from first-hand experience, this poem tells the story of the death of a soldier in hospital. The placing of screens around the dying man's bed denote his impending demise, but when this happens, he is replaced by yet another wounded man.

The screens are placed round the young soldier's bed in order to afford him some privacy and dignity and also to protect the other wounded men in the hospital ward from witnessing his death. The hospital ward must be kept quiet, so the nurses play cards, instead of listening to music, while the young man dies. We are informed of the solider's extreme youth and the fact that his life has hardly begun. The author tells us where the soldier was wounded, which makes this poem easier to date. (The attack at Suvla Bay was part of the ill-fated Gallipoli campaign and took place in August 1915). The continuous flow of wounded men is also mentioned as the author points out that this bed will soon be taken by another.

This poem seems quite harsh: the man is not named or even described in any detail which gives him a sense of anonymity; the nurses play at cards while the man is left to die alone; the contrast is made between the red colour of the screens and the whiteness of the sheets that cover the dying man, demonstrating that the innocence of his youth has been surpassed by what he has witnessed in the war, including death and destruction.

The description of the soldiers' injuries, being given in the weight of the lead shot, makes his wounds seem quite mechanical or technical, and less human. The mention of the Union Jack, which will cover him when he is dead, is the only hint at patriotism in the poem, although it is unclear whether the poet views his death as glorious or wasteful.

Finally, the soldier dies and is replaced by another wounded man, which is, again a mechanical way of looking at the situation. The author points out that the nurses (and other patients, for that matter) will be able to make some noise again, meaning that their lives will be able to return to normal. This affords a sense of insignificance to the soldier's death. The regret expressed in the final line, although this could be interpreted as ironic, seems almost light-hearted and the reader certainly does not gain the impression that the author has been adversely influenced by the death of this soldier. This might seem harsh, but could also be interpreted as a nurse's means of remaining detached from the suffering which surrounded her; or equally, as a way of showing, through satire, the monotonous nature of hospital life: as one soldier dies, he is replaced by another who will probably die too.

WHAT REWARD?

This short poem contrasts the "reward" for example, the mourning and, in some cases, over glorification of those who have died, and the care and attention given to those who have been physically maimed, compared with those who have suffered in a more hidden, psychological manner.

Winifred Letts seems to be saying that those who have given their sanity have made the greatest sacrifice of all. The dead are seen as glorious; the maimed can rest and will be looked after and lauded as heroes. However, the young men who emerged from the war with deep psychological scars, for whom life would never be the same again, were treated very differently. These men were less tolerable to a society which found mental illness somewhat embarrassing. Sometimes these men were locked away; they were certainly never paraded as heroic figures who had given as much, if not more, than their physically wounded comrades.

It should also be noted that, at this stage, there was a limited understanding of the mental breakdown which such traumas could cause, and men who suffered thus were often accused of shirking their responsibilities.This poem cries out against the injustice of this situation: these poor men are no less deserving of our thoughts than those more "acceptably" or "conventionally" wounded.

What Reward? could be compared with Siegfried Sassoon's *Glory of Women*, which describes how proud and pleased those at home are when soldiers are wounded (provided that the wound is not in an embarrassing place), or even killed, and how such men are treated with deference and respect. The public, Sassoon points out, react with disbelief at the idea of a man becoming mentally broken by his experiences and shy away from the belief that such things could even happen.

Both poets are stating that no matter what the wound is, or how it is gained, all the damaged soldiers are worthy of equal remembrance and praise.

OLIVE E. LINDSAY

BIOGRAPHICAL DETAILS

There are no verifiable biographical details available for Olive E. Lindsay.

DESPAIR

There were two main battles around Bapaume: the first was in the spring of 1917; the second came in the spring and summer of 1918, as the area was initially captures by the Germans during their Spring Offensive, then subsequently re-taken by the British army.

In this poem, Olive Lindsay is describing the effect of losing someone, presumably a husband or lover, in or near Bapaume. She relates the sensation that, with his death, a part of her has died too, and also that the supposedly living part of her has no more feeling than a piece of wood. There is a definite impression here that, given the chance, she too would choose to die. In the second verse, Olive Lindsay continues with this theme, that she has lost the 'best' part of herself, to the point where happiness is now only a 'dim remembrance'.

In the final verse, the poet suggests that by giving half of herself, she has made a sacrifice and placed it, effectively, at the feet of Christ. The notion here is that, by making such a sacrifice, her soul will, essentially, rise up again - or 'return' and allow her to rebuild her life. The title of this poem is most appropriate, signifying the abandonment of hope and the despondency which many must have experienced at the time.

AMY LOWELL

BIOGRAPHICAL DETAILS

Amy Lawrence Lowell was born on February 9th 1874 in Brookline, Massachusetts, the youngest of the five surviving children of Augustus Lowell and his wife, Katherine Bigelow Lawrence. Augustus Lowell was the treasurer of a cotton factory, while Katherine was a keen musician, and the family was a prominent one within the town. Amy's two eldest brothers, Percival and Abbot both went on to have illustrious careers themselves: the former as a renowned astronomer; the latter as a historian and President of Harvard University, from 1909 to 1933. One of Amy's sisters, Elizabeth Lowell Putnam, went on to become involved in pre-natal care.

In common with her two sisters, Amy was initially educated at home by a governess, after which she attended local private schools. However, she did not go to college as her parents did not believe that a formal further education was necessary for girls. Despite this, Amy broadened her mind by reading widely and travelling in America and Europe, where she first developed an interest in poetry.

In 1895, Amy's mother died and not long afterwards, Amy's engagement to a man from Boston (whose identity the family kept a secret) was broken off, after he fell in love with someone else. In order to recover from this disappointment, Amy travelled to Egypt and undertook a strict diet, so as to lose weight, although her regime was so extreme that it nearly killed her. Following her father's death in 1900, Amy purchased the family home, and another in New Hampshire and, thus settled, she began to write poetry in earnest, publishing her first pieces in Atlantic Monthly magazine in 1910.

Two years later came the publication of Amy's first collection of verse, entitled *A Dome of Many-Colored Glass*, although this did not meet with critical acclaim.

Nonetheless, Amy was happy, as she had just met Ada Dwyer Russell. The two women were reputedly lovers, although whether their relationship was physical remains doubtful. They certainly lived and travelled together, and it was Ada who accompanied Amy on her trip to London, to where she had journeyed specifically to meet Ezra Pound, who would go on to influence her writing style, becoming a major critic of her work. Amy became involved with the Imagist movement, often helping and encouraging other poets, although Pound eventually found her involvement overbearing.

By 1916, Amy was writing prolifically, either poetry of her own, reviews, essays or editing anthologies. In the early 1920s, she began work on a two volume biography of John Keats, which was published just before her death, from a cerebral hemorrhage in 1925. Amy's posthumous publication, *What's O'Clock*, which was edited by Ada Dwyer Russell, was awarded the Pulitzer Prize for poetry.

CONVALESCENCE

This poem first appeared in Amy Lowell's publication entitled *Sword Blades and Poppy Seed*, which was published in May 1914 - three months before the First World War even began. Therefore, although we may analyse this poem, it cannot really be done in the context of First World War literature, even though the poem, due to its title, appears to be about someone who is recovering their health, following a serious injury or illness. In the preface to her volume of poetry, Amy Lowell comments that the poet 'must constantly find new and striking images, delightful and unexpected forms', and one can see here that she has used metaphors of the sea in this 'striking' fashion, to describe the man's struggle back to fitness.

This sonnet opens with a description of a 'dragging vastness' which, given the title of the poem, we may assume to be pain or illness, for which the sea is a metaphor. It would seem that this illness or pain is holding the man back, perhaps preventing his recovery, or at least delaying it. Lowell describes this hindrance as 'sinuous seaweed strands' which makes it easily comprehensible, as most readers would be able to imagine the sensation of paddling through seaweed and becoming entwined.

The man, it would appear, manages to free himself from his bonds and fights his way to the 'beach', which is presumably a metaphor for a feeling of safety and wellness. However, then the 'shells' shift beneath his feet and he falls back into the water, by which we may assume that his momentarily improved health has now deteriorated again and he is back in the clutches of pain.

He seems to go 'up, and down' although his general movement is 'forward', no matter how slowly, and gradually he moves further up the shore towards the glowing 'poppies'. Now instead of waves and seaweed, he must contend with weeds, which 'clench' around him. However, now that he is on the metaphorical dry land, the danger seems to have passed, and the sun shines cheerfully down on him once more.

Given the metaphors used here, one might easily suppose that the subject's illness has involved a fever, as he seems to have drifted between health and illness. I do, however, have to ask why this poem has been included in Catherine Reilly's *Scars Upon My Heart*, since that is supposed to be an anthology of Women's writing from the Great War, which is now studied at A-Level in the United Kingdom and in which, clearly, this poem has no place. I can only imagine, that the mention of the word 'poppies' deluded the said editor into believing that this poem had some connection with the First World War and it was thus erroneously included.

Rose Macaulay

BIOGRAPHICAL DETAILS

Emilie Rose Macaulay was born on August 1st 1881 at Rugby in Warwickshire, where her father, George Campbell Macaulay was a master at Rugby School. Among his students was the young Rupert Brooke, whom Rose Macaulay reputedly met. Rose was the second child of George and his wife, Grace. Margaret was born in 1880, followed a year later by Rose, then a third sister, Jean in 1882. Aulay was born the following year and, finally, William in 1885. Rose spent much of her early childhood in Italy, although she was educated in England - firstly at Oxford High School for Girls and then at Somerville College, Oxford, where she studied Modern History.

Her first novel was published in 1906, not long after she left university and from then on, she wrote prolifically, publishing novels, biographies and poetry. During the First World War, she worked initially as a nurse, before joining the propaganda Department.

Although Rose Macaulay never married, she did have a long-term relationship with former priest Gerald O'Donavan, who was married. Their affair lasted from 1918, until his death in 1942. Like Vera Brittain, Rose Macaulay spent the years between the wars promoting peace and she became a member of the Peace Pledge Union. She was made a Dame in 1958, not long before her death.

PICNIC

This poem was published in Rose Macaulay's volume of work entitled *Three Days*, which first appeared in 1919, although the contents had previously been reproduced in other periodicals. The date given as the subtitle refers to the subject of the piece, rather than when it was written. In this case, the setting of the poem is the build-up to the launch of the Third Battle of Ypres, which is also known as Passchendaele. This involved the massive bombardment of the German lines by British artillery, which was often so loud that it could be heard in England.

The poem opens with a description of how a group of people have been enjoying themselves, picnicking in a wood. Rose Macaulay names the place concerned as Hurt Wood, and there is such a place, just south-east of Guildford in Surrey. In the second verse, she goes on to describe the wider surroundings of this area, from where it would be perfectly possible to see the Surrey countryside and the South Downs.

Her description of her own life seems peaceful and calm, but she goes on to shatter this by her reference to the sound of guns, which has been carried on the wind. However, although she and her friends can clearly hear the guns, the sounds have no impact on their behaviour, other than their comments on the clarity of the noise and the suggestion that the direction of the wind might indicate rain.

In the second section of the poem, Rose Macaulay points out that in the past, she and her friends have been angry, upset and sorry about the conflict and its consequences, but that now it has been going on too long and its horrors have become too commonplace for them to retain any real interest. Everything seems so remote, but also their fear and the knowledge of what is being done in the war, has forced these civilians to build themselves a protective metaphorical 'wall', which shields them from the knowledge and acceptance of these deeds.

In the third and final section, the real meaning becomes clearer. Rose Macaulay begs the guns to be 'still' and the wind to stop carrying their sounds. It would, at first appear that she is implying that, providing they don't know about the war, they can carry on, blissfully ignorant, as though none of it affects them. Then, right at the very end, she acknowledges that the noisy truth of the conflict fills civilians with fear that they will lose their protective 'wall' and be left exposed to all the frightful horrors.

This is a poem which is, at once, serious and laden with irony. Even in the title, there is an element of cynicism, as a 'picnic' not only refers to an informal outdoor meal, as described quite literally here, but also to something being easy or straightforward. In addition, there is no saying whether Rose Macaulay is referring here to her own feelings or those of civilians in general, who she might be choosing to criticise for their self-interest and callousness.

THE SHADOW

This poem, like *The Picnic*, also appeared in Rose Macaulay's volume of poetry entitled *Three Days*, which was published in 1919. The opening of the poem appears to suggest an air raid by a Zeppelin, which seems to cast a 'shadow'. This tells the poet that the sky will soon be alight and that bombs will fall on the town below, 'smashing' everything in sight. This awakens 'fear' in the people, but the poet suggests that this is insignificant, as this is only a small proportion of the 'fear' that is affecting all the young men of the world. She goes on to describe how people react to this threat and recalls a previous raid, when people had been killed and a great deal of damage done. However, the fires which were caused by the raid were nothing, she asserts, when compared to the 'pain' which is affecting the 'young men' at that time.

In the final verse, Rose Macaulay questions whether the 'blood' of civilians is more or less valuable than that of the soldiers, whose own blood is being spilt in 'heaps of mire'. Eventually she is forced to recognise the possibility of her own death, but here again, she doubts the real significance of it and states that her own experiences and, by extension, her own death, are only a tiny proportion of the 'shadow' which afflicts the 'world's young men'.

The meaning of this poem is fairly obvious, as Rose Macaulay ponders the real importance of civilians and their fears, pains and deaths, when compared to those being suffered in the trenches. This is a fairly common theme among the female war poets, many of whom sought to underplay their own role and heap all of their praise and attention on the troops. A lot of them were also quite angry at those civilians who believed that being involved in an air raid was comparable to being at the front.

Nina MacDonald

BIOGRAPHICAL DETAILS

There are no verifiable biographical details available for Nina MacDonald.

SING A SONG OF WAR-TIME

This poem was one of many published in 1919 in a collection by Nina MacDonald entitled Wartime Nursery Rhymes. This one should be thought of in conjunction with Sing a Song of Sixpence, with which its rhyme and metre match exactly.

The poem is written from the perspective of a young boy, who notices many changes in his life as a result of the war. So, for example, he must eat 'bread and margarine' for his tea, instead of bread and butter; there is no 'cake' or 'jam' and no money to buy toys. His mother does all of the housework, because their 'maid' has gone to work in a munitions factory. His nurse never seems to have time for him, because she spends her days 'sewing shirts for soldiers'.

In the final verse, 'Archie' takes a wider perspective, noting that all the 'girls' are doing something for the war effort, before his final statement that, since the war started, everything has been turned upside-down.

This is an interesting, child's-eye view of the war and how it affected his life. Although these hardships seem quite insignificant when compared to many of the situations which were affecting adults, the child's perspective makes it easy to see how, on the home front, everyones life changed and that most of the changes were unwelcome.

Florence Ripley Mastin

BIOGRAPHICAL DETAILS

Florence Ripley Mastin was born in 1886, in Wayne, Pennsylvania. Her family moved while she was still an infant to Pierpont, New York. She graduated from Tappan Zee High School in 1903 and then attended Barnard College. Her first book of poetry, Green Leaves was published in 1918.

She taught for 38 years at Erasmus High School in Brooklyn and several of her former students expressed their gratitude for her teaching and the way in which she influenced their future work.

A member of the Poetry Society of America, her work was published in The New York Times and other national newspapers and magazines. She died in 1968.

AT THE MOVIES

This poem depicts a scene being played out on a cinema screen, showing ranks of British soldiers marching towards battle. Such films were made and shown during the First World War as propaganda and to show how well the men were doing at the front. As a means of encouraging America to enter the war, the films were also exported to the USA. The scene described here shows the men as gallantly marching forwards, just as they have done for the last twelve months.

In the second verse, this description continues as one of the soldiers raises his hat to the camera, making brief eye-contact with the audience. His eyes show how young, brave and keen he is, which tells us that he is marching towards, rather than away from the battle. However, the film suddenly ends and the poet is reminded that this is not a story, but reality.

This is a poem of contrasts, not least of which is that one would normally go to the cinema, or picture-house, to be entertained and even while there, the audience find it easy to forget the harsh real world, being shown to them on the newsreels, and imagine that everything before them is a 'movie'. Florence Ripley Mastin, as a 20 year old at the time of writing this piece, was clearly impressed in this way, momentarily forgetting reality. She enhances this contrast by her use of language. So, while we know that the film would have been in black and white, she introduces tones of these colours to depict the more realistic elements of the film. The grass is, therefore, 'dark'; the invisible, but imagined battle is 'grey'; the soldier's hat is 'dusty'; and the final white screen is 'ghostly'. She contrasts these slightly depressing tones with a more cheerful depiction of the soldier himself. His hair, rather than being merely fair or blond, is 'bright'; and she admires his 'eager... young and bold' eyes. These latter descriptions give the soldier an air of a movie-star, which also enhances the sense of unreality which grows as the audience watch the film. The final line of the poem, however, shows that, having remembered that the scenes are factual, rather than fictitious, she also recalls that this young man may have been marching to his death and her heart turns 'cold'.

CHARLOTTE MEW

BIOGRAPHICAL DETAILS

Charlotte Mary Mew was born on November 15th 1869 in London. She was the third child of architect Frederick Mew and his wife Anna. Her oldest brother, Henry, was born in 1865, followed by Frederick in 1867, although he died at the age of just two months, having contracted an infection. After Charlotte's birth, another brother Richard was born in 1971, then two years later, Caroline Frances Anne (always known as Anne) came along. Christopher (who was christened David) was born in 1875, although he too died in infancy, early in 1976. In December of the same year, Richard, who was by now five years old, also died of Scarlet Fever. Charlotte's final sibling, another sister, Freda, was born in 1879. Both Henry and Freda seem to have suffered from mental illness, and both were eventually committed to lunatic asylums.

Charlotte was educated at Gower Street School and in 1894, she published her first story. 1897 brought further tragedy into her life, as her father died, leaving the family in a fairly dire financial situation. In 1901, Henry, who had been in a lunatic asylum since 1888, also died and all of these events combined to make Charlotte's mother increasingly dependent on her two daughters, Charlotte and Anne.

It is really not very surprising, given her difficult and often tragic upbringing, that Charlotte's own personality was affected. She had quite an unusual appearance and seems to have suffered from depression. Writing proved to be her one real solace and by 1909, her work was being more widely noticed. However, privately she remained desperately unhappy: a situation which was not helped by her romantic advances towards fellow writer May Sinclair, being rejected. Miss Sinclair then went on to cruelly humiliate Charlotte in public for having made these advances in the first place.

Despite the potential scandal, Charlottes poetry continued to be popular, and was soon brought to the attention of Thomas Hardy and Siegfried Sassoon. In 1919, when Sassoon had become Literary Editor of the Daily Herald, he learned that Charlotte and her family were having financial problems, so offered to pay her for articles and reviews.

Charlotte's mother died in 1923, leaving the two sisters alone. They continued to live together; neither of them married and they remained constant companions. Finally, in June 1927, there came a tragedy from which Charlotte would never recover: Anne died from cancer of the uterus and liver. Charlotte was completely overwhelmed by her grief. She rarely slept and her nerves were seriously affected. She became convinced that Anne had actually been buried alive; she saw 'black spots' in Anne's studio and was certain that these had somehow contributed to her sister's illness - these 'spots' turned out to be specks of soot. Upon her doctor's advice, on 15th February 1928, Charlotte was admitted to a nursing home to be treated for a nervous disorder. Just over one month later, on 24th March, Charlotte took her own life by drinking half a bottle of disinfectant. At the inquest into her death, her doctor said that following Anne's death, Charlotte had become obsessed that she was surrounded by the germs which she believed had killed her sister.

Charlotte Mew was described in one obituary as a 'poet of rare quality', although she never fully appreciated this herself - always having had a low opinion of herself and her own abilities. Others did not share her viewpoint and many in the literary world mourned her death, and hoped that she had finally found the peace she so obviously craved.

THE CENOTAPH

Charlotte Mew begins this poem by remembering the wasted land, which will not have had time to re-grow in the ten months since the end of the War. She perceives those fields as one great, deep grave, visited for evermore by those with justifiably proud remembrances of lost loved-ones. At home, however, those who have suffered the deep, slow pain of losing someone close, also need an outward memorial to the dead - this comes in the form of the Cenotaph.

At the foot of this memorial, these mourning people leave flowers, many brought from gardens at home, to demonstrate their grief and remembrance. Charlotte points out that this is the place where those who have no grave can be mourned - they lie with thousands of others in the battlefields, but they can be remembered with flowers and tears here at the Cenotaph.

Memorials, such as this, will appear in market-places all around the country. Throughout the year, while market traders go about their business, the memorials will overshadow them, through the eyes of God and the nation's dead youth.

In July 1919, the original temporary Cenotaph was unveiled as part of the national Peace Day event. There was such an huge public outpouring of grief that the steps of this wood and plaster construction were spontaneously covered with flowers, left by those in mourning. The decision was taken that a permanent memorial should be constructed and work began almost immediately. Charlotte Mew's poem, written in September 1919, reflects this sense of overwhelming loss and the need for a central place or monument upon which the mourning public could focus their grief.

Charlotte Mew demonstrates in this poem some commonly-held sentiments among her generation: gratitude for the sacrifices made by so many, and sadness at the huge waste of life. She appreciates the losses which are being felt by so many whilst demonstrating her own sense of pride in the victory those losses have achieved.

This poem provides an excellent commentary on the events of that time - memorials were being considered and constructed around the country to commemorate the dead and missing of the War; when the Cenotaph was unveiled, people travelled from all over the country to show their respects, often bringing flowers from home to lay in remembrance.

At the end of this poem, however, the tone changes. Charlotte accepts that, for many, life goes on as before. People will continue to go about their daily business, but she seems to have a low opinion of these men and women, referring to them as 'whores' and 'hucksters', which implies an element of compromised principles and a lack of morality on their part. Such people are, she maintains, looked down upon by both God and the dead, whom she regards as having been murdered. She does not state who it is that she considers to be responsible for the fate of these young men, but makes it clear that the loss of so many cannot be ignored or regarded as accidental.

In the same way as the construction of the cenotaph changed the face of Whitehall and formed a permanent reminder of what had happened, Charlotte Mew seems here to be implying that everything has changed - the face of the world has been altered by the cataclysmic events of the War.

MAY 1915

Although the dated title of this, and Charlotte Mew's other poem June, 1915, imply that they were written at that time, it is likely that neither was published until 1929, after Charlotte Mew's death. Therefore, to date these poems with any great degree of accuracy is almost impossible.

This short poem essentially speaks of the hope that the war will soon be over and peace will, once again, dominate over pain and death. Even to those who are currently overwhelmed by grief, there must be some hope of a brighter future, although that time has not yet come.

The months of April and May 1915 saw heavy fighting at the Second Battle of Ypres, made famous by the first use, by the Germans, of Chlorine Gas. This battle, which lasted a little over a month, saw many British losses - the dead amounted to nearly 60,000. Charlotte Mew's poem is a reflection of the sadness many felt at that time, yet is tinged optimistically with hope for a brighter future.

Although this poem could be interpreted, quite literally, as a hope for a new Spring, new growth and the re-birth of the earth, it is also open to a slightly different interpretation. The woods, which are described as 'blackened', could be a reference to the dead soldiers, and rather than literally meaning the fallen or broken trees, there could be an implied meaning here of the wounded men, who wait patiently, because that is all they can do, for their health to return, and, ultimately, for peace to come again. In this new, fearful and uncertain world of theirs, the only things of which they can be sure are their natural surroundings.

Then, her thoughts turn to those at home, who sit, blindly oblivious to everything which is going on around them, because they are consumed by grief for their lost loved-ones. Even for these, she asserts, there must be some hope that the world will survive and begin again.

This is a poem of hope, tinged with uncertainty - although she hopes for spring, she seems to be questioning whether or not it will come. Written about - and possibly during - a time when there was little hope for an early conclusion to the hostilities, this poem may seem to contain a slightly unrealistic aspiration. However, the hope for peace was all that many women had to keep them going in the face of such heavy losses.

To equate the coming of peace with the arrival of Spring is a metaphor used by many poets, such as Edith Nesbit in *The Fields of Flanders* - which was also written in 1915, and Sara Teasdale in *'There Will Come Soft Rains'*.

At the end of this poem, although Charlotte Mew still talks, hopefully, of more promising times, she acknowledges that for those suffering and mourning the death of a loved-one, such hopes are impossible to realise. These people are not even aware of their surroundings or what is happening around them, let alone being able to look, with any degree of hope, towards the future.

JUNE 1915

This poem asks a relatively simple, yet unanswered, question - essentially, how can everyday life carry on as before, given the destruction of the world which carries on all around, despite the passage of time.

This is a simple, yet effective, poem which asks how anyone can be expected to think of everyday events during these times. Only for innocent young children is there any continuation of normality. The passage of time, the blossoming of a new flower, are insignificant events when compared to the dreadfulness of the war.

For everyone else, the only things that matter are either surviving one's grief, or dreading the arrival of bad news. She compares the young child reaching out his hand to touch an early rose-bud to the distance of the stars. Both are seen as fearless, yet, to the adults, both the child and the stars are distant - almost incomprehensibly unaware of what is happening around them.

It is almost as though witnessing the fear and suffering of those at home has become too much for Charlotte, whose early life was greatly affected by death and illness - perhaps watching others grieving for a lifetime had become more than she could bear, making her long for the innocence of childhood - an innocence which she probably never experienced fully herself.

Finally, she wonders how important the war is, or should be, to the young child whose innocence is so short-lived. She appears to be asking why he shouldn't be allowed to enjoy his childhood? Why should death and destruction dominate absolutely everything?

This poem bears some comparison with *Lament* by Wilfrid Wilson Gibson. Gibson's beautifully moving poem asks similar questions: namely, how can those who survive the war ever be expected to carry on a normal life again? The main difference between the two poems is that Gibson appears to be saying that if the survivors of the conflict truly understand and appreciate the sacrifices being made on their behalf, their lives can never be the same again. Charlotte Mew, on the other hand, suggests that, while the lives of the adults are, naturally, dominated and affected by the war, why should the children suffer a similar fate? There is enough fear and unhappiness without allowing the sweet and short-lived innocence of youth to be lost forever.

ALICE MEYNELL

BIOGRAPHICAL DETAILS

In February 1844, Charles Dickens and his friend Thomas Thompson attended a concert in Liverpool, where both men were somewhat captivated by the young pianist, Christiana Weller. The next day, they called upon Miss Weller at home and Dickens wrote to her afterwards, including with his note a short poem, in which he only half humorously, expressed his desire to change her name, presumably to his own. Upon his return to London, Dickens sent her gifts and even wrote to her father of his great admiration for Miss Weller's 'great gifts and uncommon character'. A few days later, however, he received a letter from his friend, Thomas Thompson, whom he had left behind in Liverpool, which stated that that gentleman was also romantically interested in Miss Weller. Dickens, putting his own feelings to one side, urged his widowed friend to pursue Miss Weller, then aged nineteen. Thompson, who was in his thirties, was a man of independent means, but despite this, his advances towards Miss Weller were not appreciated by her parents.

Thompson continued to write to his 'Christie' of his devoted attachment, while Dickens worked on appeasing her parents. Eventually everything was arranged amicably and Thomas Thompson married Christiana Weller in 1845. They had two children: Elizabeth, who was born on 3rd November 1846 in Switzerland and Alice, whose birth in London took place on 22nd September 1847. Much of their childhood was spent travelling in Italy and they were educated almost entirely by their father. He taught them geography, history and literature, while their mother bestowed upon them a keen interest in the arts and music.

Occasionally the family would return to England for visits but did not live there with any degree of permanence until 1864, when they settled on the Isle of Wight. Alice, who was almost seventeen, and her slightly older sister, soon began to partake in, and enjoy, a social life which had hitherto been impossible. Croquet parties, concerts and dancing filled their lives, and Alice found herself at the centre of much attention from male admirers. Despite this, she also suffered from bouts of unhappiness, which seemed to stem from boredom. Her sister, Elizabeth, had taken up painting, but Alice lacked an occupation.

Always deeply religious, Alice converted to the Catholic faith in 1868, following which, the family moved back to Italy, partly so that Elizabeth could study under Giuseppe Bellucci and also to restore Alice's spirits, which were flagging in England. Alice began to write poetry, which was greatly admired, although it still reflected her melancholy tendencies. Elizabeth's career was taking off, resulting in the family taking a house in London, so that she could continue her studies. Here Alice began to attract the attention of poet and critic Coventry Patmore and John Ruskin, who in 1875 offered her unstinting praise for a volume of poetry entitled Preludes, claiming that some of her verses were 'the finest things I've seen or felt in modern verse'. In the summer of 1876, both Elizabeth and Alice were invited to visit Alfred Tennyson, which experience they both found somewhat daunting. By this stage, Elizabeth was beginning to gain a reputation for her military paintings and her piece entitled The Roll Call was exhibited by the Royal Academy in 1874. This painting was subsequently purchased by Queen Victoria and remains to this day at Buckingham Palace.

In the winter of 1876, following a holiday in Italy, Alice was introduced to a young journalist and writer named Wilfrid Meynell, who was already familiar with Alice's poetry and expressed a desire to meet her. He became a regular visitor and correspondent and their engagement was announced on 1st January 1877. Even before their marriage, which took place the following autumn, they made plans to start their own magazine.

Elizabeth was also married, in June 1877, to Major William Francis Butler. Alice and Wilfrid Meynell settled down to married life at Inkerman Terrace in Kensington, where they both embarked, in much greater earnest, upon their literary careers, focusing on journalism. In 1879, their first child, Sebastian, was born, and the following year saw the arrival of a daughter, Monica. A young nurse, May Wigley, was employed to look after the infants, enabling Alice and Wilfrid to continue with their work. In 1881, the family moved to Phillimore Place in Kensington and Wilfrid was offered the editorship of the Catholic periodical entitled The Weekly Register. Alice helped him with this task, as well as contributing to The Spectator and the Saturday Review.

The children and domestics quickly and easily slotted into the Meynell's routine which was simplified by the fact that they both worked from home a great deal of the time. In 1882, Everard was born and, despite their already hectic schedule, the following year, Wilfrid launched a monthly magazine of his own, entitled Merry England, through which came the discovery of many other writers, such as Francis Thompson and Hillaire Belloc. Other contributors, apart from the Meynell's themselves, included Katharine Tynan and Wilfred Blunt. Francis Thompson would go on to become a close friend of the family.

Madeline and Viola Meynell were born in 1885 and 1886 respectively, followed by Vivian, who died in early infancy. In 1881, Alice's father had died and she used her inheritance to purchase a plot of land at Palace Court in Paddington, where a house was built, into which the family moved in 1889. The following year saw the arrival of Olivia, followed in 1892 by the final child, Francis.

By this time, Alice had, as well as continuing with her journalism, become a much appreciated and widely published essay-writer and published a book of essays and articles entitled The Rhythm of Life in 1893, which met with great critical acclaim. Within the house at Palace Court, there was a large library, which housed an enormous long table, where the Meynell's worked. The children could often be found scattered about this room, on the floor or under the table itself. They produced scrapbooks and their own newspaper, as well as writing and drawing. Quite often, one or more the children would accompany their father when he visited the Westminster Press, to supervise the production of the Weekly Register. As such, and unusually for the times, the children were not kept hidden in the nursery, but mixed with the adult friends of their parents.

Alice and Wilfrid Meynell had a very happy marriage and, even when separated only for short periods of time, would write letters and send each other small tokens of their love. Visitors to the house, at regularly literary evenings, included Katharine Tynan, W.B. Yeats, Oscar Wilde and Aubrey Beardsley.

By now a much older children's nurse-cum-cook, Harriet Slark, had been engaged, although Alice Meynell always kept a close eye on her children herself, which she maintained was as much for the protection of the nurse, as it was for the children. Over the next few years, more essays and poetry collections were published and Alice's fame continued to rise. In September 1901, Alice embarked on a lecture tour to America. However, although she should have returned by Christmas, due to the illness of her travelling companion, Agnes Tobin, she ended up being away from home for eight months, only returning in April 1902. She then began to take more seriously, her work in the field of literary criticism and, at the artist's request, wrote the introduction to a book of pictures by John Singer Sargent.

In 1905, the family moved once more, to Granville Place. This was mainly because Wilfrid was now acting as literary advisor to a firm of publishers and wanted to have a home nearer to their offices. The house at Palace Court was not sold, however, but let out. Francis Thompson, who had become a semi-permanent lodger with the Meynells, made this move with them. By now the children were more independent, which enabled Alice to travel more and she often returned to Italy over the next few years, to revisit the places where she had been so happy as a child.

In 1907, Francis Thompson, who had been an almost constant presence in the family for nearly twenty years, died of tuberculosis, followed by Alice's mother in 1910. By this stage, three of Alice's children were married and that year also saw the death of Sir William Butler - Alice's brother-in-law - leaving her sister, Elizabeth, distraught.

During this time, Alice also became closely involved with the Women Writers' Suffrage League, which had been founded by Cicely Hamilton in 1908. In 1911, Wilfrid purchased a property at Greatham in West Sussex, and the family divided its time between there and London. Alice was at the house in Greatham in the summer of 1914, when war was declared, which filled her at once with a mixture of fear and patriotism, common to many mothers at the time. Greatham remained a bolt-hole of serenity and peace, kept that way specifically to ease the fears of Alice's many grandchildren. Here Viola made jam with her friend Eleanor Farjeon and many literary figures attended luncheon parties.

In July 1916, came the first terrible news to hit the family, as Madeline's husband, Percy Lucas, a Second Lieutenant in the Border Regiment, was killed in action at the age of 36. Everard, who was married by now, enlisted in 1917, joining the Artists' Rifles. Francis, the youngest son, was a conscientious objector and was exempted from service by a Tribunal. He did, however, serve with the non-combatant corps, apparently attached to the Royal Fusiliers. Alice continued to divide her time between London and Greatham: in the former she found the air raids daunting, but winters at Greatham were cold and damp.

When the armistice came, Alice was on a train, travelling between the two houses. The 'wild hooting' of the train's whistle announced the arrival of peace. By this stage of her life, Alice had become much weaker and suffered greatly from severe headaches. Everard also suffered from ill-health after the war, which was diagnosed in 1921 as consumption. On doctor's advise he, his wife and their four young children left for America in July of that year. Alice continued to write although her health had by now deteriorated quite seriously. Wilfrid was a constant companion throughout her final illness which began in the autumn of 1922. Her children visited her, but eventually, she decided that she wanted them to remember her as she had been; not weak and dying, but happy and strong.

She did not fear death, although right up until the moment of its coming on 27th November, she 'passionately' wanted to live.

Alice Meynell would appear to have been the epitome of refinement, style and intelligence, who treated everyone equally and with fairness. She never knowingly caused pain or embarrassment to others and showed a tolerance of all the failings of human nature which was quite uplifting.

LORD I OWE THEE A DEATH

The title of this poem is taken from a phrase made by Richard Hooker, a 16th Century Anglican priest and theologian. Here Alice Meynell uses this phrase to introduce her poem and also to outline its central theme, which is the feeling of indebtedness which she feels towards those who are sacrificing their lives. It might also be that, although she speaks of a general feeling of thanksgiving, she is also offering her own appreciation for the survival of her sons. The 'debt' to which she refers, in either case, cannot be underestimated. It should be offered meekly or ashamedly, but with pride. Alice Meynell's suggestion that the debt should be paid 'in gold' is not a literal reference to paying money, but means instead that the obligation is so valuable and so weighty, that its worth is greater than gold itself.

SUMMER IN ENGLAND, 1914

In the opening verse of this poem, Alice Meynell implies that in the summer of 1914, which has often been referred to as 'golden', there was such a different atmosphere to normal, that even the 'light' seemed to have changed. She suggests that the sun appears to have coloured-in the houses, giving them a pearlescent quality and that the sky, having seen the 'world', brings a new lease of life.

The second verse deals, in the same glorious tones, with the countryside; the bumper harvest, made better still by the war weather. There is an atmosphere of liberality, coupled with romance here, which hindsight and the title of the poem, teaches us is about to be shattered.

In the third verse, the atmosphere changes. Now Alice Meynell makes direct comparisons between the prosperous beauty of home and the carnage of war. Interestingly, although her subject has changed, the languages which she uses remains similar, so the dead soldiers are described as a 'wet corruption' because they have been brought to death by dishonest means, but also because they will decay and putrefy. These descriptions, which remind the reader of the beauty in verses one and two, despite their real meaning, provide a much starker contrast than would have been achieved by more direct and descriptive language.

The fourth verse provides a link between the harvest and the birds and animals which derive food from it. Now, however, there is a startling change of tone and Alice Meynell tells us that there are men who have been 'shot through the eyes'. This description is followed by the suggestion that 'love' would not wish to see what men are doing to one another, which implies that the poet finds mankind's actions to be inexcusable. She is not criticising individuals here, but mankind as a whole.

Finally, Alice Meynell quotes or rather paraphrases from the Bible (John, Chapter 15, verse 13), which says 'Greater love hath no man than this, that a man lay down his life for his friends'. She seems to question this sentiment and states that those who don't fight should not rebuke themselves, because the men who are dying are doing so for and with the love of Christ. The ending of this poem is not really surprising, given Alice Meynell's devout Catholicism. She probably would have believed that the 'kiss of Christ' would be sufficient reward for a dying man. Interestingly, there were many, many men who believed that they were not fighting for God, King or Country, but for their fellow soldiers - those very 'friends' of the Biblical quote, for whom they were happiest and most honoured to lay down their lives.

RUTH COMFORT MITCHELL

BIOGRAPHICAL DETAILS

Ruth Comfort Mitchell was born on July 21st 1882 in San Francisco, California, the oldest child and only daughter of John S Mitchell and his wife Florence Mowatt. Ruth's three younger siblings were all boys, named Mowatt, Standish and Douglas. John Mitchell was a hotel keeper and the family would spend their summers in Los Gatos, California, where they and Ruth's grandparents both had summer homes.

It was in the Los Gatos Mail that Ruth had her first poem published in 1896, and this encouraged her to continue writing. She mingled in literary circles in San Francisco and it was thus that she came to be introduced to William Sanborn Young, who at that time was travelling around America, having just sold his grain business. They were married in October 1914, and moved to New York so that Sanborn Young could study photography, while Ruth continued to write, publishing her first volume of poetry, *The Night Court and Other Verse* in 1916. She continued to write poetry, prose and plays and then, in 1917 the couple moved back to Los Gatos, into their newly built house, named Yung See San Fong House, or Young's Home in the Heart of the Hills, which is a fusion of pagodas and western layouts.

Here Sanborn Young was able to pursue his conservationist activities, growing almost everything they needed to survive. Ruth continued to write, producing more poetry and novels during the early 1920s. In 1925, Sanborn Young was elected to the California State Senate, largely due, it is believed, to his wife's political campaigning. He remained in office for the next thirteen years, focusing on conservation and the legislation to control narcotics, the bill for which he eventually helped to write.

Ruth also became involved in politics, serving as a Republican National Committeewoman for eight years. Through their political ties, the Youngs became friends with President Herbert Hoover, who was a frequent visitor to their Los Gatos home, as were other prominent figures including Robert W Service, Gertrude Stein and the actresses Joan and Constance Bennett.

Following the publication of John Steinbeck's novel *The Grapes of Wrath* in 1939, Ruth wrote a rebuttal entitled *Of Human Kindness*, which was published the following year. Steinbeck, oddly enough, lived in Los Gatos at this time, but the two could not have seen things more differently, for while Steinbeck paints a harsh and miserable image of the American Depression, where dignity is the only thing left for the helpless Joad family in their unremitting fight to sustain themselves, Ruth tries to portray a more positive image of the ranch owners in this situation, showing them treating their workers fairly and with a 'kindness' that would have seemed alien in Steinbeck's novel. Needless to say, it is Steinbeck's novel that has stood the test of time, while Ruth Comfort Mitchell's offering is all but forgotten.

After this, Ruth wrote less and was found dead in her bath in February 1954. Sanborn Young outlived her by ten years.

HE WENT FOR A SOLDIER

This poem was first published in 1916, but was probably written the year before, making it an extremely early, graphic anti-war poem - especially from the pen of an American, given that that country was not involved in the conflict at the time. With that in mind, the subject of the poem, the boy who volunteered may well have been from another country, and the remaining content of the poem, presumably came from newspaper reports, letters and the poet's imagination, as very few writers and poets were writing in this tone at that stage of the war, with the possible exception of Charles Hamilton Sorley. In fact, this poem was more likely written in response to the enthusiastic early war poetry which many women were writing at the time, not so much perhaps, the obvious jingoists like Jessie Pope, but maybe poets like Katharine Tynan Hinkson, whose Joining the Colours offers a very different perspective of the early war, which while sad, shows none of the harsh realities of the conflict.

Ruth Comfort Mitchell's poem opens with a description of 'Billy' marching away to war, with around twenty other young men, presumably from the same town or village. They are happy and carefree, healthy and slightly embarrassed by the attention that they are receiving from all the 'pretty girls' who have come to wave them off. There are patriotic references here to flags, but these are clean 'new' flags, which is deliberately pointed out as a reminder to the reader of the contrast between these and the torn and blood-splattered standards that form part of the battlefields, especially in ancient times, when knights fought. These fine flags, flowers and young girls seem out of place to Billy, who seems unsure, at the beginning of the second verse, as to why everyone is making so much 'fuss'. However, as the parade continues, he becomes more settled and it all becomes 'part of him'. The music seems to play a significant role here, for not only does it assuage Billy's fears, but the poet personifies some of the instruments and sounds, calling them 'bold' and 'boasting', thereby allowing them to pass these characteristics on to the marching soldiers, who appear to become more 'brave' as they continue on their way.

The third verse signifies a change of tone, as now Billy is no longer travelling to war, but is right in the midst of it. Now he does not look upon war as something brave and honourable - in fact he regards those sentiments as a 'joke'. Instead, he realises that war is all about death and dying like 'animals', not knights in shining armour. It is not about the sweet smell of 'pinks' and 'roses', but about the 'warm blood stench', which lingers where so many have died. And instead of fighting under a 'knightly' code of honour, Billy 'fights like a rat', which suggests fear, cunning and self preservation above all else.

By verse four, Billy is no longer fighting, because now he lies dying. He poet harkens back to the beginning of the poem, where the 'blithe young score' of men had marched away with Billy. Now, however, they are a 'ghoulish score' , who have been left to die in No Man's Land. All around Billy, the ground is covered with blood and 'gore', so much so, that even the leaves have turned 'red'. Billy is now no longer even a 'boy', or a 'rat', but is described as a 'thing', which is the ultimate degradation, suggesting that he is no longer human, or is not recognisable as such. It is no longer the 'pretty girls' who are crying, but Billy himself, because he is in agony and all the while, the 'sickening sun', which now just makes him burn with thirst, 'grins down' on him to remind him of all the summers that he will miss.

The fifth verse opens with a startling reminder that Billy was always a bit uncertain what it was all about, suggesting that he doesn't really understand why he went to war, or why he is dying. The poet, having sowed this seed of doubt, tells us that there is only a 'part' of Billy left, and that this is 'ghastly', which serves as a gruesome reminder of the terrible injuries that were inflicted during the First World War. Meanwhile, all around him, other wounded 'things' are 'crawling' about, as the 'crows' wait overhead to pick at their bodies.

In the final verse, the format and tone change completely as now the poet seems to address herself to God, perhaps in prayer, wondering how much longer the war can be allowed to continue. She seems to believe that, as long as men (and women) go on telling glorious stories about the war, young men, like Billy, will be deceived into believing them. She accuses them of being boastful and superficial, before changing the pronoun employed to include everyone in doing the 'devil's' work, suggesting that all men must share the blame for allowing the war to happen and continue.

This is an unusual and powerful poem, especially given the date of its composition. The regular rhyme and rhythm, as well as the jaunty style contrast with the subject and especially with the naming of Billy and the repetition of the last line of each verse, except the final one, reminding us every time of Billy's youth and familiarity. There is also an implicit feeling of deceit in this poem, as though Billy was tricked into volunteering by the 'attitudes' and 'platitudes' of his elders, when he really had no idea what it was all about.

HARRIET MONROE

BIOGRAPHICAL DETAILS

Harriet Monroe was born on 23rd December 1880, in Chicago, Illinois, the second child of lawyer Henry Stanton Monroe and his wife, Martha Mitchell. Harriet had three siblings, Dora, who was three years older, then Lucy and William, who were five and eight years younger, respectively. As the family moved in well-connected social circles, Harriet's sisters both married well, although Harriet herself remained single. Dora married a successful architect, John W. Root, while Lucy married William J. Calhoun, who became Minister to China under President Taft.

In childhood, Harriet attended the Dearborn Seminary in Chicago and then the Visitation Convent in Georgetown, just outside Washington D.C. Once her education was completed in 1879, she returned to her family and continued to live at home, or with family members for most of her life. Harriet initially found employment as a freelance journalist, working mainly for the *Chicago Tribune*, although she also wrote plays and poetry, some of which appeared in magazines.

The family's social connections enabled Harriet to gain literary commissions, such as the composition of an Ode for the opening ceremony of the 1892 Columbian Exposition. In the 1890's, Harriet sued the New York World magazine for publishing her poem without first gaining her consent. This was a test case, regarding an author's right to control their own work. She won her case and was awarded the sum of $5,000 which she used to travel around Europe. This and later visits to both Europe and China, to visit her sister Lucy, convinced Harriet of the need for a new poetic magazine, which could better represent the voices of the poets themselves. Thus, in 1912, she launched *Poetry* magazine, using money from Chicago businessmen to pay all contributors for their work, as well as run the magazine itself. For the first two years, Harriet worked at *Poetry* as its editor, unsalaried, continuing with her job at The Tribune to make ends meet. However, by 1914, this had become too much, so she resigned from The Tribune and took a salary of $50 per month from the magazine. By this time, the magazine's reputation had grown. Alice Corbin Henderson became associate editor until her health failed in 1916, forcing her to leave. Ezra Pound offered to find poems from European poets and submit them for publication. Yeats, H.D. (Hilda Doolittle), Pound, Amy Lowell, T.S. Eliot and Vachel Lindsay were all regular contributors.

The years of the First World War were to prove the magazine's most fruitful under Harriet Monroe's editorship and the 1920's saw much more difficult times, as there was greater competition from other journals and *Poetry's* stance began to appear somewhat old-fashioned. However, the Depression of the 1930's brought an unexpected revival, finishing off many of the magazine's competitors and allowing Poetry to capture a new generation of poets.

Harriet Monroe worked tirelessly throughout these turbulent times, taking little rest, other than to occasionally visit her sister in China, or to attend writers' conferences. It was while travelling back from a P.E.N. Conference in Buenos Aires, that Monroe suffered a stroke and died in Arequipa, Peru on September 26, 1936. The magazine which she founded, is still published today.

ON THE PORCH

This poem was first published in 1917, although it was probably written during the previous year. It opens with a relatively serene and secure impression of the poet lying on a 'screened in' porch, sheltering from the rain, which patters overhead. Despite the inclement weather, there is no sense of cold here and, indeed, we are informed that this is 'summer rain', which does not trouble the poet, who remains 'snug and dry'. However, the final line of this verse suggests a slight change in the atmosphere, as rather than listening to birds singing, she describes them as complaining. This may be an actual reference to the birds, who might not like the rain, but it may also be a metaphor for the people who moan about the war.

In the second verse, the atmosphere changes more obviously as the poet appears to be overwhelmed by thoughts of the war, which 'wash' over her, like waves. Everything within the outset of this verse has a very depressing and downcast air: the gun is 'huge' and 'blind', which suggests that it kills with indiscriminate menace; the train is 'armoured' as it is filled with men who are armed, going to fight and kill and die. There is the sense here, that these thoughts and images are dragging the poet 'down', even as her mind turns towards the army that is 'proudly swinging' beneath the 'gay flags' both of which suggest honour and good cheer. However, this thought is quickly dashed by the notion that the supposedly 'glorious' dead are not really respected or esteemed: they are piled up 'like rags'.

Then in a sudden change of tone, the author creates a temporarily, more calm atmosphere again. Now she paints us a rose-tinted image of 'gardens of lovers', where everything seems pretty in 'the light of the sun'. However, this too is soon shattered by the remembrance that all of this is really 'broken' and 'undone' by the 'black surges of thunder': the war.

The poet then repeats the lines from the beginning of the second verse, showing that she still feels a sense of overwhelming defeat in the shadow of the conflict. She then reiterates the content of the first verse, which shows that, for her, along with many others on the home front, nothing has really changed. Despite her serenity in her safe, secure porch, however, there is no escaping from the war and its harsh consequences, which seem to affect everyone - even those who do not appear to be directly involved.

Like many female poets, and many American poets, there is an element of distance within these lines, in that one almost senses that the poet is describing events as they are happening to someone else. Monroe had, however, travelled widely in Europe, which experience may have given her a slightly different insight into the effects of war on that continent, which she contrasts with the comparative security of her own situation.

EDITH NESBIT

BIOGRAPHICAL DETAILS

Edith Nesbit was born on August 15th 1858 in London. She was the youngest of the four surviving children of John Collis Nesbit and his wife Sarah. Mary, Alfred, Harry and Edith also had a half sister, Sarah, from their mother's first marriage. When Edith was four, her father, who owned and ran an agricultural college, died suddenly and her mother decided that the family should move to a warmer climate, as Mary was suffering from tuberculosis. Initially they moved to Brighton, on the south coast, before Mary and her mother re-located to France. Edith and her brothers were sent to boarding schools in England, she and Alfred, for example, attended the Brunswick House School. Edith was not happy at school and longed for the holidays, when she could be reunited with the rest of her family.

Mary Nesbit died in 1871, so Sarah returned to England, living first in the country and then, in 1875, finally moving back to London. In 1877, Edith met Hubert Bland, who was a bank clerk, with whom she immediately fell in love, despite the fact that she was engaged to another man at the time. She and Bland were married in April 1880 and their son, Paul, was born the following June. This was not the only unconventional aspect of their marriage, as Hubert had at least three children by two other women. Edith forgave her husband and accepted his children and their mothers into her own family.

She and herbert had two more children together themselves - Mary, who was born in 1881 and Fabian in 1885. Throughout their marriage, Edith was the main breadwinner, as Hubert was frequently out of work. She wrote poetry, short stories and novels and both she and Hubert joined the Fabian Society. In 1899, Edith really discovered her métier, when she wrote *The Story of the Treasure*

Seekers - a book for children. Her happiness at the success of this book was short-lived and tempered by the death, in 1900 of her youngest son, Fabian.

Within the next six years, Edith had written some of her best-loved stories, including *Five Children and It*, *The Phoenix and the Carpet* and *The Railway Children*. In between, she also wrote many short stories and fairy tales.

In the spring of 1914, Hubert died and although their marriage may have been unconventional, Edith was devastated. Two years later, however, she found happiness again, when she met Thomas Terry Tucker, a marine engineer. Edith's family did not approve of Tucker, but he was utterly devoted to her and they married in February 1917. Within a few years, Edith became ill and died on 4th May 1924. She is buried at St Mary in the Marsh in Romney Marsh, Kent.

Edith Nesbit's life had many unorthodox aspects, not least of which was her acceptance of her husband's infidelities and the resultant children: a generous action which many would find impossible. Her reasons for this probably stem from her own loneliness as a child - a theme which can also be seen in her books for children, where youngsters, although separated from one or more of their parents, are always reunited in the end. One also gets the impression from her books that she deeply missed her own father and that she did not want her husband's children to share that lonely experience.

Upon reading her stories and her war poetry, one cannot help but imagine Edith Nesbit as a sensitive, loving and generous person, who felt deeply the suffering of others. Her stories, many of which have been adapted for television and film, have brought happiness to millions of children - and adults - placing their author justifiably, in the same class as J.M. Barrie, Rudyard Kipling and Beatrix Potter.

THE FIELDS OF FLANDERS

This poem opens with a description of how 'the fields' had looked during the previous spring. Having been written in 1915, and based in 'Flanders', this poem would have been referring to the consequences of the Second Battle of Ypres, which took place in April and May of that year. Edith Nesbit would, therefore, have been recalling the earlier spring of 1914, when there was no war and everything had been 'normal'.

In the second verse, she goes on to describe the fields as they are now: there are no flowers, just 'black crosses' and it would seem that nothing lives. The third verse appears to be a further account of the changing 'fields of Flanders', but here the poet has used personification and is really referring to the men. They are the 'tree of life', with 'noble' ideas and 'hopes', all of which have been 'trampled' into the ground, just like the flowers and trees themselves.

There is a slight change of tone in the fourth verse, as Edith Nesbit begins to look forward to a new spring, a fresh start and the renewal of life and hope, although she also realises that the reminders of the war and death will always be present. In the final verse, Edith Nesbit suggests that there should be some punishment for those who are responsible for the destruction of her country - by which she means the men, rather than the physical country itself. She then pleads with God to help her, and others, on the day of 'reckoning', as their debt to those who have sacrificed themselves, is too great to be contemplated.

This is a beautiful and moving poem, which captures one of the most common sentiments in non-combatant poetry of the First World War, namely, gratitude. Many women dealt with this issue, as did some men, such as G. K. Chesterton and Wilfrid Wilson Gibson, both of whom wrote eloquently on the subject. Chesterton, for example, in *The English Graves*, points out that the sacrificing soldiers were really just 'simple' men, who loved their lives and their heritage. He states at the end of this piece that the men had 'died to save their country and they only saved the world.' Gibson echoed this sentiment in his poem *Lament*. Although he served in the army, Gibson's eyesight was too poor to enable him to go on active duty, although this did not prevent him from writing some of the most realistic trench-life poetry of the whole conflict, purely from his imagination. Lament, on the other hand, is a description of his reality and here, he wonders how he will ever be able to enjoy life again without feeling 'the heart-break in the heart of things'.

Edith Nesbit, like most other poets who wrote on this topic, acknowledges that life will eventually return to normal again, but at the same time, admits her own feelings that the debt owed to that generation of men will never be repaid. Many others wrote similarly: Edith Nesbit, just did it better.

SPRING IN WAR-TIME

This nature poem describes the sense of loss felt at the passing of a loved-one, presumably a boyfriend or fiancé, and of the experiences which the survivor will no longer be able to enjoy.

This is a poem which tells of lost love and regret. The descriptions of spring-time experiences evoke images of new life, which at the end of each verse are extinguished with the realisation that these activities will either never happen again, or will never be the same. This couple will no longer walk down lover's lane; the violets have lost their scent; they will never build a home or family together.

Each verse describes a different event in the spring - the blossoming and regrowth which occur in that season are contrasted with the knowledge that life, for this woman, has effectively ceased. The everyday occurrences and observations of one left at home, are made extraordinary because she now views them, not with happiness or hope, but with regret for what might have been.

There is a great, but almost unspoken, contrast in this poem between birth and death; beginnings and endings. Spring sees the earth being reborn and coming back to life after the cold winter. War, on the other hand, demonstrates the finality of death - it is as if the earth itself is dying, or is certainly, in mourning.

The final verse shows that this soldier has only recently perished: no flowers have yet grown on his grave, so the writer perceives no sense of hope, or fulfilment of the past and is, as yet, unable to look forward.

This poem is reminiscent of *Perhaps* by Vera Brittain which, similarly, recounts events which the writer feels she will either never know, or will never enjoy again, because her fiancé has died.

This acute sense of loss and loneliness, represented by both these poems, shows the deep and mournful pain and hopelessness which many have experienced as a result of war.

Eileen Newton

BIOGRAPHICAL DETAILS

There are no verifiable biographical details available for Eileen Newton.

LAST LEAVE

A simple poem, which evokes the feelings of sorrow and fear, associated with the imminent departure of a loved-one. Eileen Newton brings these emotions to life, by the simple process of trying to ignore their existence, such denial being a common practice with which almost every reader could associate. The fact that this poem is called 'Last Leave' and is set in the autumn of 1918 could lead one to conclude that the person with whom she shared these brief moments of happiness, died in the last few weeks of the war, although that supposition is really just conjecture. Nonetheless, the honest simplicity of this poem makes it easy for the reader to sympathise with the poet and sense that all might well soon be no more than a happy 'memory'.

REVISION

From the content of the poem, we may assume that it was written after the end of the war and probably around 1925. The subtitle also tells us that the poem was written for Armistice Day. It opens with a reference to the traditional two minutes of silence which is observed on Remembrance Day, although to the poet, this period of time seems so short that the two minutes seem more like 'two moments'. She has decided, it would seem, that during this time of reflection, she will not dwell on young dead men, or red poppies or the war and all the damage it has done. Instead, she says, she will recall more personal memories of a final spring day spent with her beloved. She will remember the sun shining down between the trees and the evening star ('Hesperus'), beaming in the deep blue sky. She goes on to state that, by remembering such happiness, and releasing her own heart from the bonds of hatred, she is able once again to hear his voice and to understand that, although he is dead, their division from one another is not permanent, because their love is ever-lasting.

This is a truly beautiful poem, which captures the despair of loss, coupled with the release of hope and forgiveness which have taken many years to come about, but have finally allowed the poet to realise that love is the most powerful emotion and through that, she can learn to accept the devastation of her loss and remember, gratefully, only the happy times which she and her beloved were able to share.

Eleanour Norton

BIOGRAPHICAL DETAILS

Very little is known about Eleanour Norton, although she may be better known as the Honourable Eleanour Trehane Norton. Born in 1881, she was the daughter of John Richard Brinsley Norton, 5th Lord Grantley, Baron of Markenfield and his wife, Katharine Buckner McVickar. Eleanour lived in London and died in 1951.

IN A RESTAURANT, 1917

This poem opens with a description of a restaurant scene, where many soldiers are, it would seem, enjoying an evening out while on leave. Eleanour Norton's description of the soldiers as 'khaki knights' gives the poem an air of medieval jousts, conjuring up images of honourable men in armour, fighting for the hand of a fair maiden. In the second verse, the poet alludes to one of the soldiers, who had loved London life, although his enjoyment seems so long ago, that she wonders whether the time should really be measured in 'centuries', rather than just years. In the final verse, she reveals that he is no longer present because he has been killed in the war.

This is a poem which epitomises the changes which took place for some young women during the war. Gone were the days of carefree parties, for the simple reason that many of the participants were no longer alive.

Carola Oman

BIOGRAPHICAL DETAILS

Carola Mary Anima Oman was born on 11th May 1897 in Oxford. She was the second of three children born to historian Sir Charles William Chadwick Oman and his wife Mary. Carola spent a happy childhood in Oxford, where her father was Professor of Modern History at All Soul's College, living initially at 39 St Giles Street and then, in 1908, moving to Frewin Hall. Carola's older sister Dulce had been born in 1894, while her brother, Charles was four years younger than her. All three children were friends with the Cannan family (including fellow war poet May Wedderburn Cannan), who lived nearby and were of similar ages.

While her siblings were sent away to boarding schools, Mary Oman decided that Carola's nature was not suited to a formal education and she was sent instead to Miss Batty's School in Oxford. Both at the time, and later, Carola came to resent the restrictions which she believed had been placed on her by this decision. By the time Carola left Miss Batty's in 1914, she had already written several historical plays.

During the First World War, Carola, like many other young ladies of her class, became a VAD nurse and served both in England and France. Her first collection of poetry, entitled *The Menin Road and Other Poems*, was dedicated to May Wedderburn Cannan and published in 1919.

In April 1922, Carola was married to Gerald Foy Ray Lananton. He had served in the First World War, as a Captain with the Royal Horse Artillery and had been badly wounded, thus negating the possibility of fathering any children. Nonetheless, Carola and Gerald were very much in love and lived happily together until his death in 1952. He was knighted in 1946 for work done during the Second World War, thus making Carola's official title Lady Lenanton.

Throughout their marriage and afterwards, Carola continued to write many books, including historical novels, biographies and history books for both adults and children. Following her husband's death, Carola continued to live at their home, Bride Hall in Ayot St Laurence, Hertfordshire, until her death in June 1978.

AMBULANCE TRAIN 30

In this short poem, Carola Oman describes a scene at a railway siding, in which stands an ambulance train. The poem is set in the spring of 1919, when there were no more wounded soldiers to transport and, although this ought to have signified a reason to be more optimistic, the atmosphere created here is one of dull oppression. The train, clouds and sea are all 'grey'; the day is 'pale' and there seems to be no life in the 'harbour town'.

At the end of the poem, we learn the reason behind this sombre atmosphere: the train is being used to transport the 'occupying army' into Germany. There is no colour here and, certainly, no sense of victory, which is probably quite an accurate representation of the feelings of many who served in, and survived, the conflict. It became very difficult for them to see the end of the war as a conquest, because so much and so many had been lost.

BRUSSELS 1919

Presumably set in spring 1919, as the 'lilac tree' is just beginning to sprout new leaves, this poem describes the atmosphere in Brussels, as the city begins to revive itself after the war. Carola Oman relates the ways in which life has returned to normal, although she acknowledges that the only thing missing is the soldiers, who seem to only slowly drift back home again.

In the third verse, she mentions the colour 'red' three times, which reminds the reader of the blood which has recently been spilled on Belgian soil. The final verse offers an explanation for the absence of the soldiers, who it would seem, are now ghosts and have joined the spirits of previous wars.

This poems shows how difficult it was for the people of many nations to rebuilt their shattered lives after the war, even if their towns and cities could be reconstructed.

May O'Rourke

BIOGRAPHICAL DETAILS

Born in 1898 in Ballymena, before moving to Coomber near Belfast, May's father worked as a Supervisor of Inland Revenue in the Civil Service. Her family eventually moved to London and then on to Dorset. She was educated by the Sisters of Sainte Marie at Maumbury House and became secretary to Thomas Hardy in March 1923, becoming friends with both Thomas and his second wife Florence - who had previously been his secretary herself.

THE MINORITY 1917

This poem opens with a description of a young woman who is beautifying herself. However, the poem is not addressed to her, but to a man - presumably a non-combatant, but also probably an older man, who cannot fight. There is no sense of disapproval of the man's presence, which there probably would be, if he could have been serving in the forces, but had chosen not to. This woman, it would seem, belongs with the man, although that is mainly because all the other men have gone away 'to die' on her behalf. She tries to carry on as though nothing has changed; to laugh and enjoy herself, except that this is only really a form of defence against facing the truth and acknowledging the losses, which it would appear have confronted so many others.

The poet suggests to the man that he is a 'fool' if he fails to realise the importance of his place, which has been made sacred simply by the fact that he is replacing young, brave, dead men, or men who have been maimed or wounded or suffered the mental torture of shell-shock. This man, she asserts, seems brightly coloured when compared with the grey, drab memories of soldiers, and he is able to be romantic and frivolous because he has forgotten the young men already.

The final sentence in this poem suggests that the younger men have passed on the mantle of caring for the women at home to men such as this, but there is also a slight implication here that he is not really worthy of their trust. The 'minority' of the title suggests eligible men, of whom in 1917, there would have been an ever diminishing number.

EMILY ORR

BIOGRAPHICAL DETAILS

There are no verifiable biographical details available for Emily Orr.

A RECRUIT FROM THE SLUMS

In this simple poem, the poet questions why someone 'from the slums' should want to serve their country. She lists many things which the country could be said to have failed to do for its poor, from a lack of education and housing, to the prospect of the poor-house. Despite these sad degradations, however, the poet asserts that the slum-dwellers will 'answer the call' because they regard England as their 'mother' and, therefore, they will not fail.

This is a somewhat romanticised notion of the reason why many many poor men chose to volunteer for service. Of course, a number of them would have felt loyal and patriotic, but just as many offered their services because life in the army afforded them shelter, decent food and better wages than they could earn elsewhere. That is not to belittle their courage, but simply to state a fact.

Jessie Pope

BIOGRAPHICAL DETAILS

Jessie Pope was born on 18th March 1868 in Leicester. She was the fourth of the five children of Richard George Pope, a commercial traveller, and his wife Elizabeth (née Windover), a former governess and innkeeper's daughter. Jessie was educated initially at Craven House in Leicester and then, after the family moved south to Hornsey, she attended the North London Collegiate School. By the turn of the century, only Jessie and her younger brother Frank remained at home and the family had settled at 8 Willow Road, Hampstead. Richard Pope was now a hop seed merchant with several employees, while Frank had become a stockbroker's clerk. Jessie, meanwhile, had turned her hand to writing and had published several articles in Punch magazine, as well as newspapers such as the Daily Mail, the Daily Express and the Evening Standard. Her style was generally humorous, although she could tackle serious topics as well, such as female suffrage. In addition, Jessie wrote stories and verses for children, publishing several books between 1907 and 1915. Her most famous pre-war literary achievement was the editing of Robert Tressell's novel *The Ragged Trousered Philanthropists*, which she cut from its over-long original length of around 250,000 words to approximately 100,000, as well as persuading publisher Grant Richards to produce the book the following year.

In 1911, Jessie's father died, so she and her widowed mother moved to Totteridge Road, Whetstone, North London, living in a house named "Hillside". The beginning of the war saw Jessie, in common with many other published poets and authors, turn her hand to propaganda poetry, which was widely read at the time and was enormously popular with the general public in the early stages of the conflict. Initially published in newspapers and magazines, Jessie's poems were then brought together in three collections, *War Poems* (1915), *More War Poems* (1915) and *Simple Rhymes for Stirring Times* (1916).

As the conflict progressed and the harsh realities of this new, attritional warfare began to hit home, Jessie - and those like her - found that the jingoistic style of her poetry lost its popularity. She returned, instead, to writing childrens' stories, her resolute good humour leaving her under no illusion as to her abilities as a war poet. After the war, Jessie wrote a novel entitled *Love on Leave* which was published by Pearson in 1919 which was reviewed at the time as a romantically charged piece of fiction in which the heroes and heroines fell into each other's arms at every opportunity!

Jessie continued to write childrens' stories and poetry during the 1920s. Then at the age of sixty-one, having been single all her life, she married Edward Babington Lenton, on May 11th 1929 at Mutford in Suffolk. Lenton, a retired bank manager, was no stranger to Jessie, as he was also her brother-in-law, having married her sister Elsie (Elizabeth) on 4th April 1896 (Jessie's signature can be seen as a witness on their marriage certificate). Elsie and Edward had lived together in Devon, where they had their only child - a daughter named Violet in 1897. They moved to Ivy House, Fritton in Suffolk, and it was here that Elsie died on 30th April 1928, after 32 years of marriage. Violet herself had married in the same church as her father and Jessie, four years before her father's second marriage, to Cecil Thomas Ashworth Beevor, son of a solicitor and a former lieutenant in the Royal Field Artillery during the First World War. Jessie moved into her late sister's former home after her wedding and she and her husband lived happily at Yarmouth before moving to Devon, where Jessie died at Broom Hill House, Chagford on December 14th 1941. Edward Lenton died within six months of his second wife.

THE CALL

This poem shares a similar theme with much of Pope's other work, particularly *Who's for the Game?* Here, she levels accusations of cowardice against those who choose not to enlist.

Pope uses strong, stirring language in her attempt to whip her readers into a frenzy of nationalistic pride and encourage them to 'do their bit'. She asks a series of questions, urging young men to join up, rather than protect themselves by staying at home. The constant questioning involved in this poem is reminiscent of a nagging wife and has the effect of wearing down the reader to the point of submission

She gives enlistment and fighting an air of jollity, mentioning banners, drums, processions and victory, while suggesting that even to take part in a battle must be a thrilling honour for those involved. Against this, at the end of each verse, she creates an image of those who are left behind as cowardly, biting their nails, saving their own skin.

Once again, Jessie Pope demonstrates here a lack of understanding, goading others into fighting, and dying for not just their country, but their Empire. Victory seems assured in this poem - no mention is made of defeat, injury or death.

The Call is extremely similar in tone, style and content to *Fall In* by Harold Begbie which was first published in The Daily Chronicle in late August 1914. This is a propaganda poem which was soon set to music. In fact, a whole merchandising campaign was created around popular verses and songs such as this - badges and posters were produced and sold. Begbie's poem is, in many ways, even more disturbing than Pope's. She speaks of loyalty, heroism, patriotism and even 'fun' as being the positive aspects of the war, with the only negative being cowardice. Begbie, on the other hand, urges men to fight for fear of what others will think of them if they do not - hardly a sound reason for sacrificing one's life

Although there is no date given for the composition of *The Call*, the fact that Pope mentions Sir John French in the first verse means that it was definitely written prior to December 1915, when French was replaced by Sir Douglas Haig as Commander in Chief of the British Expeditionary Force. This was prior to the introduction of conscription, and many poets were either officially employed, or saw it as their duty to rally men to join the fight.

THE NUT'S BIRTHDAY

This humorous verse details how the war changed even the simplest of things, such as everyday tasks like choosing birthday presents. The poet recalls, in the first two verses, how the previous year, before the war, 'Gilbert's' 22nd birthday had been marked by the giving of expensive but pointless fripperies, bought by his loved-ones for the simple reason that he didn't really need anything anyway. This year, however, they have sent him practical gifts for his birthday, because he is fighting in the trenches. These gifts, although comparatively inexpensive, have shown more thought and consideration on the part of his loved-ones, and have also been greeted with great pleasure and gratitude by 'Gilbert'.

A simple verse, the message here is, basically, that the war is teaching people better values, which is possibly an optimistic interpretation.

SOCKS

Jessie Pope did not write exclusively in an ardently patriotic fashion. Her poem Socks, has a completely different tone. There are definite elements of sorrow and regret in this poem which tells of a wife or mother sitting by the fire knitting socks and thinking of her loved-one. She remembers his departure and how he had been close to tears, but this is not said as a criticism, more as an appreciation that he had tried to put a brave face on his sorrow. She worries about him - simple things like whether he's warm enough, and whether he is finding a soldier's life too arduous.

The sudden noise of the paper-boy makes her start - it reminds her of the dreaded knock of the telegram-boy. The woman wonders where her soldier is now, and what he's been doing. The poem ends with the woman optimistically hoping that he'll come home and tell her all about his adventures.

Throughout the poem, Pope ends each stanza with a reference to knitting instructions and the inclusion of these can be interpreted in several ways. Women frequently knitted socks and other items of clothing for the men at the front - not just their own families, but often these garments were sent out en-masse from women's groups. Many women, who for whatever reason were unable to contribute directly to the war-effort, saw this as their way of helping the men at the front, so Pope could simply be reminding us that women were not idly sitting at home, but were doing whatever they could to help the soldiers. Alternatively, she could be pointing out the monotony of life for the women at home - the repetitive knitting pattern symbolises this, and maybe she is making a comparison here between his adventures and potential sacrifices, and her (comparatively) meagre contribution to his well-being. As a third alternative, the knitting could also be seen as an occupation which keeps the woman from thinking about her worries and fears - something which keeps her going, and banishes unwelcome thoughts which might otherwise prove too distracting.

Socks is a far more realistic poem than *War Girls*, for example. Although both paint a picture of female life during the war, Socks at least allows that women should be allowed to worry about their men, while getting on with life.

WAR GIRLS

War Girls has a very different tone from many of Jessie Pope's other works. Although still proud and patriotic, the subject matter is not the same. Here, she is not addressing herself to would-be soldiers, goading them to fight for their country, instead this poem is a celebration of the role of women in the war. Pope describes various jobs which, in the absence of men, women have undertaken - for example, the ticket collector, lift operator or driver. She speaks of the pre-war woman as though she were trapped, and has only now gained her freedom. This was, indeed, quite true. Many women, called upon to work for the first time, discovered that staying dutifully at home had, in fact, been a very unfulfilling way of life. At the same time, however, she reminds us that these women must still fulfil their household or womanly duties with a warm heart, and also that many of them are resourceful mothers. The women, she says, are also loyal, having no time for affairs of the heart and thinking only of the return of their fighting men.

This poem is a rose-tinted, optimistic portrayal of what was often a harsh reality: for example, women were not always treated very well by their employers and they, quite often, had to do dangerous work. In addition, Pope makes no mention of the widowed wife or mother. She speaks of the return of the soldiers as a certainty, but her men will be marching, not in wheelchairs or on stretchers. In common with many of her other poems, death is not seen as a necessary consequence of war - in fact it is not even mentioned.

Jessie Pope is often accused of fuelling the jingo-women; the minority of women who gave out white feathers to men who had not joined up. Quite often, these men had been unable to enlist, either because their work was considered important to the war-effort, or because their health was deemed too poor for them to serve. *War Girls* makes no mention of these women, celebrating instead, those who chose to work, in place of the men, at various tasks not normally allocated to women. However, she also makes no mention of the women who did other war work, such as VAD's, ambulance drivers etc.. As such, it appears that this poem is an attempt to praise only the women who took over the men's work. However, in reality, many of these women were, in fact, not so ready to give up their work and return to their previously subservient way of life when the men returned from the war.

Although this poem is less controversial than *Who's For the Game?* or *The Call*, its lack of realism makes it less appealing than perhaps it might have been.

INEZ QUILTER

BIOGRAPHICAL DETAILS

Very little is known about Inez Quilter, other than the fact that it is believed she was born in 1904 and died in 1978. As such, she would have been a schoolgirl during the First World War.

SALL

This poem has the subtitle of "(In Aid of the Wounded Horse)", which tells us the subject matter.

Written by an 11 year old girl, 'Sall' is about a 'plough horse', who explains her situation to the reader. The most valuable aspect of this poem is its reflection of the child's perspective of the war. In Nina MacDonald's *Sing a Song of War-time*. We can see that children, evidently, saw the war very differently from adults. This can also be seen here as, with a child's innocence and simplicity, Inez Quilter puts an eloquent case for some of the unsung heroes of the war - the horses..

Dorothy Una Ratcliffe

BIOGRAPHICAL DETAILS

Dorothy Una Clough was born at Preston in Sussex, in the summer of 1887. She was the oldest of the four children of George Benson Clough, a barrister, and his wife, Rose. By the turn of the century, the family had moved from Sussex to Oxshott in Surrey. Dorothy was educated initially in England and then also in both Germany and France, following which she began writing poetry, prose and plays.

On 21st September 1909, Dorothy married Charles Frederick Ratcliffe-Brotherton and they moved to the Yorkshire Dales. The couple were divorced in October 1931. Dorothy then married Captain Noel McGrigor Phillips, who had served in the Royal Engineers in the First World War. Captain Phillips had already been married and had two children, Cynthia and Ivor. He died in 1943 and four years later, Dorothy married Alfred Charles Vowles, who adopted her married name of Phillips.

Dorothy had become an expert on the dialects of Yorkshire and wrote widely on the subject, as well as continuing to write novels and plays throughout her life. Alfred died in 1965, followed by Dorothy, two years later.

REMEMBRANCE DAY IN THE DALES

This poem, which due to its title, we may assume was written some time after the end of the war, offers a mother's perspective of the loss of two of her sons. Although there is no evidence that Dorothy Una Ratcliffe had any children - and even if she did, they would not have been old enough to fight in the First World

War - it would not have been difficult for her to imagine herself in the role of a grieving mother.

The reference to 'The Abbey', in line two might give a clue as to the date of composition, as it was in 1920, on 11th November, that an unknown British warrior was buried in Westminster Abbey as a symbol of the many men who had died, but who had no known grave. Within the context of this poem, we may assume that the same could be said of 'Jack' and 'Willie', as the poet does not mention a grave, only states where they would have chosen to be buried themselves.

The recollections of the delights of 'Jack' and 'Willie' are, however, somewhat diminished by the irregular and slightly jarring rhythm and rhyme of this poem and, in particular its last line, which does scant justice, in its informality, to the representative of so many, who was deservedly 'buried among the Kings'.

Ursula Roberts

BIOGRAPHICAL DETAILS

Ursula Wyllie was born in 1887 in India, the youngest of five children. Her father, Robert, was a Lieutenant-Colonel in the Indian Army. Of her three brothers, one appears to have served in the First World War. Ronald, the youngest of the three, was already an officer in the Royal Garrison Artillery and was attached to the General Staff during the war. In 1909, Ursula married the Reverend William Corbett Roberts, who was fourteen years older than her and they lived, initially and throughout most of the First World War, in Northamptonshire, where he was Rector of Crick. The years between the wars were spent in London and then in various parishes in the south-east. Ursula wrote mainly novels, articles and poems, sometimes using the pseudonym of Susan Miles. William died in 1953, while Ursula survived until 1975.

THE CENOTAPH

This poem must have been written after 1920, when the Cenotaph in Whitehall was unveiled. The setting is, presumably, Armistice Day, as we are told that the 'relatives of dead heroes' are waiting to place their wreaths. The poet, or narrator, is on an omnibus and describes the reactions of some of the other passengers to the scene which is taking place outside.

Their silence is broken by a 'plump woman', who as she prepares to leave the bus, declares that she would not be prepared to 'stand in a queue' just to be publicly distressed, although she is quite prepared to accept that others might. The poet seeks to recall this woman's tolerance, when she becomes impatient with those who choose public displays of grief.

It is unclear whether Ursula Roberts is being ironic or realistic here. She may be suggesting that everyone could do with demonstrating a little more tolerance, or she may be alluding to a sense that she has grown weary of public grief.

Margaret Sackville

BIOGRAPHICAL DETAILS

Lady Margaret Sackville was born on Christmas Eve, 1881 in Mayfair, London. She was the youngest of the five children of Reginald Windsor Sackville, 7th Earl de la Warr, and his wife Constance. Reginald had been baptised Reginald Windsor West, which he later changed to Sackville-West and then to Sackville. Margaret was second cousin to Vita Sackville-West.

She spent a fairly idyllic childhood in Sussex, although this was marred by the death, by drowning, of her oldest brother, Lionel in 1890 and then her father's death, six years later. Margaret wrote poetry from an early age, and in 1897, was 'discovered' by the poet William Scawen Blunt. From then on, she regularly published poetry in newspapers and magazines and in 1900, produced her first collection, entitled Floral Symphony.

Her literary career took off. In 1912, she became friends with the Labour politician, Ramsay MacDonald, for whom their relationship was more than simple friendship, as he proposed marriage several times. His offers were always refused, although recently discovered letters between the two reveal that they may have been lovers, but that marriage remained socially and religiously impossible.

During the First World War, Margaret took a firm anti-war stance, joining the Union of Democratic Control, which was opposed to military influence in government and had been co-founded by Ramsay MacDonald. The Union opposed censorship and conscription and had close links with other organisations, such as the Quakers.

In her poetry at the time, Margaret was highly critical of women who supported the war, writing a notable poem, *Nostra Culpa* ('Our Fault'), which decried the mothers of men, who allowed them to fight and said nothing. Her only remaining brother, Gilbert, who had inherited his father's title and become 8th Earl de la Warr in 1896, fought in the Royal Naval Volunteer Reserve as a Lieutenant aboard HMML California. He was killed on 16th December 1915, off the Italian coast and is one of only three Commonwealth dead buried at Messina Town Cemetery.

After the war, Margaret moved to Scotland, remaining there until 1936, whereupon she moved firstly to London and then to Cheltenham, where she died in 1963.

A MEMORY

This poem appears to be written from the perspective of a soldier, who has witnessed some of the horrors of the war. The scene is a village, presumably in Belgium, where some of the civilians have been killed. Women weep, bodies lie in the street and, although there has been some shelling, the place now seems strangely quiet. These people are not soldiers and, therefore, it is difficult for troops to see such sights and not be haunted by them. The poet suggests, in fact, that the soldiers find episodes like this even more disturbing than being in a battle.

This is a fairly self-explanatory poem, presumably written on the basis of newspaper reports or other accounts, as the poet had no first-hand experience of the war. Her portrayal of the soldiers' sensibilities also coincides with her own anti-war sentiments, as well as providing a romanticised image of the troops involved.

SACRAMENT

Margaret Sackville was of the Roman Catholic faith and a 'Sacrament' is a religious act, which outwardly demonstrates evidence of inner spirituality, such as in a marriage ceremony, baptism or Mass (Holy Communion) at which bread and wine are consumed, representing the body and blood of Christ. In this poem, Margaret Sackville likens the world to an altar, at which the people are kneeling. They want to partake in the Eucharist and ask for the bread and wine, but then decry the offerings which are being made, because they are the results of so many sacrifices. The poet associates the bread and wine with the bodies and blood of the soldiers, rather than of Christ and also hints that God is in some way responsible for their deaths. She implies that everyone shares in the suffering and, in addition, hints that the sacrifices are wasted, in that they are 'crumbled' and 'poured' away.

Aimee Byng Scott

BIOGRAPHICAL DETAILS

Very little is known about Aimee Byng Scott. She was born Aimee Byng-Hall in 1868, the daughter of General C. H. Hall. In 1894, she married Major-General Sir Arthur Scott. Aimee published many poems and plays, in some of which she used the pseudonym Alec Holmes.

JULY 1st, 1916

Aimee Byng Scott came from, and married into, the military. Her husband, Major-General Sir Arthur Scott, had entered the army in 1881 and had risen through the ranks, serving in South Africa. In the First World War, he was in command of the 12th (Eastern) Division on the Western Front, from 1915-1918. On 1st July 1916 (the opening day of the Battle of the Somme), this Division was in action, attached to the Fourth Army, under Sir Henry Rawlinson.

In her poem, Aimee Byng Scott initially describes a peaceful, early morning scene, where poppies grow in the forests and cornfields, while there are larks singing above. In the second verse, however, although the setting is the same, it is now night time: there are no more poppies, only gunfire; the corn and the trees are dead and the war has trampled nature into submission.

This is a fairly basic nature poem, showing the effects which the war was having on man's natural surroundings, but making no mention of the consequences for the men themselves.

MAY SINCLAIR

BIOGRAPHICAL DETAILS

Mary Amelia St Clair Sinclair was born on August 24th 1863 in Rock Ferry, Cheshire. She was the youngest child and only daughter of William Sinclair, an East India Merchant and his wife, Amelia. May, as she became known, had five older brothers, who were aged between eleven and two when she was born. By the end of the 1860s, William Sinclair's business was floundering and in the early 1870s he was declared bankrupt

Over the next ten years, although her brothers attended grammar schools, May was educated largely at home, although she did briefly attend Cheltenham Ladies' College. Meanwhile her father had turned to alcohol and died in 1881. During the course of the next few years, Mary's brothers also died, probably from an inherited heart condition, starting with Harold in 1887 and ending with Joseph in 1905. Both Joseph, and May's oldest brother William, left children and May took on the responsibility of raising them. She had, meanwhile, begun writing, publishing her first book in 1886, using the pseudonym of Julian Sinclair, followed by another, Essays in Verse, which was published in her own name, in 1892.

As her brothers departed, either through marriage, or death, May was left alone to look after her mother in their small flat in Hampstead. Her feelings of entrapment and frustration were evident in her writing at the time. More books followed and, after her mother's death in 1901, May, now aged 38, moved to Kensington. She was becoming a regular feature in London's literary circles, her social group including W.B. Yeats, Thomas Hardy and H.G. Wells.

A keen supporter of the women's suffrage movement, May Sinclair also became interested in psychoanalysis and included these topics in some of her novels. In

1913, May was introduced to Charlotte Mew and, although it has been widely reported that the two women shared an 'intense' friendship, it would seem that Charlotte Mew made the mistake of declaring her love for May: a sentiment which was rejected. It is alleged that May then publicly humiliated Charlotte Mew for having made such an approach, which had a detrimental effect on the, already fragile, personality of Miss Mew.

During the First World War, May Sinclair worked as secretary and treasurer for Dr Hector Munro's volunteer ambulance service, although Munro soon replaced her. Over the next few years, she continued to write, earning a reputation as one of the best and most widely-read female authors of her time. By 1920, she had been to develop Parkinson's disease and wrote little from then on. She died on 14th November 1946.

FIELD AMBULANCE IN RETREAT

The subtitle to this poem appears to mean something like 'Painful Road, Sacred Road'. May Sinclair opens the poem with a description of a road, lined by 'tall trees', flowers and canals. She goes on to explain that this road in Belgium was once used to move 'corn from the harvest', but now the 'few' farmhands who are left, stand to one side of the road to allow the Red Cross ambulances to pass. She likens the gathering of the corn, which has been cut down, to the harvesting of the wounded men.

In the third section of the poem, Sinclair describes how, under the trampling of the mens' feet, the road becomes like 'dust'. The men seem despondent and 'proud' at the same time, as they withdraw from the field of battle. At the same time, the ambulance is also 'in retreat', as it must take its cargo of wounded away from danger, although there is also a sense of regret that the perils of war are at an end. It is as though the ambulance drivers feel 'safety' in retreat, and yet this security actually leaves them feeling more ill-at-ease. The men in retreat are themselves overtaken by the ambulance, which can obviously travel faster, therefore, leaving them behind.

This is a poem of mixed messages and metaphors, which describes, it would seem, the retreat from Mons in late August 1914. May Sinclair had joined a volunteer ambulance service and spent a brief time in Belgium. She may well have witnessed the retreat itself and, therefore, might have been struck by the ambiguity of the situation, where men marched exhausted, pursued by the Germans, and knowing that at some point, they would have to turn back and fight again (which they did on September 5th at the First Battle of the Marne). The retreat was carried out in a very orderly manner, there was no panic, but the human cost of holding off the German army to allow the Allied retreat, was enormous.

Edith Sitwell

BIOGRAPHICAL DETAILS

Edith Sitwell was born on 7th September 1887 in Scarborough. She was the oldest of the three children of Sir George Reresby Sitwell, fourth baronet, and his wife, Lady Ida, who was the daughter of the First Earl of Londesborough. Her brothers, Francis Osbert and Sacheverell were born in 1892 and 1897 respectively.

While Osbert and Sacheverell would later recall happy childhoods, Edith's recollections of their parents were less favourable. Unlike her brothers, who went to Eton, Edith was educated mainly at the family home, Renishaw Hall in Derbyshire, by a series of governesses.

During her teenage years, Edith became interested in poetry and, in 1913, she had her first poem published, in the Daily Mirror. This minor success encouraged Edith to leave home, which she did, in the company of her governess, Helen Rootham. The two women shared a flat in Bayswater during the First World War, in which both of Edith's brothers served.

In 1916, Edith began editing a poetry anthology entitled *Wheels*, which was produced annually until 1921. This influential series featured many up and coming poets, including Wilfred Owen, Nancy Cunard, Iris Tree, Edward Wyndham Tennant, Aldous Huxley and all three Sitwells.

Although Edith Sitwell never married, she did have a relationship with Russian painter Pavel Tchelitchew, which only ended when Helen Rootham became ill, with cancer. The two women moved again, settling in Paris, where Rootham died in 1938.

When the Second World War began the following year, Edith returned to England, moving back to the family home, now occupied by Osbert and his lover, David Horner. The Second World War saw her produce some of her best-known poetry. She was made a Dame in 1954 and converted to the Roman Catholic faith the following year. For the last seven years of her life, Edith Sitwell was confined to a wheelchair and died in December 1964.

THE DANCERS

This poem conjures up several bizarre images in the mind of the reader. Initially, it seems that Edith Sitwell is describing a macabre dance party on a blood-stained floor, where people enjoy themselves, regardless of the war. One could be fooled into thinking that she is alluding to real people dancing in London, while young men die in France and that the blood is, somehow, representative of their guilt or complicity.

In verse three, however, the real meaning becomes clearer, as she literally explains that the subjects of the poem are the flies which plague the battlefields. Edith Sitwell paints a horrendous picture of these creatures enjoying the results of the battle, 'dancing' over the corpses. No longer could one think of them as just surviving, but rather they delight in their surroundings.

This is quite an unusual poem for a woman to have written at the time and it demonstrates Edith Sitwell's unorthodox nature.

CICELY FOX SMITH

BIOGRAPHICAL DETAILS

Cicely Fox Smith was born on February 1st 1882 in Cheshire, the youngest of the four children of Richard Smith, a barrister, and his wife Alice. She was educated at Manchester High School for Girls and both she and her sister Margaret took a keen interest in poetry. Margaret went on to write essays, but Cicely's first love was always poetry. Her oldest brother, Richard, followed their father into the legal profession, while the second son, Philip, became a painter.

Such was Cicely's passion for poetry, that she published her first volume of poetry in 1898. Many more books, of both poetry and prose followed, but the subject upon which she most frequently based her work, was adventure on the high seas. Due to this subject matter, Cicely wrote under the name of C. Fox Smith, or sometimes just CFS. Some of her books were written in conjunction with her sister, who used the pen-name Madge S. Smith. Cicely never married and died on April 8th 1954, at the age of 72.

THE CONVALESCENT

This poem is written in a conversational, colloquial style, portraying that the narrator and subject of the piece is probably a ranking soldier, rather than an officer. The setting is either a hospital or a convalescent home, where the wounded men, who no longer needed full hospital care, could be sent to recover from their injuries, before going home on leave.

The poem opens with a description of the facilities that have been made available to the men, which to a working class man would probably have seemed quite palatial. Despite this, the man longs to go home and frequently asks the 'sister' when he will be released. She seems a little surprised, but he explains that, although the home and its staff are not at fault, he really just wants to go home. He goes on to recall details about his home and how these memories have helped him at various times during the conflict. He also thinks about other, simple things, which he has missed since being away from home. Finally, he thinks about the prospect of his homecoming and how the neighbours will be pleased to see him; he thinks that his wife will probably cry and that his children - one of whom is clearly a baby - will be delighted to see him too.

This seems like quite a jolly poem, as the man looks forward to going home, despite his wounds, which are not described. This sense of cheerfulness is enhanced here by the informal language and also by the repetition of the last line in each verse.

MARIE CARMICHAEL STOPES

BIOGRAPHICAL DETAILS

Marie Charlotte Carmichael Stopes was born on 15th October 1880 in her mother's home town of Edinburgh. She was the older of the two daughters of Henry Stopes, a wealthy master brewer from Colchester in Essex, and his wife, Charlotte. Another daughter, Winifred, was born three years later, by which time the family was living in London. Marie was initially educated at home, before being sent to St George's in Edinburgh and then the North London Collegiate School. Her father was a keen amateur archeologist and this sparked an interest in Marie, who studied science at University College, London. She went on to a career in palaeobotany, the study of fossil plants, studying botany in Munich. In 1904, she became assistant lecturer in botany at Manchester University, before travelling to Japan in 1907, where she spent two years researching and writing.

Marie's choice of occupation was extremely unusual for a young woman at that time but, despite her firm allegiance to the Womens' Suffrage movement, she also wanted marriage and children. In 1911, she married a Canadian botanist, Reginald Ruggles Gates, although she retained her maiden name. Despite the fact that their relationship seemed happy on the surface, there were underlying problems and in 1916, Marie successfully applied to have the marriage annulled, on the grounds that it had not been consummated. She claimed that she remained completely innocent with regards to the physical aspects of marriage. Gates contested this statement, with accusations as to Marie's fidelity, citing her relationships prior to their marriage and one romantic friendship with a lodger afterwards. Nonetheless, the court was convinced by Marie's statement and she and Gates parted acrimoniously.

Despite her claimed innocence upon sexual relations, by 1914, Marie had already begun writing a manuscript based on sexual behaviour and feelings. In

1917, she met Lieutenant Humphrey Verdon Roe, a wealthy officer in the Royal Flying Corps, who was also involved in the design and manufacture of aircraft, having co-founded A.V. Roe & Company (AVRO), with his brother. Marie and Humphrey were married in May 1918, shortly after the publication of her bestselling book, *Married Love*, to which Humphrey gave both moral and financial backing. This book and its sequel, *Wise Parenthood*, published later in 1918, dealt with the taboo subjects of ovulation, menstruation, sexual desire, the sexual problems facing married couples and, latterly, contraception - in that she advocated, vociferously, that sex within marriage should not be seen purely as a means of procreation.

These books were an overnight success, but were also extremely controversial. In addition to her literary success, Marie was now pregnant and, at 38, was delighted. Her child, a son, was stillborn in July 1919 and, although distraught, she and Humphrey continued with their plans to open a birth control clinic in a working class area of North London. Here she advocated that women should take responsibility for their own pregnancies, deciding upon the timing and quantity of children they were going to have. There was also a standing policy that only those who were already, or about to become, married would be given advice. Marie believed that it was beneficial to both the parents and their children, that all pregnancies should be wanted and planned.

All of this proved unpopular with the establishment, especially the church. In 1924, Marie gave birth to a son, named Harry, who was her only child. Following his birth, Marie's relationship with Humphrey became difficult, although she attributed their sexual problems to a wound which he had received during the First World War.

Other scientists and doctors were now becoming more interested in birth control, but Marie refused to co-operate with them, becoming more professionally isolated. Despite her protestations regarding the joy of married love, her own marriage was floundering and she became romantically interested in other men. In approximately 1938, Humphrey wrote to her, giving her his permission to take a lover - although it has been alleged that Marie dictated this letter herself.

In 1947, two years before Humphrey's death, she also became estranged from her son, Harry, as a result of his engagement to Mary Wallis. Mary, the daughter of Barnes Wallis, the inventor of the 'bouncing bomb' which was used in the famous Dambusters Raid of 1943, had myopia, which Marie claimed, as a hereditary defect, made her an unsuitable match for Harry. This episode demonstrates one of Marie Stopes's more radical perspectives. She believed in

Eugenics - that the human species may be improved by discouraging reproduction by persons who have hereditary defects. As a result of Harry's marriage, Marie disinherited him and they only managed a partial reconciliation shortly before her death, from cancer, in October 1958.

NIGHT ON THE SHORE

The setting and supposed date of this poem are given as a subtitle, although given the content of the second section of the poem, it was probably written retrospectively, some time later. The poem opens with a description of a scene in which the narrator and an owl watch the clouds and the sea, in a 'cosmic' experience which seems to leave the narrator somewhat dumbfounded.

In the second section, Stopes changes the scene and, although there is still a tent, it would now appear to be in an army camp. The problem with the given date of the poem ensues, as on 6th August 1914, the soldiers would not have been 'scanning the horizon for their foes', as few, if any, British troops had arrived in France or Flanders and barely a shot had been fired. The poet goes on to describe how men seem eager to fight and kill, blaming these feelings on some deep-set 'rage'.

This is a confused poem, which says little and means less and which, like much of Marie Stopes's verse, leads one to believe she should have stuck to science and left literature well alone.

Muriel Stuart

BIOGRAPHICAL DETAILS

Muriel Stuart Irwin was born on 20th March 1885 in London. She was the oldest of the three daughters of Thomas Lennox Irwin, a barrister, and his wife, Elizabeth. Muriel attended Croydon School of Art and also began writing, using the pseudonym Muriel Stuart. In 1912, she married a man named Minnitt, but he died within a few years. By the mid-1920s, she had published five collections of poetry and was beginning to make a name for herself. Then in 1927, she married Arthur William Board, a publisher, with whom she had two children. From then on, she wrote no more poetry, although she did write a play *The Marriage Bond*, which was produced in the West End in the 1930s. She and her family lived quietly in Berkshire and she died on December 18th 1967, at her daughter's home in Lyme Regis.

FORGOTTEN DEAD, I SALUTE YOU

The first two verses of this poem deal with the pre-war experiences of a man who has died. These experiences revolve around the natural world, as the poet describes birds, flowers, the wind, rain and many other everyday feats of nature, which the man will no longer be able to enjoy. At the end of these first two verses, Muriel Stuart questions whether anyone remembers the man.

In the third verse, she answers her own question, as she asserts that no-one commemorates him. She paints a sad and lonely picture of him lying, abandoned in a grave, while others are able to carry on living, because of his sacrifice. Stuart then makes a comparison between this man's death and that of Christ, before going on to urge the survivors to remember the man, for the simple reason that he died for them.

This poem has a fairly common theme of gratitude and remembrance and, although Stuart speaks only of a single man, it may be assumed that she was referring to the dead in general, rather than one particular person.

MILLICENT SUTHERLAND

BIOGRAPHICAL DETAILS

Lady Millicent Fanny St Clair-Erskine was born on 20th October 1867 at Dysart House, Fife. She was the oldest of the five children of Robert Francis St Clair-Erskine, 4th Earl of Rosslyn and his wife, Blanche. In 1884, on Millicent's seventeenth birthday, she was married to Cromartie Sutherland-Leveson-Gower, Marquess of Stafford, who in 1892, would succeed to the title of 4th Duke of Sutherland. He was sixteen years older than Millicent, but she was by no means out of her depth, quickly establishing herself as one of the greatest of the many London society hostesses.

Their first daughter, Victoria, was born within ten months of the marriage, although she died before her third birthday. Three more children followed: George in 1888, Alastair in 1890 and Rosemary in 1893. When Cromartie inherited his father's title, he also became the owner of estates in Scotland, Staffordshire and Shropshire, as well as his own property, Stafford House in London. As well as proving a great success in London society, Millicent was also becoming more politically aware and became interested in workers' rights and the revival of traditional Scottish industries. In addition, she wrote novels, plays and poetry, with varying degrees of success.

In 1913, the Duke died at the age of 62 and the following year, Millicent married Brigadier General Percy Fitzgerald. At the beginning of the First World War, she established a Red Cross Ambulance unit and served in France, winning awards from France, Belgium and Great Britain for her services. Her daughter, Rosemary, also served with the Red Cross during the conflict.

By the end of the war, her husband's womanising had taken its toll and the couple were divorced in 1919. In October of the same year, Millicent married

Lieutenant-Colonel George Ernest Hawes, although they too divorced in 1925. At the beginning of the Second World War, Millicent was living in France and found herself a prisoner of the advancing Third Reich. She managed to escape through Spain and Portugal and saw out the war in America. Once Paris was liberated, she returned to live there, and died in France in August 1955.

ONE NIGHT

This poem was, it would seem, written while Millicent Sutherland was working at the British Hospital in Dunkirk. This is a simple verse of rhyming couplets, in which the poet imagines herself, during a break from her duties, having a conversation with the moon. During this discussion, the moon tells her of all the various things it has seen: from dead and dying men, to sinking ships.

We may assume that this poem was set in the winter, as the moon alludes to the snow covered ground. At the end of their conversation, the poet returns to her hospital ward.

This simple poem provides quite an insight into the poet's personality. She saw service in France throughout the war, but makes hardly any reference here to her own work, alluding instead to the suffering of others.

C.A.L.T.

BIOGRAPHICAL DETAILS

There are no verifiable biographical details available for C.A.L.T.

YMCA

Although the name of the poet is unclear, we may assume that these are the initials of someone who worked with the YMCA during the conflict. That organisation, which was established in America in the middle of the nineteenth century, set up huts during the First World War, which served food and drinks to soldiers as well as providing entertainment. The YMCA huts could sometimes be found in quite close proximity to the front lines.

In this poem, set in August 1915, the poet describes her feelings on serving tea, scones, 'Horlicks' and other such refreshments to the five hundred or so 'Tommies' who pass through the canteen. She thanks each soldier that she sees, with a heartfelt gratitude, for his bravery. The work done at canteens like this was an essential boost to morale and men would often use this brief respite to write letters home, or enjoy some peace and quiet. Another poet who wrote of similar war work was May Wedderburn Cannan and although this poem might lack some of Miss Cannan's literary prowess, it is heartfelt and honest, nonetheless.

SARA TEASDALE

BIOGRAPHICAL DETAILS

Sara Trevor Teasdale was born on 8th August 1884, the youngest of the four children of wealthy St Louis merchant John Warren Teasdale and his wife, Mary Elizabeth Willard. Sara was significantly younger than her siblings, her oldest brother George being twenty years her senior, while even her nearest brother, John was a full fourteen years older. In between these two brothers, Sara had a sister, named Mary. However, as all three were so much older, Sara was effectively raised as an only child and was kept very protected and isolated by her parents, who encouraged her to keep herself hidden away from society. This was partly born out of their own fear that Sara might fall 'victim' to the more Bohemian side of St Louis society, which went contrary to their own more Victorian values. Thus, Sara's upbringing was rather stifled, creating within her some very unrealistic notions as to romance and marriage.

In line with this rather Victorian childhood, Sara was educated at a private girl's school named Hossmer Hall, although even her education began late, as her parents decided she was too sickly to attend school until the age of nine. Following a mere four years at Hossmer Hall, Sara's formal education was considered to be complete. However, by this time, she had already discovered her passion for poetry, a hobby which her parents encouraged, deeming it a suitable pastime for their daughter. By her early twenties, Sara was no longer regarding writing as a hobby, but as a profession, which she undertook with regimented discipline, publishing her first volume of work, *Sonnets to Duse*, four years later.

Further volumes of poetry followed at regular intervals, totalling six during her life time, and one which was published after her death. Many of her early poems feature themes centred around death and depression, much of which was caused by the continued stifling atmosphere at home, which contradicted Sara's artistic talents and desires. As Sara's poems progress, it is possible to see that she gained greater freedom and more experience of life and that this was translated into her work. Even here, however, there was a conflict, as Sara longed for love and marriage, while simultaneously desiring her own freedom, realising that the two were not usually compatible.

Between 1911 and 1914, Sara was allowed to travel - initially as a curative, following a bout of depression - but then to visit friends in New York, Chicago and even Europe. During these visits, she met other poets, including Harriet Monroe and Vachel Lindsay, with whom she fell in love. Despite this, and against the advice of her friends, Sara married Ernst Balthasar Filsinger, the son of German immigrants in 1914. Filsinger, a wealthy businessman in his own right, was far more in the mould of respectable husband that her parents would have expected her to choose. Vachel Lindsay, who himself later married, remained a close friend of Sara's until his suicide in December 1931.

Sara's marriage was not a happy one, as she soon came to realise her disappointments in her anticipations of love and romance - especially given her choice of a somewhat sedate husband. Filsinger travelled a great deal, while she relied greatly upon her ill health to keep her at home, thus enforcing her desired independence from her husband. Eventually, she made this permanent and sought a divorce in 1929. After this, Sara Teasdale wrote little poetry, but turned her attention instead to writing a biography of the nineteenth century English poet, Christina Rossetti. Research for this project necessitated two trips to England and upon her return from the second of these, Sara suffered from a slight stroke. A fear of possible paralysis as a result of any further strokes filled Sara with dread and she committed suicide on January 29th 1933, by overdosing on sleeping pills.

SPRING IN WAR-TIME

This poem was first published in Sara Teasdale's 1915 volume of poetry entitled *Rivers to the Sea*, making it quite an early war poem - especially by an American poet. Within that volume, the poem is preceded by another piece entitled *Dusk in War-Time*, which runs as follows:

A half-hour more and you will lean
To gather me close in the old sweet way -
But oh, to the woman over the sea
Who will come at the close of the day?

A half-hour more and I will hear
The key in the latch and the strong quick tread -
But oh, the woman over the sea
Waiting at dusk for one who is dead!

Here, Teasdale shows sympathy and support for the women of Europe who, at this stage of the war, shared a very different fate from their American counterparts.

In *Spring in War-Time*, however, the theme is different, as here, the poet examines the commonly studied topic of how life can be expected to continue as normal, in the midst of such a terrible war. Spring is frequently chosen to represent this theme as it demonstrates the coming of new life and new beginnings, which contrast with the harsh finality of war and death.

The poem opens with a reference to the fact that spring feels as though it is 'far off', although it is clearly close enough for the 'scent' of it to be recognisable. However, the poet then seems to wonder how the spring can have the 'heart' to make her usual annual appearance, in a world so full of grief.

In the second verse, time appears to have moved on just a little, as now the days grow longer, signalling the onset of the warmer months. Once again, however, the element of doubt creeps in as she wonders how the lengthening of the daylight hours can still be taking place, since this is what allows the men to fight - and this should surely go against nature. The poet seems to make the assumption that it is the 'daylight' that gives the soldiers the opportunity to fight, which isn't really the case: night time was just as dangerous in the trenches. However, most of the fighting on the Western Front did take place during the spring, summer and autumn months, but rarely during the winter.

The third verse has a repetition of this same idea: that spring is imminent , but that the poet is somehow surprised by its inevitable arrival, given the surroundings, which are dominated by death. There is a repetition of the personification from verse one here, in which the poet suggests that the season has a 'heart'. Her description of the graves as 'new' not only reminds us of the recent deaths of soldiers in war, but also implies, by omission, that older graves of civilians, are perhaps, less important or less worthy.

In the final verse, we see, possibly, the real source of the poet's sadness. Having recently married herself, and found that relationship somewhat disappointing, Teasdale might well have found her thoughts turning more easily to the days when lovers could walk together, dreaming romantically of what their future held. Her own situation was not destroyed by death, as were so many others, but she may well have found it possible to empathise with those who had lost more than their ideals of love and romance. Her blank description of death as simply 'grey' is automatically depressing, although rather non-descript and this contrasts with the images of spring which have gone before.

Overall, this is a rather disappointing poem as it covers ground which has been covered by many other poets, before and since, including Vera Brittain and Edith Nesbit in her poem of identical title. Here, Nesbit covers exactly the same ground, wondering how it will be possible for spring to ever appear again, now that her beloved is dead. The difference between the two, and the thing that makes Nesbit's version more affecting, is that her poem is more personal: she is the one who has lost a loved one and who now cannot smell the violets, or see the blossom, or hear the birdsong without him. Although Nesbit suffered no such loss herself, she writes as though she did and we can feel this in her words - a sense which is lacking in the much more aloof form of Teasdale's writing.

THERE WILL COME SOFT RAINS

This poem opens on an optimistic note as the poet alludes to the coming of spring. She remarks on the rainfall and the fresh, clean smell which spring rain tends to leave in its wake. Then she mentions birdsong and the frogs which sing, both of which may refer to courtship or mating rituals as both of these species use their voices to attract a mate. This is followed by a reference to the white blossom which is found on plum trees during the spring. All of the items mentioned in the first two couplets describe the arrival of spring and all of the positive aspects of that season. Even the rain, which might have been given a negative association, is seen as beneficial.

In the third couplet, Sara Teasdale continues with her spring-time aspirations, but one could argue that her descriptions have become slightly more sinister here. She refers to the robin's plumage as a 'feathery fire' which may be a reference to its colour but could also be interpreted as an allusion to the fire of battle. Equally, her description of this bird sitting on a 'low fence-wire', may be literal, but could also refer to the barbed wire of the battlefields. Also in this couplet the reason for the singing has changed. The robin is not making a mating call, but is singing simply on impulse - because it can. The inference here, especially when taken with the poet's other possible references to battle, is that the robin, unlike man, has no cares: there is nothing to prevent his enjoyment of the moment.

The fourth couplet continues this reference to battle as she directly mentions the war for the first time. However, as before it is seen as something that has no impact on the birds. They continue with their lives and rituals regardless of whether there is a war on, or not. After that, she asserts that not only does the war have no influence on the birds and trees, but that mankind itself is so insignificant that they would not worry if man died out entirely. The spring would still arrive and everything would be just as though man had never been there at all.

This nature poem examines the not uncommon theme that, regardless of the war and the devastation which mankind is bringing upon itself, nature will continue to thrive. Many of these poems, such as *A Girl's Song* by Katharine Tynan Hinkson and *Spring in War-Time* by Edith Nesbit, are about how nature seems to appear the same, while everything else has changed. Sara Teasdale, on the other hand, looks at the normally hopeful season of spring from the perspective that man's self-destruction will have no effect whatsoever. There are a number of ways of interpreting this: she may be implying that nature is more powerful than man, or she may be arguing against man's stupidity in his own ruination. She certainly seems to be saying here that despite man's feelings of superiority, mankind is insignificant when compared with nature.

Lesbia Thanet

BIOGRAPHICAL DETAILS

There are no verifiable biographical details available for Lesbia Thanet.

IN TIME OF WAR

This poem opens with the poet's reminiscence that, in her innocent childhood, when she was 'at play', she had dreamt of great romance. As part of this dream, she had anticipated that, if war should come, she would urge her 'beloved' to do his duty and fight to protect her.

In the second verse, however, the tone changes, as the poet is no longer thinking of childhood fantasies, but of reality. The lover of whom she speaks is not a figment of her imagination, but a real person who is at once ordinary and beloved. In other words, he is not a fantastic or romantic hero, but an average man who is, nonetheless, very much loved. Now that her love is real, rather than imagined, however, she no longer feels so brave about sending him to war and instead, just prays for his safe return.

Like many First World War poets written by women, there are many contrasts within this piece, mainly related to the difference between a peacetime perception of war and the reality of facing the loss of a loved-one. In peacetime, or childhood, war seems glorious and adventurous: a time for heroes and splendid deeds. As an adult, however, when faced with the truth about war, death and loss, everything seems very different.

This poem is sometimes compared with *At The Movies* by Florence Ripley Mastin and there are similarities between the two. Both poets note the contrast between the perception of war and its reality. Their subject is slightly different in that Florence Ripley Mastin bases her interpretation on a film, while Lesbia Thanet uses childhood dreams to represent the 'fantasy' element. Both of them, however, have a similar message as the realistic side of war. Florence Ripley Mastin describes her heart as growing 'cold' to show how the prospect of loss frightens her. Lesbia Thanet describes the facts of war as making her 'blind with fear'.

These poems, along with many other home-front pieces, show the war from the perspective of a woman who is forced to wait and wonder, hoping that she will be lucky and her fears will be unfounded.

Aelfrida Tillyard

BIOGRAPHICAL DETAILS

Aelfrida Catherine Wetenhall Tillyard was born on October 5th 1883 in Cambridge. She was the only daughter of Alfred Isaac Tillyard, a Classics master, and his wife Catherine. She had three brothers, Henry, Eustace and Conrad, although the latter died at the age of two. Aelfrida was mainly educated privately, with two other local girls, before going to Switzerland for a year to complete her education. Throughout, Aelfrida's main preoccupation was literature and she wrote biographies, poetry and prose for both adults and children.

At the age of 21, she met Constantine Cleanthes Michaelides and they quickly became engaged to be married. In 1906, Michaelides, a diplomat, changed his surname to Graham and he and Aelfrida were married the following year. They had two daughters named Alethea and Agatha, but his work kept them apart and they were divorced in 1921.

During the First World War, Constantine was Consul in Amsterdam and Lyons, as well as having a short spell at the Foreign Office in London. Aelfrida's younger brother, Eustace, served as a Captain in the 1st Battalion, 4th Royal Lancashire Regiment, landing in France in May 1915.

Throughout her life, Aelfrida had been deeply interested in religion and in the mid 1920s, she became more serious about this. She regularly visited convents to retreat from society and between 1936 and 1946, she lived permanently at the Convent of the Sacred Cross in Monmouthshire, where she became a life-tertiary, adopting the name Sister Placida. After the Second World War, she returned to Cambridgeshire, where she continued to work within the church until her death in December 1959.

INVITATION AU FESTIN

The title of this poem translates as 'Invitation to the Feast', which is meant ironically, as the poem itself is about the hardships on the home front. It would seem that civilians have been told that they can help the war effort by eating less, so the meal which Tillyard describes here is made up mainly of scraps and items which most people would not normally consider to be edible. In order to be 'patriotic', the table bears nothing frivolous or extravagant, and nothing may be wasted. From the ironic tone of this poem, one could assume that Tillyard thought these efforts were an unnecessary hardship.

A LETTER FROM EALING BROADWAY STATION

The subtitle of this poem shows that this 'letter' was from Aelfrida Tillyard's brother, Eustace Mandeville Wetenhall Tillyard, who served during the First World War as a captain in the 1st Battalion, 4th Royal Lancashire Regiment. The poem is dated October 11th 1914, when Eustace was probably still in training, as he did not embark for France until May 1915. It would appear that one of his 'duties' is to help guard Ealing Broadway station and we may imagine that he has written a little to his sister, explaining this and that she has transposed his words into a poem.

While on duty, he evidently thinks about his time at University (Newnham College is a Women's College at Cambridge), his friends in barracks, and the reasons why he enlisted. In October 1914, Belgians were being evacuated from Antwerp and it would seem that Eustace feels frustrated at being given such a mundane task as guarding a London railway station.

Aelfrida Tillyard has turned his thoughts into quite a simple poem, with a straightforward metre and rhyming pattern, which compliments the subject.

Iris Tree

BIOGRAPHICAL DETAILS

Iris Tree was born on 27th January 1897, in London. She was the third and youngest daughter of Herbert Beerbohm-Tree, an actor-manager and his wife, actress Helen Maud Holt. Iris's older sisters, Viola and Felicity were, by the time of their sister's birth, quite used to their parents' enforced absences and parties with the famous. Herbert already owned the Haymarket Theatre and within months of Iris's birth, he opened Her Majesty's Theatre as well.

The childhood of these three girls was the stuff of fairytales. They attended the theatre regularly, always going backstage afterwards and mingling with the stars. Viola, the oldest of the three, soon became involved with the 'Corrupt Coterie' - a group of young intellectuals, mainly the children of the 'Souls', a similar group from an earlier generation. In 1904, Herbert founded the Royal Academy of Dramatic Art (RADA) and five years later, received a knighthood.

Viola secretly became engaged to Alan Parsons in 1912, just before going to Italy, where she was joined by Iris, now 15 years old. The freedom which Iris found during this visit was too great a temptation and she embarked on several love affairs. Luckily, Viola and she returned to London before any damage was done and in July 1912, Viola and Alan Parsons were married.

Herbert had always been a womaniser and his obvious indiscretions caused his wife great distress. She was involved in a car accident, which permanently disfigured her, causing Herbert to be, at least, a little more discreet in his philandering.

By the beginning of the First World War, Iris was studying at the Slade School of Art and was living in a shared flat with Nancy Cunard, where the two young women could behave as wildly as they chose, away from the glare of their disapproving parents. In 1915, Iris accompanied Herbert on a trip to America and while in New York, she met and fell in love with a painter named Curtis Moffat. By early 1916, the couple were married, and they initially lived in Havanna. Following the birth of their son, Ivan, they returned to England in early 1918, by which time Herbert was dead.

The young Moffat family moved into their own flat, but within six years, Iris and Curtis were separated and Ivan spent most of his time in the care of his grandmother, while Iris resumed her wild ways with Nancy Cunard. In 1925, Iris accompanied her old friend Diana Cooper (née Manners) on a tour of America and fell in love again: this time with an Austrian nobleman named Friedrich Ledebur.

Although Iris was still married to Curtis Moffat, she moved in with Ledebur and, before long, was pregnant with his child. She returned to London and sought the help of Diana Cooper, who suggested that she and her husband, Duff Cooper, could adopt the child. Iris was relieved at this suggestion and readily agreed, but then changed her mind a few months later, much to Diana's disappointment.

In February 1928, Iris gave birth to another son, named Christian, although everyone called him 'Boon'. Following her eventual divorce from Moffat, Iris and Friedrich were married in 1934, after which they lived a nomadic existence. Ivan lived either with his grandmother or with Viola and Curtis Moffat also remarried.

When the Second World War started, Iris and Friedrich moved to America, where they both had affairs while touring with a theatre group. After the war, Iris returned to Europe, her marriage over. She initially went to Paris where Duff Cooper was British Ambassador, and spent some time with Diana, before visiting London and Italy. She and Friedrich divorced and he remarried, but Iris found it difficult to settle. She visited Boon, who was studying medicine and then Ivan, who had become a successful screenwriter, working on movies such as Shane (1953), Giant (1956) and D-Day the Sixth of June (1956). He gave her enough money to rent a house at Cadaques on the Costa Brava, although even here she could not settle and ended up in a studio flat in Cagnes, lent to her by Curtis Moffat's widow, Kathleen.

By this stage, due mainly to her lifestyle, Iris had become extremely ill and Boon was summoned from Switzerland. He advised surgery and suggested that this should be carried out in London. Diana Cooper made all the arrangements and, within a few days, Iris was in a London hospital, having a large part of her colon removed. Following this, Friedrich arranged for her to live in a small villa in the South of France, but as her health continued to deteriorate, Iris moved back to London,where she died in April 1968.

OF ALL WHO DIED IN SILENCE FAR AWAY

This anti-war poem, essentially demonstrates the effects of death on those left behind, together with the public perception of grief and mourning at times of war. It displays many emotions which were commonly felt during the First World War, such as anger at the waste of life and the futility of the war, as well as regret for lost dreams.

The poem begins by telling us that the dead have met their end in silence a long way from home. This is said, despite the fact that war is rarely silent, because at the time of their deaths, there would have been no-one present to mourn them. In war, it seems, there is no time to sympathise because people are either busy fighting, or controlling the war, or arguing about the politics and conduct of each battle. Therefore, it seems as though the men are dying unnoticed.

Each dead soldier is perceived as small, since there are so many of them that they have almost become insignificant as individuals. This is contrasted with the greatness of the love they gave and received during their lives. While they lived, the men had control over their futures and they made plans. It is as though their hopes and dreams were like a flock of sheep and the men were shepherds, driving their lives forward, with purpose. Now, all is lost - their hopes, like them, are buried.

Looking back over their lives, Iris remembers how much the dead men were loved by their mothers who fed and cared for them. The intensity of a mother's love is so great, she says, that it is as though she had become the centre and focus of her son's world and he, in turn, gave her life a sense of meaning and completeness. Now, though, he has gone and she is left alone - her life is empty.

Next, our attention is drawn towards a more romantic scene of passionate young love. These young men were adored and the implication here is that many of them may have become secretly engaged before going to the front, placing a glittering jewel on the hand of their beloved. (This would not have been an unusual suggestion for Iris Tree to make as both she and her two sisters had either become secretly engaged or married). This passion has now been suppressed because the men are dead and instead of being bound to their lovers by marriage, they are bound to the earth by death.

There follows a sudden angry cry for this to stop - not just the killing, but the mourning, and the constant reminders of death. Iris goes on to tell us that those who mourn cannot always openly show their grief, possibly for fear that it will overwhelm them, but also because many, particularly in Iris' social set, were often told that they should not show their emotions, but that they should keep them hidden. The bright clothing and coloured flags represent the outward appearance which people were 'supposed' to display, while the black of mourning shows the reality which must be kept secretly locked inside, away from prying eyes. Ironically, at least one of the bright colours - a reddish orange - only serves as a reminder of spilled blood, which flows out like the train of a wedding dress and reiterates that such dreams of future contentment will remain unfulfilled.

Another outward sign of mourning would be to weep, but once again, emotions must be kept in check. The quote which follows in the poem, demonstrates the futility and waste of the war, together with the notion that the dead are somehow capable of happiness. Iris shows her view of such platitudes by reminding us that, being dead, the soldiers can neither cheer themselves, nor hear the cheering of others. She also suggests that the dead men do not understand why they died and why those they loved and left behind are not supposed to weep for them.

The first line of the last verse echoes the beginning of the poem, except that now the men have also died in darkness. This follows on from the previous verse: the darkness representing the unknown, while also introducing, for the first time, an element of fear. This emotion is only allowed a very brief acknowledgement as Iris quickly reminds us that, although the men are gone, they have left behind a wealth of love and memories. Love, she asserts, can overcome everything - even grief - so the roses on his grave are not 'blood-red', but 'passion-red', proving that love is more powerful even than death. Also, although he lies beneath the ground with his arms folded across his chest, rather than open in a loving embrace, he looks forward to a new day. It is also interesting to note the alteration in the pronoun used from 'they' and 'them', to 'his', which makes the ending of the poem even more touching and personal.

Written in 1917, this poem demonstrates the poet's anger at the waste of so many young lives and she suggests that neither those who fight, nor those who are grieving really understand what it is all for. This reflects her own pacifist opinions, but also demonstrates an immense depth of understanding and sympathy for both the dead and the mourning. The use of irony in this poem, particularly in the first and sixth verses, shows that she had little time for politics, rhetoric or 'socially acceptable' behaviour, when compared to human suffering.

In many ways, this poem could be compared to *When You See Millions of the Mouthless Dead* by Charles Hamilton Sorley. Both poets agree that the dead cannot speak or hear, and also that they are, to a certain extent, no longer the property of the living - they belong to death. Unlike Iris, however, Sorley suggests that to mourn is pointless, since the only people who could ever appreciate such an emotion - the dead - cannot do so, simply because they are dead. This serves to demonstrate a difference between the poetry of a non-combatant, written at a distance from the war, and that of a serving soldier. Sorley does not romanticise or sentimentalise about the war or death, or their effects on those left behind. He seems, in fact, to view death as a natural consequence of battle. Iris Tree, on the other hand, asserts that no death should go unnoticed or unmourned, and that the grieving process is a necessary means of recovering from the loss of one so beloved. Neither poet is glorifying the war - they simply view its cost from different perspectives. In Sorley's poem, the most powerful force is death. To Iris the overriding emotion, as well as the soldier's most notable legacy, is not honour, victory or sacrifice - but love.

AND AFTERWARDS, WHEN HONOUR HAS MADE GOOD

This angry poem questions the validity and cost of the war, regardless of victory or defeat. It begins as though half-way through a debate, which suggests that this is a topic which is often, or even continually, being discussed, without necessarily reaching a conclusion. The poet initially asserts that even though a victory might seem desirable, honourable and just, any happiness that follows with be unfounded, since the fight itself was so damaging and costly. She also questions whether those fighting really know, or remember, why they went to war, and whether, if they do, those reason still seem justified.

When the war is over, Iris implies that the British, represented by the bulldog, will relinquish their grip on Europe and revert to their old Imperial ways. The Germans (whose national symbol, used to represent their Kings and Emperors, was the eagle) are portrayed as vanquished and fleeing the battlefields to return to their abandoned families in their devastated country. The poet could be demonstrating a sense of irony here: she may be implying that these stereotypical images of victor and vanquished will be irrelevant, since both sides will have ruined their countries because they will have killed off a generation of men, and also that both sides will return to their old habits - making one indistinguishable from the other, despite their proud national emblems.

Iris appears to reserve her anger most, however, for the leaders and commanders when she ironically asserts that these men should not feel any sense of shame over the course and conduct of the war. They are held up as representing the pride of the nation, which they have in fact killed, and that may explain why they seem worried and nervous. She implies that they are stained with the blood of the men for whose deaths they should be held responsible.

In the second stanza there follows a more direct series of questions as the poet asks what victory will achieve. She asks whether the old hatred between nations will be vanquished; whether such costly undertakings, bearing equally disastrous outcomes, will be a thing of the past; whether there will be any greater freedom as a result of victory. Being as these questions have an ironic tone, one may suppose that she does not expect an answer. This may be because she believes that the war will have solved nothing.

Maybe, she implies, the result of the war will be that the cost will prove too great: so great, in fact, that the only victors will be the gods, who will consume everything - riches, earth, power - leaving just a scent of humankind, a ritual offering of all the suffering and sorrow.

This poem was written in 1917 and is a bitter indictment of the war - its conduct, ethics and perceived outcomes. The use of questions enables the poet to demonstrate how ironic the situation is: the questions remain unanswered, partly because the war is still going on, but also because Iris does not believe that there are any answers - the end cannot justify the means. She is obviously starting to wonder whether, when it is all over, anyone will actually remember why it began. Iris also seems to believe that victory or defeat is irrelevant since no good can ever result from such evil.

The bitterness and anger of this poem, which reflects Iris' pacifist beliefs, make it reminiscent of much of Siegfried's Sassoon's poetry. Indeed Sassoon and Iris' Uncle Max met during the war, while Sassoon was on leave, and went on to form a close and lifelong friendship. Whether or not Sassoon's work had any influence on Iris is unknown as she spent almost the entire war abroad. The mood and tone of this poem, however, undoubtedly share similar traits to many of Sassoon's more bitter and satirical verses.

Alys Fane Trotter

BIOGRAPHICAL DETAILS

Alys Fane Keatinge was born in 1863 in Ireland. She was the third of the four children of Maurice Keatinge, the Principal Registrar of the Court of Probate in Ireland, and his wife, Ellen. Alys's siblings were Richard, born in 1851, Eleanor, born 1853 and her younger brother Gerald, born 1872.

Following their father's retirement, the family moved to London with a substantial number of domestic servants. In 1886, Alys met and married Alexander Pelham Trotter, a civilian engineer and editor of Electrician magazine, from Woodford in Essex. Their first child, a daughter named Gundred, was born in 1889 in Kensington, followed by a son, Alexander Nigel in 1895.

Shortly afterwards, the family moved to South Africa for a brief time, but were back in England by the turn of the century, living in Chiswick. While in South Africa, Alys wrote and illustrated a book entitled *Old Houses of the Cape*, which was published in 1899. During their absence, Gundred went to live with her maternal grandmother, Ellen Keatinge in Oxford, presumably to avoid disrupting her education. Upon their return, Alexander Snr., was appointed Electrical Advisor to the Board of Trade.

In 1913, Gundred married Horace Courthope Beck in Kensington and shortly afterwards, Alys and Alexander moved to Coates Farm, Fittleworth in Sussex, although they also retained a property in London. Upon the outbreak of war, Alexander Nigel, who was a Lieutenant in the Royal Scots, having joined them in 1912, went to France with the BEF and died of wound received, probably at La Bassee, on 12th October 1914, at the age of 20. In 1918, Alys published a volume of poetry entitled *Nigel and Other Verses*, which was dedicated to her son. Alys Fane Trotter died in 1962.

THE HOSPITAL VISITOR

In this poem, Alys Fane Trotter describes a visit to some wounded men in hospital. She related taking them small gifts and how one particular man showed her the stump where his leg used to be. In brackets, she explains her feelings of pride and gratitude, which gives this piece an informal and conversational tone.

In the second verse, she more generally describes the courage of the men; their self-effacing attitudes and good humour, despite their hardships, which they do not acknowledge. They undergo different medical treatments, without complaint and show no sign of self pity or glorification. Instead, she asserts, all they really want is to be able to 'get about a bit'.

If this poem alludes to a genuine event, the reader must certainly acknowledge Alys Fane Trotter's own courage, being as she had lost her only son in the first few months of the war. She makes no mention of her own loss, however, and focuses only on the quiet suffering of the wounded men.

Like many First World War poems written by women, the theme here is gratitude, although here this is thinly disguised in the poet's appreciation of the attitude of the wounded soldiers.

Katharine Tynan

BIOGRAPHICAL DETAILS

Katharine Tynan was born on January 23rd 1861 at Whitehall Dairy Farm in Clondalkin, County Dublin. Her parents, Andrew Cullen Tynan and Elizabeth Reilly Tynan had twelve children. They were a Catholic family and Andrew Tynan, as well as being a dairy farmer, was also an entrepreneur.

Katharine was educated at the Dominican Convent of St Catherine of Siena in Drogheda. Throughout her childhood, she was plagued by eye ulcers which would, in later life, lead to extreme short-sightedness. She left the convent in 1875 and immediately began writing, with her first poem being published in 1878.

In 1884, Katharine met and fell in love with Charles Gregory Fagan, an Oxford graduate and fellow poet. His untimely death the following year led her to write some very touching and emotional poetry which demonstrated her heartfelt loss.

From this time until her marriage, Katharine became a prominent member of the Celtic Revival movement which sought to reinstate traditional Irish values in literature and the arts. She became a close friend of the poet and dramatist William Butler Yeats, with whom she maintain correspondence until her death. She also frequently met Charles Stewart Parnell, the prominent Irish politician and Home Rule campaigner.

Given her Catholic upbringing and proud Irish roots, it came as quite a surprise to her family when in 1893, she married protestant writer and barrister, Henry Albert Hinkson. In fact many of her close family objected so strongly to the marriage, that Katharine was estranged from them and she and Henry moved to

England. They lived in or around London until 1911. During this time, Henry struggled to earn a living at either of his professions so Katharine turned her hand to writing novels and newspaper articles to ensure they had an income.

In 1897, Katharine and Henry's first child Theobald Henry was born. Two years later, he was followed by another son, Giles Aylmer. Finally in 1900 a daughter was born. Pamela Mary Katharine Tynan Hinkson would eventually following in her mother's footsteps, becoming a writer. In 1911, the family returned to Claremorris, County Mayo where, two years later, Henry was appointed Resident Magistrate. This change in status and, more importantly, income enabled Katharine to devote more time to writing poetry. This was particularly so during the First World War, when the publication of her poems led her into correspondence with other anxious or bereaved families.

Both of her sons fought in the First World War. They both held the rank of Lieutenant. Theobald was in the Royal Irish Regiment, while Giles served with the Royal Dublin Fusiliers. This was an understandably difficult time for Katharine, who, together with Pamela, felt isolated in safety in the west of Ireland. They felt that the war was a remote series of events, which barely touched local lives, and yet, with Theobald and Giles both on active duty, they craved information and involvement.

Several of Katharine's friends experienced the heartbreak of losing their sons, but Katharine was lucky and both Giles and Theobald survived. Her happiness and relief were short-lived, however, when on January 11th 1919, just two months after the end of the war, Henry died suddenly at the age of 53. Katharine was devastated and the depression which had haunted her intermittently throughout her life, returned.

Eventually, Katharine rallied and she and Pamela enjoyed many visits to England and the Continent. She also continued to write both novels and poetry, until her death in Wimbledon on April 2nd 1931.

THE BROKEN SOLDIER

The first verse of this poems creates an image of a soldier, who has been maimed and partially blinded in the war. Despite his injuries and hardships, however, he refuses to be unhappy and sings cheerfully while he works.

Next we discover that this soldier is working in the gardens at the Hall. He has been given light work to do, since he has lost one of his hands. His face is scarred, but he keeps working busily and singing while he does so.

While the soldier sings, his fellow gardeners stop their work to listen to him. They are not maimed and are more physically attractive than him, but, while they worry about insignificant things, his carefree soul shines through.

The soldier, although damaged, seems courageous and handsome because his inner being has remained untouched by his experiences. As he continues with his gardening, throughout the day, he carries on whistling and singing like a bird.

This is a poem of appreciation, tinged with sadness, but also rejoicing at the strength of human nature. The maimed soldier has obviously lost a great deal, yet has managed to remain cheerful. He also brings joy to those he works with, even though they are obviously much better off than he is. The favourable comparison between him and the other gardeners shows that his strength of character is more important than his appearance.

There is irony in the title of this poem: the soldier is physically broken, like damaged goods, he is no longer handsome, like the whole men he shares his time with, yet the description given of him makes him seem much more of a man than they are. Therefore, while he may be maimed and physically incomplete, he appears much happier than them. He has nothing to worry about, possibly because he is now safely out of the war. He may also feel grateful that he, at least, survived and one may presume, due to his injuries, that he has seen some heavy fighting, and probably the deaths of many of his comrades.

The Lady of the house, like the poet herself, obviously sympathises with the soldier, and has found him work within her grounds. This appears, in itself, to make the soldier happy. Katharine Tynan makes frequent references to birds in this poem: larks, linnets, thrushes and robins are all mentioned by name. This helps to give the impression that this soldier is as happy as these birds. The war may have broken his body, but his mind and soul remain undimmed.

This poem has a very different tone from *Joining the Colours*, for example. Here, there is no doom, no death and no foolish hysteria. This poem has a much lighter note and, in making such a favourable comparison in the nature of the broken man compared with his whole colleagues, the poet is demonstrating her gratitude for what the soldier has sacrificed and yet still remained cheerful.

In the very final line of *The Broken Soldier*, comes the truth: the broken soldier may be free of worries and responsibilities, yet he is trapped in a broken body, like a bird in a cage. He may sing and appear contented but he'll never fly again. The soldier's freedom has been taken from him: this has been his sacrifice.

Tynan appears to be saying that he has given his freedom so that the other whole young men may be free to worry about the simple things in life. He may still be alive, but what quality of life can he expect? If he is indeed trapped like a caged bird, one's sympathy, like Katharine Tynan's should be very great indeed, for what could be worse than having the capacity to understand happiness without the freedom to enjoy it?

A GIRL'S SONG

This poem begins with a description of two rivers, the Meuse and the Marne: the trees that overhang them and the green grass on their banks. There is here a reminder that the grass is given its lush colour by the bodies that lie underneath it.

In the second verse, a young French girl appears, wearing a red rose which she has picked from the ground above these graves, without acknowledging the reason for its colour. This leads us into the third stanza where the narrator asserts that the rose gains its colour from the blood of her dead lover; the yellow colour of the corn comes from his hair. However, all she has to give are tears, like the rain; and sighs, like the wind.

Next, she urges the rivers, the sheep, and even the dew to pass by her lover soundlessly, so as to not disturb his sleep. Realism creeps back into the fifth verse as she acknowledges that the earth which covers him has sealed his lips and destroyed his handsome features. She wishes she were dead too, and able to rest peacefully beside him.

In the final verse, there is recognition that spring will come again - that the earth will be reborn and life will, once again, be carefree. This realisation is tempered, however, by the fact that in making his grave look beautiful she must acknowledge the other countless dead and all must count the cost.

Judging from the title, this poem is written from the perspective of all the many young women who lost husbands or lovers. The impression given is that this poem was written after the war, or at least with a view to the end of the war, since the French girl is able to walk by the river and pick flowers, the sheep are free to roam and the narrator herself has been able to visit her lover's resting place and build a cairn.

The tone of this poem is sorrowful, demonstrating an almost overwhelming grief. The girl attributes the quality of all the beautiful things she sees - the grass, the rose, the corn - to him. Because his dead body feeds the earth, she asserts that he is responsible for the beauty that surrounds this area where he now lies. In this way, it might be said that she gives him a certain element of immortality, and also that she manages to find some justification for his death.

Although Katharine Tynan shows a clear understanding of the grief experienced by such young girls, this was not gleaned from her own sorrows. By the time the First World War started, she was in her early fifties and would have feared for the lives of her two sons, rather than a husband or lover. The rivers Marne and Meuse saw many fierce battles and their banks would have formed the final resting place for many young men, and therefore the focus of grief for many young women.

Three times during this poem, Tynan refers to the dead as sleeping, which is a rose-coloured, optimistic way of looking at death. This was fairly common amongst poets, both male and female, who, for various reasons, seem to have preferred to think of the dead as resting. For example, May Wedderburn Cannan in *'Since They Have Died'* writes of the dead in this way. However the tone of Cannan's poem is different - she urges the living to remember the dead fondly and with smiles and states that only thus may they find true contentment. Katharine Tynan's language is just as optimistic - she dreams of spring and peace, yet the tone is more sorrowful - the grief more real.

The spring to which Tynan refers is more likely metaphorical since one is given the impression that the war has already ended, and the flowers are, once again, in bloom. Therefore the change brought by the coming of another 'spring' is more likely to be that the girl can learn to live with her grief and accept it, along with all the others who have suffered similarly.

JOINING THE COLOURS

The first verse of this poem creates an image of extremely young men, marching cheerfully to war. This scene, we know from the sub-title, is taking place in the very early days of the war, yet Katharine Tynan is, unusually for that time, referring to these men as cannon-fodder. She compares the sight of them marching to a wedding procession and then reminds us that each of them, somewhere, has a mother.

In the second verse, she contrasts the happiness of these men with their dull surroundings, which implies that they are walking through the streets in a poor district of Dublin. The happiness exudes from the men rather than their surroundings; there is no flag-waving or crowds cheering them on their way. Katherine Tynan makes it clear that there are many men going, and as they pile into the trams, they sing cheerfully. They are too carefree and happy to need courage, which gives the impression that the soldiers believe they are immune to death. Yet, finally it is pointed out that they are journeying into darkness, into the unknown, or the unthinkable - to a place from which there is no return.

These soldiers to not merely sing, they use instruments too - anything which will make a noise and make their departure more celebratory, even though they are going to their deaths. Nothing can save these men - not even love. This is presumably a reference to a mother's love since the youth of the men is pointed out throughout the poem. Ordinarily, it could be assumed, that a mother would willingly sacrifice her own life to save her child, yet here, no mother can save her son.

Finally, in praising their courage and exuberance, Katharine Tynan sympathises with the young girls too. Their lives will also change when all the young men have gone. There will be no-one left for them to kiss - or, by extension, to marry. The soldiers, she claims, have appeared as though from a mist, to serve their country at this vital time; as though by magic they have materialised, yet they will disappear just as quickly, never to return.

Joining the Colours is subtitled *"West Kents, Dublin, August 1914"*, which gives the poem an implied date. This is confirmed by the fact that The Queens Own (Royal West Kent Regiment) was in Dublin that August. It formed part of the 5th Division which helped to make up the original British Expeditionary Force which went to France in the first few days and weeks of the First World War. That this poem was written at that time, while not impossible, is unclear. The scene is that of early August 1914, the sentiment of doom and certainty of death could imply that this poem was, in fact, written retrospectively. This is not certain, however, since many people were aware of the tragic consequences of going to war before the conflict had even started, so dating this poem accurately is almost impossible.

The poem itself contains a series of mixed messages: the soldiers are happy and carefree, yet they are destined to die. In the midst of this happiness we are reminded of the things that the young men will miss - weddings, kisses, romance and the love of their mothers. Their deaths will cause great changes to those left behind: their mothers and sweethearts will suffer too. The soldiers are obviously very young and the implication throughout is that they should have had their whole lives ahead of them, but now are doomed. This mixture of feelings probably represents the poet's sensation of pride mingled with foreboding and anxiety, which was commonly felt at the beginning of the war.

The soldiers' enthusiasm to join the fight was quite usual in the early days. There existed an element of nationalist pride which, coupled with the certainty that the fighting would be all over by Christmas, encouraged young men to join up so as not to 'miss out'. In all probability it was only the mothers of these young men who fully appreciated the magnitude of their impending losses. Youth, by its very nature, gives one a sense of invulnerability or immunity to danger. There is no sense of imminent defeat - these men are marching to glorious victory.

Katharine Tynan, quite harshly, refers to the young men as foolish. Very few people were aware of what the coming four years of war would bring, or even that the war would last that long. Yet she seems almost angry with the soldiers for their lightheartedness while throwing away their lives in such a reckless fashion.

The poem also contains many repetitions of the same words used to represent youthfulness and boyhood, and the cheerful mood of the soldiers. This is done to reiterate the message of wasted youthful lives. The 'colours' of the title refer to the flags of a battalion. The King's (or Queen's) colour - for example the Union Flag; and the Regiment Colour. These, in previous wars, would have been carried into battle, but as the ways of fighting wars made this less practical, the colours were still carried around with each regiment, but not necessarily displayed. The whistles, pipes and mouths organs are noteworthy also. Music was a frequent accompaniment to military marching; but there is here also the possible implication of the ordinary soldier with his mouth organ and the officer with his whistle, piping the men into battle, as the officer's whistle was the signal for the men to go 'over the top'.

The overall tone of this poem is sadness. These happy, enthusiastic young soldiers, so keen to fight and win glory, are doomed. No mention is made of survivors, as though none are expected to live. Nothing can save these men from their fate. The poet seems angry at the waste of life, while grateful for their courage in facing up the challenge ahead of them.

VIVIANE VERNE

BIOGRAPHICAL DETAILS

There are no verifiable biographical details available for Viviane Verne.

KENSINGTON GARDENS (1915)

In this poem, the poet offers a description of Kensington Gardens in London, at some point during 1915. She describes trees, people, grass, ducks, dogs and statues and, at the very end of the poem, compares these sights with the war. This simple message is portrayed with extreme clumsiness, where words have been used, it would seem, for no other reason than that they fit the rhyme pattern or metre of the poem. It tells the reader almost nothing: the language used is overly elaborate and unnecessary, leaving one with a feeling of dissatisfaction.

Alberta Vickridge

BIOGRAPHICAL DETAILS

There are no verifiable biographical details available for Alberta Vickridge.

IN A VAD PANTRY

This poem appears to provide a homage to the pots which are used every day in a hospital and then washed and dried by the humble volunteer. 'Blue and white' refers to a particular type of traditional china and these 'pots' are evidently quite old and worn and clearly see regular service.

In the second verse Alberta Vickridge wonders why no-one ever wonders about the fate of the 'pots', before going on to relate the effects which the pots can have on the patients in hospital and likening this to the cup which Jesus is reputed to have used at the Last Supper.

This is one simple explanation of this poem. However, it may also have a secondary meaning, in that the 'pots' might be a reference to the VADs themselves. Their uniforms were blue with a white apron; they were often worn out and tired, due to the hours which they were required to work. They were also unappreciated by their superiors, who were often quite critical of the young ladies who wanted to help and 'do their bit', but received little formal training.

The second verse could be interpreted as a reference to the upbringing of these young ladies, who were quite often from sheltered middle and upper class backgrounds. In addition, this may refer to the training which the VADs received before being 'sold' into service.

In the final verse, one might draw the conclusion that the poet is referring to the many services provided by the VADs which ease the pains of their patients, to the extent that they begin to take on the appearance of angels themselves.

It is really for each reader to decide what the poem means to them, and which interpretation they feel is more appropriate.

Mary Webb

BIOGRAPHICAL DETAILS

Mary Gladys Meredith was born on March 25th 1881 at Leighton in Shropshire. She was the oldest of the six children of George Edward Meredith, a private tutor, and his wife Sarah. Mary was born at the school which her father owned and ran, and this was very much a family affair, as George Meredith's cousin, Charles Mattley also taught in the school, which was in turn attended by nephews and nieces, as well as his own children, including Mary and her siblings, Alice, Edward, George, Olive and John.

At the age of fourteen, Mary was sent away to 'finishing school' in Southport. Throughout her happy childhood, Mary was greatly influenced by her father, through whom she developed a love of the Shropshire countryside. She was an extremely sensitive child, who disliked bloodsports or any form of cruelty and became a vegetarian at quite an early age.

In 1901, she became seriously ill, suffering from Graves' disease. Although she recovered, her facial features remained altered and the disease would recur later in life, such as, upon the death of her father in 1909.

Mary threw herself into her writing, which was invariably about her native county. In 1912, Mary was married to Henry Bertram Law Webb, who was four years her junior. Henry was the son of a general practitioner and also came from Shropshire, however, possibly due to Mary's earlier illness, the couple were unable to have children. Initially they lived in Weston-Super-Mare, where Henry was employed as a teacher, although they returned to Shropshire in 1914.

Over the next twelve years, Mary wrote six novels, based in and around the Shropshire countryside and way of life. Her writing was proving quite popular, but when they moved to London in 1921, Mary's health and marriage began to suffer. Henry had accepted a position at King Alfred's School and although Mary wrote her most famous novel, Precious Bane, during this time, she deeply missed the countryside.

Mary Webb died at the age of 46 in October 1927. Since her death, her work has been more greatly appreciated than it was during her life, and many of her novels have been made into films, plays and television programmes.

AUTUMN 1914

This poem opens with an autumnal description of an ash tree, which seems in itself to miss the men who have gone away. Mary Webb's description of the tree as 'scarlet-jewelled' is both appropriate and sufficient to explain what she means: namely that the leaves have turned red, because it is autumn. In addition, this brief image shows the reader who important nature is to the poet.

A man, it would seem, has gone away to the war and his wife waits for his return and recall how he had been a good man to have on the farm. Now, however, he is with the dead. This line does not necessarily mean that the man is dead himself, because he still 'marches', but the poet could be trying to point out the contrast between the 'living' things which he dealt with on the farm and the dead men among whom he now resides. In addition, Mary Webb forces us to relate the dead men with the 'harvest'.

Then, we are told that it is winter, because the leaves or 'gems' have fallen from the tree and still the man does not return. The woman calls for her son to 'come in' from playing at soldiers, but when he does, he reminds her of her husband and this makes her think that if there is another war, her son might be called upon to fight.

In the final verse, the poet seems to be asking that all the men should return from the grey pastures ('leasowes'), which are no longer green because they are covered with dead men. She urges them to come home to their simple country pursuits, ploughing the fields, rather than dying in them.

Finally, we return to the ash tree again. Now it is spring and the man has come home, returned to his loving wife and countryside.

This is a sad poem, made even more sorrowful by the benefit of hindsight. Here, in the autumn of 1914, Mary Webb clearly hopes and believes that the young men who have gone away to fight, will be home by the following spring. We, of course, know that it would be another four years before the men returned and that for men, that joyous and long-anticipated day. would never come.

M. WINIFRED WEDGWOOD

BIOGRAPHICAL DETAILS

Very little is known about M. Winifred Wedgwood, other than the fact that she served with the Devonshire 26th Voluntary Aid Detachment during the First World War.

THE VAD SCULLERY-MAID'S SONG

This simple poem, with its jaunty rhyme and rhythm shows an insight into the world of a Voluntary Aid Detachment worker. Some VADs became nurses, while others did more menial tasks, such as helping in the kitchens. Here the poet paints a picture of herself as somehow less worthy and certainly less intelligent than some of the other volunteers and yet, the tone of this piece suggests that she is happy in her chosen work.

CHRISTMAS 1916

This, like Wedgwood's other poem in this collection, is a piece which offers a description of the life of one of the more menial workers in a hospital. It would seem that this is the later of the two poems, as now she is a cook, whereas before (in *The VAD Scullery-Maid's Song*), she merely did the washing-up. Nonetheless, she still seems to derive some pride and pleasure from her work.

CATHERINE DURNING WHETHAM

BIOGRAPHICAL DETAILS

Catherine Durning Holt was born in 1871 in Liverpool. She was the second of the eight children of Robert Durning Holt, a cotton broker and magistrate, and his wife Lawrencina. By the age of twenty, Catherine was studying Natural Sciences. In 1897, she married William Cecil Dampier-Whetham, who was knighted in 1931. They had six children between 1900 and 1911: five daughters and one son. In 1917, Catherine, not surprisingly, wrote a book entitled The Upbringing of Daughters. She and William both died in 1952.

THE POET AND THE BUTCHER

This poem, which is dated May 1918, is addressed to John Milton, the seventeenth century English poet and author, whose reputation is, generally speaking, as one of the greatest authors in the English language. Milton was writing during the time of Oliver Cromwell, when England was in a great state of upheaval.

Here Catherine Durning Whetham seems to crave the influence of Milton, although this poem is also loaded with irony and she is, by no means, imply that there is really any similarity between the Civil War and the hardships of rationing.

By the time this poem was written, many everyday products were subject to restrictions. The poet describes England as being devoid of her traditions, which have been replaced by an obsession with food. She accuses the 'butcher' of being miserly and blames the situation on Viscount Rhondda (David Alfred Thomas), who was appointed as Food Controller in June 1917 (he died of heart failure two months after this poem was written).

Catherine Durning Whetham acknowledges that to indulge in 'luxuries' such as meat, means she must be a 'bad' person, but she asks that she might be allowed to forget that, presumably so that she can enjoy her meal!

This poem demonstrates the author's sense of humour, but also the underlying difficulties of life on the home front.

Lucy Whitmell

BIOGRAPHICAL DETAILS

There are no verifiable biographical details available for Lucy Whitmell.

CHRIST IN FLANDERS

Written in 1915, this poem appears to be addressed to God, or Christ. It opens with the suggestion that, for the best part, men do not really think about God, unless they have some particular need of His guidance. Man, she avers, is too busy with his day-to-day life, to take very much interest in God. Yet she goes on to point out that He has always been among the people, making sacrifices on their behalf, even though they have never noticed Him.

However, now that the men are fighting in Flanders, it would seem that they firmly believe that God is on their side and watching over them. Now, she asserts, they do remember Christ on the cross and the sacrifices which he made for the sake of mankind. Finally, she acknowledges that the men need Christ and that they know He will not let them down.

Religion played a significant role in the lives of many people during the First World War, although it should be noted that both sides believed that God was fighting with them alone! The evident popularity of this poem reflects the fact that, for many people, both in and out of the trenches, religion provided them with a crutch, with a faith which they had earlier ignored, that they would survive, or that if they didn't, their death would not mark the end, but the beginning.

Margaret Adelaide Wilson

BIOGRAPHICAL DETAILS

There are no verifiable biographical details available for Margaret Adelaide Wilson.

GERVAIS

We may assume from the subtitle that the subject of this poem was killed during the Gallipoli campaign in 1915, although his relationship to the poet is not clear. It may be that he was no relation at all, and that the poet is actually just writing about a general English schoolboy who, in the recent past, has been reading Greek mythology and now lies dead in similar lands.

MARJORIE WILSON

BIOGRAPHICAL DETAILS

Mary Wilson was born in 1885 in Torquay, Devon, the oldest daughter of Theodore Cameron Wilson, a clergyman, and his wife, Annie. Mary had four brothers and one sister and they all grew up together at Christchurch vicarage in Paignton. One of Mary's brothers, the poet, Theodore Percival Cameron Wilson, died in the First World War, having enlisted in the Sherwood Foresters in 1914. He rose to the rank of Captain before being killed during the German Spring Offensive, in March 1918.

TO TONY (AGED 3)

This poem, we might assume, was written to the poet's child and is dedicated to her brother, Captain Theodore Percival Cameron Wilson, who was killed in action in March 1918. In this beautifully simple poem, Marjorie Wilson describes her brother fondly and urges young Tony to remember him and the reasons why he gave his life.

This poem is replete with happy memories of the poet's younger brother and one can imagine that with only one year's age gape between them, they would have grown up to be very close. In 'Tony', she clearly sees reminders of the brother she has lost and, although this poem is unutterably sad, there is, at the end, at least a vestige of hope that, if the children can remember why the soldiers died, their peace will have been well-earned.

THEMES IN SCARS UPON MY HEART

The AQA examination will ask students to assess one particular aspect of the anthology, such as whether a specified named poem is typical of the collection or whether the first or last poems are suitable introductions or conclusions to the anthology, although such a question would be difficult to apply to *Scars Upon My Heart*. Alternatively, students may be asked to assess whether the collection lacks variety or coherence, or whether the poems in the anthology have little literary merit.

In order to help with some of these questions, I have initially re-arranged the anthology on a thematic basis, using eight basic themes and placing each poem within the one which is most appropriate.

LOSS/GRIEF/SACRIFICE/REMEMBRANCE

The Wind on the Downs - Marian Allen
The Parson's Job - Madeline Ida Bedford
Perhaps - Vera Brittain
Lamplight - May Wedderburn Cannan
Love, 1916 - May Wedderburn Cannan
The Falling Leaves - Margaret Postgate Cole
Afterwards - Margaret Postgate Cole
Fallen - Alice Corbin
Flanders Fields - Elizabeth Daryush
Pierrot Goes to War - Gabrielle Elliot
Easter Monday - Eleanor Farjeon

'Now That You Too' - Eleanor Farjeon
The Wykhamist - Nora Griffiths
The Fallen - Diana Gurney
The Seed-Merchant's Son - Agnes Grozier Herbertson
'For Valour' - May Herschel-Clarke
Dulce et Decorum? - Eleanor Jenkins
Reported Missing - Anna Gordon Keown
Despair - Olive E. Lindsay
The Cenotaph - Charlotte Mew
May, 1915 - Charlotte Mew
June, 1915 - Charlotte Mew
Spring in War-Time - Edith Nesbit
Last Leave - Eileen Newton
Revision - Eileen Newton
Remembrance Day in the Dales - Dorothy Una Ratcliffe
The Cenotaph - Ursula Roberts
Sacrament - Margaret Sackville
Spring in War-Time - Sara Teasdale
A Girl's Song - Katharine Tynan
Gervais - Margaret Adelaide Wilson
To Tony (Aged 3) - Marjorie Wilson

DESCRIPTION OF WAR/LANDSCAPES/NATURE

The Raiders - Marian Allen
Leave in 1917 - Lilian Anderson
Rouen - May Wedderburn Cannan
Night Duty - Eva Dobell
Nature in War-Time - S. Gertrude Ford
The Lark Above the Trenches - Muriel Elsie Graham
The Battle of the Swamps - Muriel Elsie Graham
The Lost Army - Margery Lawrence
Screens - Winifred M Letts
Convalescence - Amy Lowell
On the Porch - Harriet Monroe
Ambulance Train 30 - Carola Oman
Brussels, 1919 - Carola Oman
'Sall' - Inez Quilter
A Memory - Margaret Sackville

July 1st, 1916 - Aimee Byng Scott
Field Ambulance in Retreat - May Sinclair
The Dancers - Edith Sitwell
Night on the Shore - Marie Carmichael Stopes
One Night - Millicent Sutherland
There Will Come Soft Rains - Sara Teasdale
Kensington Gardens - Viviane Verne
Autumn 1914 - Mary Webb
The VAD Scullery-Maid's Song - M. Winifred Wedgwood
Christmas 1916 - M. Winifred Wedgwood

GRATITUDE/APPRECIATION

From a Trench - Maud Anna Bell
Drafts - Nora Bomford
To My Brother - Vera Brittain
'Since They Have Died' - May Wedderburn Cannan
Anniversary of the Great Retreat - Isabel C. Clarke
The Veteran - Margaret Postgate Cole
Subalterns - Elizabeth Daryush
Unknown Warrior - Elizabeth Daryush
Pluck - Eva Dobell
Gramophone Tunes - Eva Dobell
New Year, 1916 - Ada M. Harrison
Airman RFC - Agnes Grozier Herbertson
A War Film - Teresa Hooley
Casualty - Winifred M Letts
What Reward? - Winifred M Letts
The Shadow - Rose Macaulay
At the Movies - Florence Ripley Mastin
Lord, I Owe Thee A Death - Alice Meynell
Summer in England, 1914 - Alice Meynell
The Fields of Flanders - Edith Nesbit
Forgotten Dead, I Salute You - Muriel Stuart
YMCA - C.A.L.T.
The Hospital Visitor - Alys Fane Trotter
The Broken Soldier - Katharine Tynan

ANGER/RESENTMENT

Lament of the Demobilised - Vera Brittain
Praematuri - Margaret Postgate Cole
Women at Munition Making - Mary Gabrielle Collins
For a Survivor of the Mesopotamian Campaign - Elizabeth Daryush
After Bourlon Wood - Helen Dircks
Peace - Eleanor Farjeon
'A Fight to a Finish' - S. Gertrude Ford
The Tenth Armistice Day - S. Gertrude Ford
Non-Combatant - Cicely Hamilton
The Ghouls - Helen Hamilton
The Romancing Poet - Helen Hamilton
Nothing to Report - May Herschel-Clarke
Transport of Wounded in Mesopotamia, 1917 - Margery Lawrence
Picnic - Rose Macaulay
He Went for a Soldier - Ruth Comfort Mitchell
'Of all who died in silence far away...' - Iris Tree
'And afterwards, when honour has made good...' - Iris Tree

HOME FRONT (Including soldiers on leave or convalescing)

Zeppelins - Nancy Cunard
London in War - Helen Dircks
Her 'Allowance'! - Lillian Gard
Sing a Song of War-Time - Nina MacDonald
In a Restaurant, 1917 - Eleanour Norton
The Minority, 1917 - May O'Rourke
The Nut's Birthday - Jessie Pope
Socks - Jessie Pope
War Girls - Jessie Pope
The Convalescent - Cicely Fox Smith
In Time of War - Lesbia Thanet
Invitation au Festin - Aelfrida Tillyard
A Letter from Ealing Broadway Station - Aelfrida Tillyard
In a VAD Pantry - Alberta Vickridge
The Poet and the Butcher - Catherine Durning Whetham

RECRUITING/REASONS TO ENLIST

Over the Top - Sybil Bristowe
A Volunteer - Helen Parry Eden
The Three Lads - Elizabeth Chandler Forman
A Recruit from the Slums - Emily Orr
The Call - Jessie Pope
Joining the Colours - Katharine Tynan

CRITICISM OF OTHERS

'Education' - Pauline Barrington
Munition Wages - Madeline Ida Bedford
The Jingo-Woman - Helen Hamilton
The Deserter - Winifred M Letts

RELIGION

An Incident - Mary H J Henderson
Christ in Flanders - Lucy Whitmell

These are eight fairly common themes within this genre and, in each case, I have selected the one which I feel is most suitable, although others may disagree. In some cases, a poem might fit into more than one category and in these instances, I have listed it within the section which I feel represents its most central theme.

Re-arranging the poems in this way helps students to begin to answer many of the examination questions, which would otherwise be more difficult, because of the alphabetical, rather than thematic listing within the anthology.

EXAMINATION QUESTIONS - SUGGESTIONS AND TIPS

In this section, I am going to take each type of question in turn and make suggestions as to the ways in which students might deal with them, with examples of relevant poems, where possible.

NAMED POEM QUESTIONS

USING A NAMED POEM AS THE KEY TO THE COLLECTION.

For Example: Remind yourself of Vera Brittain's poem 'Perhaps'. To what extent to you agree that, in terms of subject matter and style, this poem is the key to the whole collection.

In this case, a poem has been referred to directly and students are being asked to assess the level to which this named poem is the 'key' to the whole collection, by referring to specific elements, such as language, content, style, etc.

Firstly, in order to answer this type of question you must ask yourself about the 'key'; whether the specified poem unlocks the collection; whether its inclusion makes sense of the whole anthology or not.

THE KEY OR NOT THE KEY

Looking at the thematic lists in the section of this study guide entitled 'Themes in Scars Upon My Heart', it is clear that, within this collection, some poems are going to be more typical than others. Where a given poem's central theme is recruitment, for example, the student could argue that this is not representative or 'key' to the whole anthology, as out of 125 poems, only 6 really cover that topic. However, where a poem's theme is gratitude for the sacrifices being made, this could be said to be far more typical.

Within each of the four main themes (descriptions, loss, gratitude and anger), some poems represent their theme better than others and it is these that the examiners are more likely to choose.

Just because a poem is seen as a 'key' poem, or one which represents one of the key themes in the collection, that does not necessarily mean it is a good, or well-written poem. Within just the theme of 'descriptions of war', which covers a great many of those in this collection, there is a wide diversity of skill on display. For example *Rouen* by May Wedderburn Cannan offers a memorable and occasionally poignant description of the poet's service in a canteen during the spring of 1915. The tone of this poem is conversational, its metre is regular and its rhyme pattern and the repetitive elements enhance the atmosphere of fond remembrance, despite the horror and unhappiness of war. May Cannan had been very happy during her brief spell of service in Rouen and reflects this by her nostalgic tones, especially in the final verse of the poem, by the end of which, her feelings are absolutely apparent. Within this same theme, one could also examine *Kensington Gardens* by Viviane Verne, which offers another, much less satisfactory description. This has nothing to do with the subject matter, as a London park during war-time can provide just as much of interest to the reader, as anywhere else. The problem here lies with the quality of the poem: the rhyme scheme is clumsy, especially in the final stanza, although throughout, the impression given is of a forced and contrived series of lines, placed together on a page for no real reason.

Between these two extremes, there is a whole range of other poems of differing standards and significance within the collection, which means that in order to answer a question regarding how far any particular poem provides the 'key' to the anthology, students must first formulate an opinion as to the overall impression of the selection.

Generally speaking, the descriptive poems do not form the bulk of the selection, as this position falls to the emotive poetry. Therefore, any named poem which deals solely with descriptions could not be said to form the 'key' to the anthology. Equally a poem which deals solely with emotions is not really the 'key', because one of the most popular themes is descriptions.

However, there are some poems which have more than one theme and this might include both a descriptive and emotional response. A good example of this type of poem would be *The Fields of Flanders* by Edith Nesbit, which offers us two contrasting descriptions, showing the changes which the war has inflicted on the landscape, but mingling this with the emotive reactions of hope for the future and gratitude for the sacrifices being made. As such, this poem could be said to provide a 'key' to the collection, because it encompasses several of the many themes.

In view of the fact that this anthology covers a wide number of diverse themes, any named poem must, therefore, demonstrate an ability to be placed comfortably within more than one topic.

WHAT NEXT?

In order to do well in answering this question, although you may not specifically have been asked to do so, students should refer to other poems, in order to fully satisfy the requirements of Assessment Objective 3, in which students need to demonstrate an ability to link between poems.

You do not, of course, have to agree with the assertion of the question, so if you feel that the named poem does not provide the 'key' to the collection, then that is fine. What you must then do, is provide an alternative which does the job better and state why your chosen text is more effective.

On the other hand, if you agree that the given text does provide the 'key', you need to back up that opinion by explaining how the language, structure and meaning of that poem is more appropriate and affecting than any other in the collection, referring to a few others to demonstrate their effects.

To be most effective when making these comparisons, students should avoid comparing the few gems within the collection, with the poems which have less literary merit, because to make such uneven comparisons belittles your argument.

EXAMPLE

If you are arguing that *Perhaps* by Vera Brittain does not provide the key to the collection, you first have to decide why not, and a personal dislike of the poem is not a good enough reason!

You could, however, argue that, although Vera Brittain's central theme of grief is reflected in many of the other poems, it is done with greater effectiveness elsewhere and then give a few examples, such as Eileen Newton's *Revision*, which deals with both the multitudinous and the individual losses, where *Perhaps* only deals with personal grief.

In addition, you could suggest that Vera Brittain's more simple rhyme scheme (abab), and metre are less thought-provoking and affecting than Eileen Newton's unusual scheme of abcddcba. You could also put forward the point that what Vera Brittain's poem lacks is the element of hope, which flows through this anthology, together with the widely-covered message that love conquers all.

Perhaps focuses on the loss, while *Revision* emphasises love, which emotion surely dominates this anthology.

Then, of course, you might choose to show how another poet demonstrates the same themes with a greater or lesser degree of success, remembering to point out in conclusion, which one you feel actually does provide the key.

VARIETY QUESTIONS

The question, in this instance, might ask you, for example, to address the variety of themes, topics, styles or moods and you will also, in these instances, be told that you can choose to refer in your answer either to two or three poems in detail, or more widely through the whole collection.

In the case of a question like this, you must first decide upon the direct answer to the direct question as to whether you feel the anthology offers enough variety.

A SIMPLE YES, OR NO?

For some students, having studied the collection closely, the answer will be a gut reaction, one way or the other, and this is entirely a matter of opinion - there is no 'right' answer.

Other students will be more ambivalent towards the poems and may, therefore, find it more difficult to form an opinion.

In either case, before reaching a final conclusion, one of the best ways to make, or confirm, the decision, is to read some other anthologies to see how other editors have handled the poems within this genre.

There is no other major anthology that deals solely with female writing of the First World War, but good alternatives include:

Up The Line to Death, edited by Brian Gardner - an anthology compiled almost two decades before *Scars Upon My Heart*, containing poems written only by men, arranged thematically.

Poems of the First World War: Never Such Innocence, edited by Martin Stephen - an anthology originally compiled seven years after *Scars Upon My Heart*, containing mainly male poetry, although there are contributions (and some of these are unusual) from female writers. The collection is arranged thematically with useful explanatory notes.

Voices of Silence: The Alternative Book of First World War Poetry, edited by Vivien Noakes - an excellent comparative anthology for students of *Scars Upon My Heart*, because it deals with a minority voice, containing the poems of some more obscure poets, including some surprising choices from both male and female poets. First published in 2006, this collection is arranged chronologically in chapters, each one also containing a description of contemporary events.

Students should not feel pressured one way or the other, by peers or teachers, who might have stronger views on whether this anthology lacks variety or not. If you are struggling to analyse this question, it might help to go through the thematic list given in our earlier chapter, looking firstly at the themes themselves. Do you feel, for example, that the emotional response of these poets has been given too much emphasis? Or are you struck by the lack of poems which fall under the heading of recruitment? Perhaps you had expected there to be less emphasis on descriptive poetry? By categorising the poems and, maybe re-organising them into larger groups, with less themes, you might be able to see a more distinct pattern emerging, as to the variety of the poems which have been included.

NOW FOR THE GOOD NEWS...

Unlike many of the questions in the examination, this is one for which students can prepare in advance. As such, you could take the time to read through Catherine Reilly's introduction, to see whether that gives you any clues.

Pay attention, for example, to her language when describing the war. She uses words such as 'gross folly', 'immense agony' and 'tragic absurdity', all of which make her feelings about the conflict very clear. This might lead you to the conclusion that her own response to the war is an emotional one, and you would then have to decide whether you feel this has affected her choices.

You could also assess Catherine Reilly's comments regarding the 'naive' elements of some poetry, during which she quotes from one such example by Rose Macaulay, which she has omitted from the anthology, preferring to show us instead, two other poems by that poet which demonstrate a more positive female perspective.

It is equally interesting that, although Catherine Reilly mentions recruitment, or 'call to arms' poetry, such as Jessie Pope's *The Call*, this is one of only six poems within the collection that deal with this theme, while over seventy three feature the emotions of grief, anger or gratitude.

You might then choose to debate whether Catherine Reilly's obvious - and some might argue necessary - desire to raise the profile of female war poetry, has clouded her judgement as to the variety and balance in the choices she has made.

In assessing this issue and by reading other anthologies you might come to the conclusion that, given the limitations of the subject matter and comparing this collection with others in the genre, Catherine Reilly has done a good job in providing a variety of topics, styles and standards for her readers. In order to really back up this theory, it would be useful to assess how other anthologists have represented the female voice.

In *Voices of Silence*, for example Vivien Noakes has included four poems by May Wedderburn Cannan, none of which are featured in *Scars Upon My Heart*. What these four poems show is an even more emotional response to the war and its aftermath than those selected by Catherine Reilly, which knowledge might lead you to the conclusion that *Scars Upon My Heart* is more a objective collection than one might otherwise have supposed.

Simply put: if you are not aware of at least some of the alternative texts and poets that Catherine Reilly had at her disposal, you cannot make an informed decision as to her choices in this selection.

WHAT NEXT?

Having done your research and, hopefully, formed your opinion, you must decide whether you want to refer closely to a small number of poems, or to the collection as a whole and, once again, this is a choice for each individual and will depend greatly upon your familiarity with the anthology and how the question is phrased.

If it simply asks you whether the anthology offers enough variety, then it is probably more suitable to refer to the whole collection.

If, on the other hand, the question relates to a more specific style or theme, then you could refer to other poems which fall within the same category, demonstrating their similarities and differences to reinforce your arguments as to their variety.

You should bear in mind that, unless the question relates to the variety of literary merit within the question, your answer should not really reflect whether you feel the poems are good or bad, but whether they demonstrate variety within the anthology itself.

COHERENCE QUESTIONS

This question will basically be asking for your opinion on whether this collection of poems is consistent and will probably ask you this in conjunction with a specific theme.

For example, you might be asked whether you feel that the anthology as a whole provides an adequate perspective of the whole war; if you feel that the collection is too biased in its negative portrayal of the conflict; or perhaps whether you believe that the mood of the anthology is too cheerful, or too sad.

Quite often, the question will be based on a quotation, either from within the anthology, or from a critic or reviewer. Examples relevant to *Scars Upon My Heart* might include:

'*The anthology shows that the view of women as ignorant and idealistic was quite false*';

'*This collection provides a moving record of women's experience of war*'; or

'*The anthology is pervaded by a horror of war*'.

You will then be asked whether or not you agree with the statement and to reinforce your argument with references to the collection, either in detail or more generally.

In order to form this opinion, you will need to be extremely familiar with the poems and their themes so as to quickly make a decision, based upon an unseen question.

So, if we take the three examples given above, these could be approached as follows:

'The anthology shows that the view of women as ignorant and idealistic was quite false'. How far to do you agree with this statement? In your answer you should refer to 2 or 3 poems in detail or range more widely through the whole collection.

To answer this question, students should first of all recognise the meaning behind the statement itself. In this case, the assertion is that women during the First World War were generally thought of as 'ignorant and idealistic' and that this anthology proves the opposite. So really, the basis of the question, if re-worded, would be: does this anthology show women as ignorant and idealistic, or not?

Having established the meaning of the question, while focusing on ignorance and idealism, students then have to decide which side of the argument they are going to portray. In order to make this decision, you need to discover whether, in your view, the majority of the poems show women in this light, or not. In some poems, women will show themselves as ignorant, in others, idealistic, some as neither and some as both and it is for you to determine how you have reacted to them. Remember that you do not have to wholly agree, or disagree with the statement that has been made, because the question asks 'how far' you agree, which might mean that you agree, but only in part.

At the same time, you will need to decide whether you are going to refer, in your answer, to the anthology as a whole, or to 2 or 3 poems more closely. In this decision, you will need to be guided by how strongly you feel about the assertion in the question. So, for example, if you strongly believe that overall the anthology does not show women were ignorant and idealistic, you could probably refer to the feeling created by the whole anthology. On the other hand, if your view of this aspect is less clear, you can argue this in your answer and might find it easier to refer to fewer poems which demonstrate your perception of the ambiguity of the anthology.

'This collection provides a moving record of women's experience of war'. To what extent do you agree with this statement? In your answer you should refer to 2 or 3 poems in detail or range more widely through the whole collection.

Here, the question is basically, does the anthology show a moving, or emotional, response to the female involvement in the war.

In order to answer this type of question - and many others - it is useful to have an understanding of what the war was really like for women. Some of this information can be found in the biographies of the poets, but further reading would provide you with useful background information for both this type of problem and the contextual linking question in Section A of the paper.

Suggested titles for further reading might include:

Roses of No Man's Land by Lyn MacDonald - this book offers an insight into the lives of nurses and volunteers, in the form of letters, diaries and interviews.

Testament of Youth by Vera Brittain - the story of Vera Brittain's life before, during and just after the war.

The Accrington Pals by Peter Whelan - a play written in the 1980s, which offers a reasonable perspective of the attitudes of working-class women.

Students then need to assess how representative of these experiences the collection is and then, bearing in mind the question, whether the content of the anthology is 'moving' or not.

As with all of the questions in this examination, students are being asked to give an opinion and you must demonstrate how well-informed your chosen viewpoint is by your references to the text. In this instances, you are being asked for an emotional response to the question and this is a very personal perspective.

To what extent do you agree that the anthology is pervaded by a 'horror of war'? In your answer you should refer to 2 or 3 poems in detail or range more widely through the whole collection.

This is a form of question where the answer really should be provided by the texts. By the time you sit your examination, you should be sufficiently familiar with the collection to form your opinion fairly quickly. Your answer is, once again, based on a personal perspective and this should be reinforced by references to the texts themselves.

In this particular instance, the emphasis is on the phrases 'pervaded by' and 'horror of war' and it is for each student to decide how far they agree or disagree with this assertion, having first established what is really meant by a word like 'horror'. This is quite an emotive word, used intentionally to force a strong reaction from the student or reader. By definition, 'horror' is more significant than fear or alarm.

In addition, you must limit your answers to demonstrate the 'horror' displayed in the poems, if there is any, as directed towards the war as a whole, rather than one particular aspect of war, such as air raids or death. Additionally, students should pay attention to the word 'pervaded' which means saturated and, therefore, that the vast majority of the poems in the collection should demonstrate a 'horror of war' if you are going to be able to successfully argue this point with relevant reinforcement.

Where a question uses a word like 'pervaded', it is really more appropriate to refer to the anthology as a whole, rather than to 2 or 3 poems, as such a small sample of reinforcement would hardly prove pervasion.

LITERARY MERIT QUESTIONS

In the case of *Scars Upon My Heart*, this question would almost certainly draw a comparison between the female poets contained in the collection and their male counterparts. It might take the form of a statement or quotation which suggests that the poetry in Scars Upon My Heart is less skillful than the poetry of the male writers of the time and, generally speaking, the question is unlikely to argue that the women's poetry is the more accomplished.

This is another question which is looking for an opinion and, in this instance, the further reading requirement would be to have studied the poetry of male writers. Here, the most useful anthology to study would probably be *Up the Line to Death*, edited by Brian Gardner, because it contains no female writers at all.

In his introduction, Brian Gardner states that his intention was to use poems which tell 'part of the whole story' and yet this does not include the female voice, even though the anthology features a chapter on the home front! He makes no mention of female war poets, although there are contributions by non-combatants such as John Masefield, Rudyard Kipling and Wilfrid Wilson Gibson, although Brian Gardner claims, erroneously, that Gibson served in the trenches for a short time.

Having read his anthology, you might begin to wonder why Brian Gardner left out the voice of women. You might assume that he had few manuscripts to choose from, or that he felt that in the telling of his story about the war, the female voice was less relevant. Or, might it be that he excluded female poetry, because he simply thought it wasn't very good?

Just to deal, briefly, with these points. Firstly, there were many manuscripts available, even in the 1960s and, two years later, when compiling the sequel to this anthology (*The Terrible Rain, The War Poets 1939-1945*), Gardner included the poems of a few women. Certainly the more major poets such as Vera Brittain, May Wedderburn Cannan and Margaret Postgate Cole had all published collections of poetry. The relevance of the female voice could also be refuted, as surely the experiences of a VAD nurse, ambulance driver or grieving widow are no less valid than those of Thomas Hardy, A E Housman or Sir Henry Newbolt, who were too old to enlist, but whose poetry has been included by Gardner, because it is representative of the patriotic expectations which existed at the beginning of the conflict. Therefore, we could be led to the assumption that Brian Gardner was just not very impressed with the quality of the female poets. However, in order to really justify that supposition, which is, after all the whole point of this question, students would need to show that the writing of the female poets is significantly worse, across the board, than that of the men.

Again, this is a matter of personal opinion and there are many who would argue that even the worst of the male poetry is better than the best of the female offering. By reading an anthology such as *Up The Line to Death* in detail, students should be able to begin to form an opinion on this aspect of the topic.

Looking through the Preface of *Scars Upon My Heart* might also prove useful and insightful as here, Judith Kazantzis demonstrates a polarising opinion on the subject. Here, she uses the argument that the female voice deserved to be heard, regardless of its literary merit, in order to refute the statements laid down by Siegfried Sassoon in his poem *Glory of Women*, in which he 'attacked women's romantic ignorance' of the war's 'real nature'. This is a somewhat spurious, but commonly purported opinion, because it shows a lack of understanding of Sassoon's situation. He had been decorated for his bravery and wounded on the field of battle and had experienced at first hand, the attitudes of women, which made him angry enough to write the quoted poem. However, he wrote another poem at around the same time, entitled *The Hawthorn Tree*, in which the narrator is a woman, whose husband or lover (or some argue, son) has gone to fight and who recalls happier times, acknowledging that her 'lad' 'would gives his eyes for just one glance' at the 'white hawthorn tree' in the lane where they used to walk together. Here, Sassoon shows great sympathy for the strength of some women, but also for their agony of waiting. So, this knowledge makes Kazantzis's argument less forceful and leads one to wonder whether there is a justifiable argument for including 'bad' poetry in an anthology, just because it has been written by a woman.

Some of the poems are, of course, more than worthy of being published, read and studied, but on the other hand, quite a few are not, so the reader or student must, in this case, assess whether the literary merit of these poorer poems has an adverse effect on the collection as a whole.

For example, as a matter of my own opinion, I have to question the inclusion of works by Marie Carmichael Stopes or Vivienne Verne, at the expense of better poems by May Cannan or Margaret Sackville. If these less worthy poems had been selected because they portrayed a different perspective of the war, then one could argue for their inclusion; but they do not. The repetitive nature of the viewpoints portrayed throughout the collection makes the poorer poems more obvious, because they fail to hold their own within the anthology, when placed next to the better pieces. For example (and remember, this is a matter of my personal opinion), both *Revision* by Eileen Newton and *Remembrance Day in the Dales* by Dorothy Una Ratcliffe fall into the category of poems about grief or loss, but the latter poem fails to capture the essence of this emotion because its rhyme scheme is too contrived and its metre is too sprightly for the subject matter. In many cases, it is the final line or sentence of a poem which is pivotal to its meaning and impression, and this proves to be so in this instance, where Ratcliffe's poem falters, but Newton's is a triumph of emotional expression.

FURTHER READING RECOMMENDATIONS FOR STUDENTS

Students are often expected to demonstrate a sound knowledge of the texts which they are studying and also to enhance this knowledge with extensive reading of other books within this genre. I have provided on the following pages a list of books, poetry, plays and non-fiction which, in my opinion, provide a good basic understanding of this topic. In addition, a small review of each book has been provided to help students choose which of the following are most suitable for them.

NOVELS

STRANGE MEETING by Susan Hill

Strange Meeting is a beautiful and moving book. It is the story of two young men, who meet in the worst circumstances, yet manage to overcome their surroundings and form a deep and lasting friendship. They are opposites: John Hilliard is quiet and reserved, while David Barton is outgoing and friendly. Despite their differences, their friendship blossoms, as the world around them disintegrates into self-destruction. Susan Hill writes so evocatively that the reader is automatically drawn into the lives of these men: the sights, sounds and even smells which they witness are brought to life. This is a book about war and its effects; it is also a story of love, both conventional and 'forbidden'; of human relationships of every variety. This is a tale told during the worst of times, about the best of men and is, quite simply, one of the best novels ever written about the First World War.

A VERY LONG ENGAGEMENT by Sebastien Japrisot

A story of enduring love, truth and determination. Refusing to believe that her fiancé can possibly have left her forever, Mathilde decides to search for Manech whom she has been told is missing, presumed dead. She learns from a first-hand witness, that he may not have died, so she sets out on a voyage of discovery - learning not just about his fate, but also a great deal about herself and human nature. Mathilde herself has to overcome her own personal fears and hardships and, out of sheer persistence and a refusal to accept the obvious, she eventually discovers the truth. Although this novel does not form part of the main syllabus reading list, it does make an interesting and fairly easy read and is useful from the perspective that it gives a French woman's viewpoint of the war.

REGENERATION by Pat Barker

This book is, as its title implies, a novel about the rebuilding of men following extreme trauma. Billy Prior is a young working-class officer - a 'temporary gentleman' - who finds himself at Craiglockhart Military Hospital in Edinburgh, having been damaged by his experiences on the Western Front. It is the job of Dr W. H. R. Rivers, to 'mend' Prior, and others like him, ready for them to return to the fighting, while wrestling with his own conscience at the same time. Interweaved into this central plot is the meeting, also at Craiglockhart, of poets Siegfried Sassoon and Wilfred Owen, who are both there to receive treatment. This mixture of fact and fiction within a novel has created some controversy, but it is a common feature within this genre and one which Pat Barker handles better than most. This is an immensely useful book - even if not read as part of the Trilogy - as it takes place away from the front lines, showing the reader the deep and long-lasting effects of battle upon men, whose lives would never be the same again. Due to some adult content, we recommend this book for A-Level students only.

THE RETURN OF THE SOLDIER by Rebecca West

Written in 1918, by an author who had lived through the conflict, this home-front novel gives a useful insight into the trauma of war and society's reaction, as seen through the eyes of three women. Chris Baldry, an officer and husband of Kitty, returns home mid-way through the war, suffering from shell-shock and amnesia. He believes that he is still in a relationship with Margaret Allington - his first love from fifteen years earlier. Kitty, Margaret and Chris's cousin, Jenny, must decide whether to leave Chris in his make-believe world, safe from the war; or whether to 'cure' him and risk his future welfare once he returns to being a soldier. A useful novel from many perspectives in that it was written right at the end of the war, and it gives a female, home-front view of the effects of the war on individuals and families.

ALL QUIET ON THE WESTERN FRONT by Erich Maria Remarque

Written from first-hand experience of life in the trenches, this novel is the moving account of the lives of a group of young German soldiers during the First World War. Remarque had been in the trenches during the later stages of the war and this poignant account of war is a must-read for all those who show an interest in this subject. His descriptions of trench-life and battles are second-to-none and his portrayal of the close friendships forged between the men make this an immensely valuable piece of literature. The fact that this, often shocking, story is told from a German perspective also demonstrates the universal horrors of the war and the sympathy between men of both sides for others enduring the same hardships as themselves.

A LONG LONG WAY by Sebastian Barry

Sebastian Barry's novel tells the a story of Willie Dunne, a young Irish volunteer serving in the trenches of the Western Front. Willie must not only contend with the horrors of the war, but also his own confused feelings regarding the Easter uprising of 1916, and his father's disapproval. Willie's feelings and doubts lead to great upheavals in his life, including personal losses and betrayals by those whom he had believed he could trust. This is an interesting novel about loyalty, war and love, although it does suffer from a degree of historical inaccuracy. In our opinion, due to the adult content of this novel, it is suitable only for A-Level students.

NOT SO QUIET... by Helen Zenna Smith

This novel describes the lives of women working very close to the front line on the Western Front during the First World War, as ambulance drivers. Theirs is a dangerous job, in harsh conditions, with little or no respite. Helen (or Smithy, as she is called by her friends), eventually breaks down under the pressure of the work and returns, briefly, to England. An excellent novel for studying the female perspective, as well as the home front.

POETRY

It is recommended that students read from a wide variety of poets, including female writers. The following anthologies provide good resources for students.

POEMS OF THE FIRST WORLD WAR - NEVER SUCH INNOCENCE
Edited by Martin Stephen

Probably one of the finest anthologies of First World War poetry currently available. Martin Stephen has collected together some of the best known works by some of the most famous and well-read poets and mixed these with more obscure verses, including many by women and those on the home-front, together with some popular songs both from home and from the front. These have been interspersed with excellent notes which give the reader sufficient information without being too weighty. At the back of the book, there are short biographical notes on many of the poets. This is a fine anthology, suitable both for those who are starting out with their studies, and for the more experienced reader.

LADS: LOVE POETRY OF THE TRENCHES by Martin Taylor

Featuring many lesser-known poets and poems, this anthology approaches the First World War from a different perspective: love. A valuable introduction discusses the emotions of men who, perhaps for the first time, were discovering their own capacity to love their fellow man. This is not an anthology of purely homo-erotic poems, but also features verses by those who had found affection and deep, lasting friendship in the trenches of the First World War.

UP THE LINE TO DEATH
Edited by Brian Gardner

This anthology, described by its editor Brian Gardner as a 'book about war', is probably, and deservedly, one of the most widely read in this genre. The famous and not-so-famous sit happily together within in these pages of carefully selected poetry. Arranged thematically, these poems provide a poet's-eye-view of the progression of the war, from the initial euphoria and nationalistic pride of John Freeman's 'Happy is England Now' to Sassoon's plea that we should 'never forget'. Useful biographical details and introductions complete this book, which is almost certainly the most useful and important of all the First World War poetry anthologies.

NON-FICTION

UNDERTONES OF WAR by Edmund Blunden

Edmund Blunden's memoir of his experiences in the First World War is a moving, enlightening and occasionally humorous book, demonstrating above all the intense feelings of respect and comradeship which Blunden found in the trenches.

MEMOIRS OF AN INFANTRY OFFICER by Siegfried Sassoon

Following on from *Memoirs of a Fox-hunting Man*, this book is an autobiographical account of Sassoon's life during the First World War. Sassoon has changed the names of the characters and George Sherston (Sassoon) is not a poet. Sassoon became one of the war's most famous poets and this prose account of his war provides useful background information.
(For a list of the fictional characters and their factual counterparts, see Appendix II of *Siegfried Sassoon* by John Stuart Roberts.)

THE GREAT WAR GENERALS ON THE WESTERN FRONT 1914-1918 by Robin Neillands

Like many others before and since, the cover of this book claims that it will dismiss the old myth that the troops who served in the First World War were badly served by their senior officers. Unlike most of the other books, however, this one is balanced and thought-provoking. Of particular interest within this book is the final chapter which provides an assessment of the main protagonists and their role in the conflict.

THE WESTERN FRONT by Richard Holmes

This is one of many history books about the First World War. Dealing specifically with the Western Front, Richard Holmes looks at the creation of the trench warfare system, supplying men and munitions, major battles and living on the front line..

LETTERS FROM A LOST GENERATION (FIRST WORLD WAR LETTERS OF VERA BRITTAIN AND FOUR FRIENDS) Edited by Alan Bishop and Mark Bostridge

A remarkable insight into the changes which the First World War caused to a particular set of individuals. In this instance, Vera Brittain lost four important people in her life (two close friends, her fiancé and her brother). The agony this evoked is demonstrated through letters sent between these five characters, which went on to form the basis of Vera Brittain's autobiography *Testament of Youth*.

1914-1918: VOICES AND IMAGES OF THE GREAT WAR by Lyn MacDonald

One of the most useful 'unofficial' history books available to those studying the First World War. This book tells the story of the soldiers who fought the war through their letters, diary extracts, newspaper reports, poetry and eye-witness accounts. As with all of Lyn MacDonald's excellent books, *Voices and Images of the Great War* tells its story through the words of the people who were there. The author gives just the right amount of background information of a political and historical nature to keep the reader interested and informed, while leaving the centre-stage to those who really matter... the men themselves.

BIBLIOGRAPHY

Violets from Oversea (Tonie and Valmai Hart)
Minds at War - The Poetry and Experience of the First World War (David Roberts)
Poems of the First World War - Never Such Innocence (Martin Stephen)
Lads (Martin Taylor)
Up the Line to Death: The War Poets 1914-1918 (Brian Gardner)
The Winter of the World - Poems of the Great War (edited by Dominic Hibberd and John Onions)
Oxford Dictionary of National Biography, Oxford University Press, 2004
Scars Upon My Heart (Catherine Reilly)
Vera Brittain - a Life (Paul Berry and Mark Bostridge)
Testament of Youth (Vera Brittain)
Letters from a Lost Generation (Mark Bostridge and Alan Bishop)
Grey Ghosts and Voices (May Wedderburn Cannan)
Portrait of a Family (Eleanor Farjeon)
Portrait of a Farjeon (Denys Blakelock)
A Rainbow Picnic - A Portrait of a Tree (Daphne Fielding)
Alice Meynell - A Memoir (Viola Meynell)

Other Titles

GREAT WAR LITERATURE STUDY GUIDE E-BOOKS:

NOVELS & PLAYS

All Quiet on the Western Front
Birdsong
Journey's End (A-Level or GCSE)
Regeneration
The Eye in the Door
The Ghost Road
A Long Long Way
The First Casualty
Strange Meeting
The Return of the Soldier
The Accrington Pals
Not About Heroes
Oh What a Lovely War

POET BIOGRAPHIES AND POETRY ANALYSIS:

Herbert Asquith
Harold Begbie
John Peale Bishop
Edmund Blunden
Vera Brittain
Rupert Brooke
Thomas Burke
May Wedderburn Cannan
Margaret Postgate Cole
Alice Corbin
E E Cummings

Nancy Cunard
T S Eliot
Eleanor Farjeon
Gilbert Frankau
Robert Frost
Wilfrid Wilson Gibson
Anna Gordon Keown
Robert Graves
Julian Grenfell
Ivor Gurney
Thomas Hardy
Alan P Herbert
Agnes Grozier Herbertson
W N Hodgson
A E Housman
Geoffrey Anketell Studdert Kennedy
Winifred M Letts
Amy Lowell
E A Mackintosh
John McCrae
Charlotte Mew
Edna St Vincent Millay
Ruth Comfort Mitchell
Harriet Monroe
Edith Nesbit
Robert Nichols
Wilfred Owen
Jessie Pope
Ezra Pound
Florence Ripley Mastin
Isaac Rosenberg
Carl Sandburg
Siegfried Sassoon
Alan Seeger
Charles Hamilton Sorley
Wallace Stevens
Sara Teasdale
Edward Wyndham Tennant
Lesbia Thanet
Edward Thomas

Iris Tree
Katharine Tynan Hinkson
Robert Ernest Vernède
Arthur Graeme West

Please note that e-books are only available direct from our Web site at www.greatwarliterature.co.uk and cannot be purchased through bookshops.

Printed in Great Britain
by Amazon

87479880R00139

HISTORY

FRANCE

Claude Lebédel

"Nowadays, the majority of young people grow up in a kind of permanent present, without any organic link between the public past and the times in which they live"
Eric Hobsbawn (British historian, specialist in contemporary history).

Translation: 5/5

Editions Ouest-France

By way of introduction

"Each period creates its own mental image of past history"
(Lucien Febvre founder of the History School called the Annales).

The sentence above provides an essential reference for any reader of a history of France and, obviously, all the more so for the person who writes it. The importance which we attribute to this or that event in our past, the place which we grant it in the chain of events which comprises our history must always be considered by taking into account its relative character. Sometimes an historical account can be the real reflection of a perhaps imaginary reality, which has nonetheless become impressed on people's minds.

Our period, at the end of the second millennium, has been marked by considerable political change. The French nation, as it has asserted itself after many centuries of development, is witnessing the disappearance of some of its essential landmarks: the signing of the Single European Act in 1986 and in 1991 the Maastricht Summit, which was its continuation and direct consequence, have caused one of the essential expressions of national sovereignty to disappear, i.e. control over its currency. Tomorrow, now that globalisation has gradually become irreversible, what will happen to one of the other essential components of a nation's life, its culture?

The regions become attached to France

Note:
- Some complex aspects concerning the bishoprics of Metz, Toul and Verdun and also Alsace have been left aside.
- Do not confuse the Duchy of Burgundy with the Earldom of Burgundy, i.e. Franche-Comté.

Knowledge of the past is an indispensable basis for understanding the present and not remaining passive when confronted with the future. In fact, for thirty years and up to a recent date, history teaching at secondary level has ceased to use the chronological framework as a point of reference; the results of a teaching method of this kind has been disastrous for the knowledge and understanding of our past. It is the purpose of this small work to attempt to supply the reader with sources of information and thought on the development of France since its origins.

The history of France has not been linear; it has been subject to many upheavals. The pages which follow will endeavour to describe and explain them. Before doing this, however, it would be useful briefly to examine three questions: first, the borders of the geographical framework, i.e. the problem of the frontiers as it has been perceived from the start, secondly the meaning of the word "France" and lastly the question of language.

Contrary to what one might believe, clear understanding of French territory arrived late. Certainly from the XVIth century onwards, kings and queens sought the proper geographical representation of the territories because a distinction had to be made between the royal domain, properly speaking, and the fiefs relating to the feudal system. The first printed map of France dates back to 1482 and lacks accuracy. Despite Colbert's efforts, the aim sought was not attained until the end of the Ancien Regime, just before the Revolution.

On the other hand, the general boundaries of what became France were fixed very early as far as the east was concerned. It was the Treaty of Verdun in 843 which outlined them in the partitioning, between his three sons, of the kingdom of Louis le Débonnaire or Pious (778-840), son of Charlemagne; it involved the breaking up of the "regnum Francorum" (Kingdom of the Franks) and western "Francie" was granted to Charles the Bald with, in the east, the so-called four rivers' boundary - Escaux, Meuse, Saône and Rhone i.e. about 330,000 km2.

As the centuries passed and with the incessant reminders of Charlemagne's empire, these boundaries were going to appear inadequate compared with the never really defined "natural frontiers" (Alps, Pyrenees, Rhine?). The original territory gradually grew during the long process which constituted French national unity.

Another question to be raised is the perception of the concept of "France". In the beginning, the term used to describe the essential part of our present national territory was "Gaul" but it was the invaders, the Franks,

Gallic oppidum: aerial view of Alésia
Determining where the site of Alésia lay has been the subject of long discussions between specialists; symbolically, Alésia represents the final victory of Roman power in the land of Gaul and the end of Gallic resistance.
Regional Committee of Burgundy for Archaeological Research, Photo: R. Goguey.

A funerary stele in Greek characters and Gallic language.
Documents in the Gallic language are few, a very serious obstacle to understanding Gallic culture.
Nîmes Museum.
Photo: D. Stokic.

A Gallic statute
Little-known portrait, which gives an idea of the face of Vercingétorix, all later representations are purely imaginary.
BNF, Cabinet des Médailles.

which gave it their name. France was first of all the combination of the Frankish lands with in particular the Ile-de-France around Paris. The expression "regnum Francorum", gave birth from 1254 onwards to the term "Rex (king) Franciae"; to be French was to recognise oneself as a subject of the King of France.

In the XVIth century, in an unexpected and legendary way, Gaul and the Gauls made their reappearance. A lawyer in the service of King Louis XII, Jean Lemaire with "Illustrations of Gaul and the Singularity of Troy" in 1511 and the poet Ronsard, with his "Franciade" in 1572, elaborated the idea that the origin of the kings of France was to be sought among the Gauls, themselves descendants of the Trojans. According to the legend, the Gauls founded Troy. After the latter's destruction by the Greeks the fugitives returned, via the banks of the Rhine, to Gaul where they rediscovered their ancestors, those who had not departed to found Troy. Francion son of Hector and Andromache was to be the ancestor of Charlemagne. The "Gallo-Trojan" concept was thereby established. Subsequently the transition was made to the notion of "our ancestors, the Gauls", so dear to teaching in the Third Republic. Indeed this had the consequence, apart from the absurdity of being used as a reference for the spread of French history in the colonies, of completely hiding one of the characteristics of France: the complexity of the mixture of its peoples. The Gallo-Roman line, i.e. the regional inhabitants subject to Roman civilisation, was in fact a Gallo-Roman and Frankish line. The Frankish component, i.e.

Liberty, equality, fraternity

This inscription on the front of public buildings dates from 1880.
It appeared, with variations, from 1791 onwards.

Germanic, cannot be dissociated from the Gallo-Roman base; this component and this base were subsequently completed by the addition of Celtic, Germanic, Burgundian, Basques and Savoyard elements.

The third question, language, now has passionate implications. The original nucleus of the Kingdom of France having been the Ile-de-France, the language spoken in the latter gradually prevailed, accompanying the characteristically centralising movement in French history, very different in its early strength from what happened in Italy and Germany. The federating language could have been Latin, constantly used in chancelleries up to a very advanced date. It was Francis I, with the Ordonnance de Villers-Cotterêts (1539), who gave the final blow to Latin as the official language by imposing French on all official documents; subsequently for more than two-and-a-half centuries there was no other provision. One has to wait until 1794 before this fundamental principle was recalled by the Convention which also imposed French upon teaching, however prescribing that the idiom of the country, i.e. the place, could be used but only in an auxiliary way.

A work of Romanesque art: the Pont du Gard
Photo: Richard Nourry.

What has come to be called the "regional languages" have had their range very strongly restricted and the problem has occasionally become acute in the contemporary period. On the other hand the desire to resist the spread through advertising, films and television and also popular songs of the English, or rather American, language has led the legislator to insert into our constitution (Article 2) the sentence, "The language of the Republic is French", and to prescribe various schemes for its protection. On the other hand the movements which, lacking a more appropriate description, have come to be termed "regional" have obtained some teaching rights and the use of these languages in their regions. The question is very delicate: for example is it really an additional asset for the inhabitants of this or that French region to be able, in addition to French, to use their regional language, whereas the latter's circulation is precisely confined to the area of the region under consideration? But inversely the maintenance of a local or regional identity can often be linked to its language.

The time has now come, however, to start the account of the history of France.

The cock, emblem of France

The sole current official emblem of France is the tricolour flag as defined by Article 2 of our constitution and not the cock.
The Latin word "Gallus" described both the inhabitant of Gaul and the king of the farmyard.
In the XVIth century French kings made this creature their emblem but it was the French Revolution which ensured the cock a definite position when minting coins.

ORIGINS – STARTING IN 987

Why 987? Because this date corresponds to the accession of Hugh Capet, lay abbot of Saint-Martin de Tours, lord elected by his peers, the counts and dukes of Western Francine; the **Capetian** dynasty reigned for 341 years with 14 kings. It started and strengthened the royal authority's movement towards unification and centralisation on the lands around the central nucleus of the Ile-de-France. The later dynasties (**Valois, Valois-Orleans, Valois-Angoulême and the Bourbons**) connected to the first through male succession, continued in the same direction.

It is estimated that more than fifty peoples lived in the territory of Gaul, the total representing perhaps about ten million persons; only fragmentary information is available about their life.

The Empire of Charlemagne (768-814)

The Roman conquests lasted more than a half-century: from 122 to 58 BC. Julius Caesar completed the process ; first of all he was beaten by Vercingetorix at Gergovia, but finally made him prisoner in Alesia.

Conquest by the Romans played a decisive role in the history of Gaul because, for more than four centuries, Roman culture and religion were deeply imbedded. Consequently an urban civilisation was able to expand based on ancient Gallic cities and new Roman cities where the Roman way of life had spread with, for example, the forum, the centre of administrative and commercial life, baths, etc. Like the other regions of the Roman Empire, Gaul also experienced the spread of Christianity.

At the beginning of the Vth century of our era a new period began which profoundly transformed the Gallo-Roman culture and civilisation. At first tentative and slow but subsequently much more violently, the barbarian peoples, i.e. those speaking a language not understood by the Romans, crossed the Rhine and the Danube – Burgundians, Franks, Visigoths, etc. In fact, the movement had been started from the third century onwards by the Germanic tribes, including the Franks, which Rome had called upon to defend its frontiers against other tribes.

Little by little the Franks who had settled in Gaul became a normal component of the struggle against the new invaders; they occupied an important place during the decline of the Roman Empire. It was a Frankish chieftain,

Mérovée, who led the struggle against the Huns; the latter led by Attila, were repulsed at the Battle of the Catalonic Fields in 451. The final disappearance of the Roman imperial system of the West in 476 did not fundamentally change the situation. The essential fact was the increasingly distinctive emergence of the Franks. Clovis asserted his authority as far as the Loire by his victory over a rival at Soissons. He converted to Christianity and by his coronation at Reims, he marked the beginning of one of the characteristic features of the French monarchy, i.e. the close links with the Catholic Church.

This beginning of the process constituting French unity could have stopped there since, on the death of Clovis probably in 511, all the Frankish lands were divided among his sons. But one of them, Clotaire, reassembled them once more, which was also achieved by the great-grandson of Clovis, Clotaire II in 613, whose son, Dagobert, founded the Abbey of Saint-Denis.

Clovis' triumphal entry into Tours in 208.
By Joseph Nicolas Robert-Fleury (1797-1890).
Castels of Versailles and Trianon. © RMN – G. Blot.

▸ The people over whom he reigned, the Franks, gave their name to the territory which they occupied. Consequently Clovis could be considered the first King of France but his almost mythical character must not be lost sight of. It was he who chose Paris as capital but very few things about him can be historically proved.

In 752, Pépin the Short, son of Charles Martel, "Mayor of the Palace" who at Poitiers in 732 stopped an Arab invasion, deposed the last Frankish king, Childeric III. It was done with the agreement of the Pope who crowned Pépin in Reims. A new dynasty was thereby founded, that of the **Carolingians** whose most famous representative was to be Charlemagne who reigned from 768 to 814.

Charlemagne's reign was important from several points of view; he revived the myth of a universal empire with his coronation by the Pope in Rome on Christmas Day in the year 800. Secondly, his reign corresponded with a veritable cultural renaissance centred in particular on the activity of the abbeys – conserving and copying manuscripts and teaching. Lastly, Charlemagne's empire extended over a vast geographic area from the Baltic to the Mediterranean, from the Oder to the Ebre. But we must keep well in mind that, since the French and German nations were still not constituted as such, Charlemagne can be considered both a French Emperor and a German Emperor; his capital was Aix-la-Chapelle - Aachen. The practise of division within the family, already noticed above in the case of the Franks, led to conflicts between Charlemagne's grandsons; the timely death of Charlemagne's two sons, Pépin and Charles

The oath of Strasbourg

This is a text of capital importance; Charlemagne's grandsons, Louis the Germanic and Charles the Bald swore in Strasbourg in 842 a joint oath, in French and German, to their troops engaged in the struggle against another of Charlemagne's grandson – Lothaire.
The following year in 843 in Verdun a partition was signed between the three protagonists, to some extent giving birth to France and Germany with, between the two, Lotharingia.

had enabled power to remain solely in the hands of Louis le Débonnaire, whose reign lasted from 814 to 840 but ended in a real partition. The **Treaty of Verdun in 843** clearly marked the birth of two entities: on the one hand Gaul, the future France between the Ocean, the Escaux, the Meuse and the Ebre for Charles the Bald and on the other Germany for Louis the Germanic. Between these two future nations lay Lotharingia (for Lothaire), which is a corridor, roughly the valleys of the Rhine and Rhone and North Italy, subsequently disputed by the two emerging nations.

To some extent Charles the Bald, 843 to 877, was the first King of France. In his reign events of major importance for the future occurred; in 847 Charles the Bald recognised the sovereignty of the great lords over Brittany, Ile-de-France, Flanders. In 877 he grouped together a series of texts, ordinances, which founded the feudal system.

From 887 a conflict for the possession of the crown developed between two families: the families of the descendants of Charlemagne and the **Capetians**, the first to be known among the latter was Robert the Strong, Duke of the Ile-de-France. The conflict was in fact always arbitrated by the great lords, possessors of power in the major regions.

It was precisely in 987 that these great lords elected Hugh Capet as king.

The partition of Verdun (843)

Charlemagne crosses the Alps to give battle to Didier, King of the Lombards in 773, by Eugène Roger (1807-1840).
The picture represents the nineteenth century passion for the beginnings of French history.
Castels of Versailles and Trianon. © RMN – G. Blot.

With hindsight, this long eight-century period can be considered in two ways: either insistence can be placed on continuity and in this case the enlargement of the royal domain is to be noted with its corollary, the struggle for central power with the great feudal lords and its consequence – the establishment of an absolute monarchy; or the accent can be placed on the major crises which the royal power underwent (Hundred Years War from 1337 to 1453, wars of religion from 1560 to 1598 and the Fronde from 1648 to 1653) with above all the fundamental crisis, which affected the heart of the political and ideological system from the middle of the XVIIIth century onwards.

Neither one of these two major lines of reasoning should be given preferential treatment at the expense of the other. External events, the ambitions of neighbouring countries and their resistance to French ambitions, often played a decisive role. The history of France has not been linear; it has been the result of a series of complex factors, which must be explained and linked to each other. Bearing these remarks in mind and with a concern for clarity, we will, therefore one after the other, study the following periods:

— from Hugh Capet (987) to Charles the IV's death without direct male successor in 1328;

— the very serious crisis which the Hundred Years' War amounted to;

— after this the accretion of royal power, despite the serious new crisis connected with the wars of religion, which Henry IV managed to bring to an end;

— with the accession of Louis XIII (1610) began an era of assertion of internal royal power combined with what has been called the "French ascendancy" abroad;

— the death of Louis XIV (1715) whose reign was the longest in the history of France, from 1661, the beginning of his personal reign, to 1715, i.e. fifty-four years, gave free rein to currents of thought, which arose in the Regency during the minority of Louis XIV's great-grandson; in latter's reign, and above in that of Louis XVI, principles up to then considered indisputable were called into question.

The Capetian dynasty and gradual assertion of royal power

When Hugh Capet ascended the throne the country was far from achieving the territorial, economic and political settlement to be found on the eve of the Hundred Years' War.

The royal domain and the lands of the grand vassals in the twelfth century

The important point is that the kings of France attempted, and succeeded, right from the start in ensuring their succession. This was done at the height of feudal times when the power of the great vassals was considerable; vast principalities or duchies were formed, taking advantage of the disappearance of central authority after Charlemagne: Aquitaine, Gascony, Normandy (where Viking invaders settled) and Toulouse.

From a date difficult to pinpoint (middle of the XIth century), new factors intervened: the improvement of cultivation techniques - the horse collar, tools such as ploughshares and pickaxes, the transition from a four-year to a three-year rotation of crops, which eliminated a year's fallow, and water-mills, contributing to population growth and hence extensive clearings. Hence also the growth of towns which was to have political consequences.

To assert their authority, the kings of France knew how to exploit the situation.

First factor: they were consecrated at the moment of their crowning and received the support of the Catholic Church which the latter never refused. A characteristic example is supplied by Louis VI (1108-1137) who relied upon Suger, Abbot of Saint-Denis. Through his consecration, the king was reputedly capable of performing miracles by touch, hence the importance rightly recorded by Marc Bloch, the great historian, to the concept of the "healing kings".

Second factor: the kings knew how to exploit the innumerable conflicts between their vassals. Little by little feudal society was established; at the head were the kings, the supreme suzerains, high above the other lords owing to their sacred character.

The formation of a society into "orders" also contributed to the accretion of royal power, since the lords and nobility were only the second order, after the clergy who came first. It was precisely the third order, "the third estate", in its urban composition which emerged as an auxiliary and often an ally of royal authority. The kings' granting new towns (the urban movement was very strong from the XII century onwards) franchise charters placed the communes outside the feudal system.

The Capetian monarchy knew how to exploit the opportunities of legal construction provided by the renewal and resurgence of Roman law. Gradually a whole series of

Philippe-August at the Battle of Bouvines, 27 July 1214 by Horace Vernet (1789-1863), specialist in battle scenes.

concepts and texts, introduced by the "jurists" of Philippe le Bel (beginning of the XIVth century), justified and strengthened the idea of the state, making fundamental progress by comparison with the feudal system. They proclaimed that the king of France was "*emperor in his kingdom*".

All this occurred while numerous conflicts and upheavals were taking place.

Internal upheavals should be mentioned first; it was not until 1242 that the king, Louis IX (Saint Louis), achieved the acceptance of the principle whereby lords possessing fiefs in France and England had to choose to whom of the two suzerains they intended to pay homage. It remains difficult to separate the internal and external aspects, for example when armed conflict broke out between Philippe Auguste and Richard the Lionheart or again between Philippe Auguste and the Flemish and English lords and Otto of Germany. In the latter case, the ***battle of Bouvines*** (1214) had particular significance: contemporaries saw it as a national victory, it has **become the cornerstone of national unity**.

An interesting example of the French kings' ability to exploit the conflicts, in which they became involved, to increase the royal domain, is supplied by the Cathar affair. In this instance Philippe Auguste and then Saint Louis took advantage of a crusade against the Albigensian heretics (Cathar) to obtain the lands (Occitania to simplify) of the Count of Toulouse; thereby a great vassal, dangerous owing to his alliance with Aragon, was annihilated.

What was the state of France at the moment when the very serious crisis of the Hundred Years' War broke out, i.e. around 1330?

France had still not attained the borders of the Treaty of Verdun and furthermore it was a mixed entity: the royal domain, properly speaking, had as its nucleus the Ile-de-France, the appendages, or parts of the domain donated to the king's children, and the large fiefs outside the domain belonging to the great vassals (de facto autonomous). There still did not exist any tax collected by the king and consequently, lacking resources, the latter did not possess an army belonging to him alone; he remained dependant on the feudal levy, a vassal owed 40 days "service" per year.

Royal power had, however, asserted itself and was recognised both internally by the majority of vassals and externally by

The feudal system

The feudal system developed from the beginning of the Xth century in France and Germany, mainly in the Rhine valley and was "exported" first of all to England as a result of the latter's conquest by the Norman, William the Conqueror, in 1066 and subsequently to the Holy Land, in our days Israel, Lebanon and Syria, as a result of the crusades. The system's zenith was achieved during the XIIth and XIIIth centuries. It was a whole series of institutions which defined the obligations and obedience of a "vassal" towards a "suzerain" in exchange for the "suzerain's" protection and support obligations towards their "vassals". The whole system was organised in the shape of a pyramid with crossed relations; a given suzerain could be the vassal of another lord; the supreme suzerain was the king who in principle only had vassals even if some of them were in reality more powerful than he.

Landmarks

1066: William the Conqueror, Duke of Normandy, conquered England and introduced the French feudal system.

1180-1223: reign of Philippe II (Philippe Auguste).

1226-1270: reign of Louis IX (Saint Louis).

1285-1314: reign of Philippe IV (Philippe Le Bel).

An example of Roman art: two knights on an historiated column of Notre-Dame-du-Port at Clermont-Ferrand (Puy-de-Dôme).
Photo Hervé Champollion.

neighbouring powers. Moreover, the king of France was now able to avail himself of a too close a partnership with the Church or more exactly with the Papacy. The conflict (1302-1305) between Philippe le Bel and the Pope Boniface VIII is revealing in this respect. It was the beginning of a Gallic policy confronting ultramontane positions, i.e. Roman. Philippe le Bel caused a French Pope to be elected and he transferred the seat of the papacy to Avignon (from 1309 to 1378). Another sign of the times: Philippe le Bel in 1302 convened the first "states general" combining the representatives of the three orders - clergy, nobility and commons.

The XIIIth century in the broad sense of the term, from Philippe Auguste to the death of Philippe le Bel, was a period of growth and change when the French nation really emerged. **Romanesque art** achieved its zenith around 1100; in the XIIIth century (the work on Chartres began in 1194) **gothic or ogival art**, owing to its pointed arches, spread. Paris was acknowledged as an intellectual centre.

The Salic Law

The Salic law was invoked for the first time in 1328 by the states general, combining the representatives of the nobility, clergy and towns: women were declared by law incapable of acceding to the succession on the death of the king.

The States-General of Paris met in Notre-Dame after the death of Charles IV on 1 February 1328; the Salic Law was mentioned for the first time.
Painting by Jean Alaux called the Romanesque (1786-1864)
Castels of Versailles and Trianon. © RMN – G. Blot.

The crisis of the Hundred Years' War

Apart from the upheavals of this long period lasting several generations (events which it is outside the scope of this small work to describe), its essential importance should be understood for the destiny of France. During the period France, threatened by internal and external causes escaped breaking up, even disappearing.

The origin of the crisis? A problem of succession to the throne of France. In 1154 Henry Plantagenet was at the same time Duke of Normandy, King of England and Lord of Aquitaine, he had married Elinor of Aquitaine, divorced from Louis VII. He remained the vassal of the King of France, but was a vassal more powerful than his suzerain. In 1328, his successor was Edward III, grandson of Philippe le Bel, through the latter's daughter.

At the same moment, the direct accession was no longer ensured in France: the three sons of Philippe le Bel died without male heirs.

Calendar from a fifteenth century book of hours: the month of August, harvest.

Close examination of the miniatures appearing on the individual calendars gives a good idea of the daily life of the time.

Paris, Museum of the Middle Ages, Cluny. © RMN, H. Lewandowski.

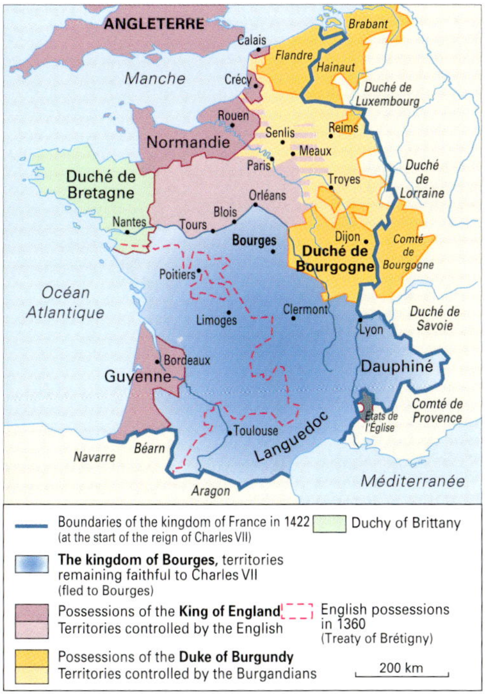

France during the Hundred-Years War

The *states general of 1328*, applying the Salic law, decided to exclude women from the succession and endorsed the crowning of Philippe III, nephew through the male line of Philippe le Bel. The King of England swore allegiance to the new king of France in 1329, retracting it in 1337 by declaring war.

Military disasters followed one after another, culminating in the Treaties of Brétigny (1360) and Troyes (1420). In 1422, the kingdom of France was confined for the time to south of the Loire. A complete reversal occurred: Joan of Arc led Charles VII to Reims to be crowned. Gradually, up to 1449 the English were expelled from France, except for Calais which remained English.

Obviously, these serious external difficulties encouraged the outbreak of internal conflicts, among which we mention only two. Etienne Marcel, provost of the Paris merchants, led the urban opposition to the king of France declaring

"The Virgin": Joan of Arc at the head of her army by Craig Franck (1874-1918). The picture is clearly inspired by the battle scenes of Uccello (1397-1475), the Italian painter. Musée d'Orsay. © RMN, G. Blot.

an alliance with the rebellious peasantry (the "jacques") and ultimately tried to deliver Paris to the English but the Parisian people objected and Etienne Marcel was assassinated (1358).

In 1388, national unity was endangered by a violent armed conflict between Burgundians and Armagnacs, supporters of the royal family. It was the beginning of a question which was to last beyond the Hundred Years' War: the problem of a very powerful vassal, the Duke of Burgundy, confronting the king of France.

In addition there was the problem of the "great companies" that is to say bands of mercenary soldiers without pay who devastated the countryside, in particular during the period of **Charles V** (1364 to 1380) whose reign achieved a recovery.

Assertion of royal power, from Charles VII to Henry IV

From the end of the Hundred Years' War onwards (no treaty has officially put an end to it), i.e. in the middle of the XVth century, the royal power was able to resume its previous policy.

The recovery of France took place in a very favourable general context; it was the brink of great discoveries, like that of America in 1492, but the XVIth century was also a time of technical discoveries, spread by the use of printing. The merchant economy developed and with it, a social class, the bourgeoisie, for whom the feudal system was a burden.

Politically it must be noted that from the end of the XVth century the system of succession through the male line was no longer questioned. The kings provided themselves with the indispensable instruments for their policy: the introduction of standing taxation from 1439 onwards and the establishment of a royal army from 1445 onwards.

Two feudal affairs were settled before 1500. First of all the problem of the *power of Burgundy*; Charles the Bold, grand vassal, wanted to institute a kingdom combining Burgundy and the Netherlands by means of mastery over Alsace and Lorraine. His death in Nancy in 1477 enabled **Louis XI** to take over the Duchy of Burgundy.

In the West the rich *duchy of Brittany*, vassal of the king of France, was behaving with great autonomy. The last duke died in 1488 with a single daughter as his successor; the latter proposed her hand in marriage to Maximilian of Austria, which fortunately for France was not successful. Finally, in 1491 she married Charles VIII leading to the incorporation of the duchy into France.

This leads us to broach the question of French external policy. One of its guidelines dates from the beginning of the XVIth century: the struggle with the Habsburgs to avoid encirclement. Mary of Burgundy's marriage to Maximilian of Austria made **Charles V's** empire formidably powerful, although at his death the division of the empire between the Habsburgs of Spain and Austria resulted in a more complex situation.

French ambition in northern and central Italy made an armed conflict inevitable. During the first part of the XVIth century **Francis I's campaigns** were numerous, particularly from 1521 to 1526, from 1536 to 1538 and 1542 to 1544. His whole "Italian policy" failed but the wars enabled the ideas of the Renaissance to spread in France. In the middle of the XVIth century with Henry II the conflict took a particular shape; already Francis I had sought, and obtained, an Ottoman alliance against the Habsburgs. With Henry II (1547-1559) began what became a constant of French policy, which Louis XIII and Louis XIV were to practise with effectiveness, seeking alliance with any force liable to weaken the adversary, for example with the Swiss Protestants of Grisons to block the Alpine route to Spanish troops going from the Milan area to the Netherlands in revolt against Spain or with the Hungarian Protestant majority rebelling against Vienna.

Charles VIII's entry into Naples, 12 May 1495, painting by Eloi Firmin Feron (1802-1876).
Castels of Versailles and Trianon. © RMN.

Charles V received by Francis I at the Abbey of Saint-Denis, by Antoine-Jean Gros Baron (1771-1835).
Francis I and CharlesV, inverterate opponents, met on several occasions, particularly when the King of France gave the Emperor safe conduct to cross France when returning to Spain.
Musée du Louvre. © RMN, G. Blot.

Scene of Saint Bartholomew, assassination of Briou, governor of the Prince de Conti, 24 August 1572, by Joseph Nicolas Robert-Fleury (1797-1890).
Musée du Louvre. © RMN.

Assassination of Henry IV and arrest of Ravaillac on 14 May 1610, by Charles-Gustave Housez (1822-1880).
The assassination occurred at the moment when Henry IV was preparing to attack Spain, resulting in the motives for internal and international orders becoming mixed up.
Castel of Pau. © RMN – R. G Ojeda.

Particularly under Henry II, but already under the Francis I, the ideas for reform launched by Martin Luther became widespread. A substantial segment of the population, belonging to different social strata, converted to the Protestant Huguenot religion. The religious problem, originally a matter of individual conscience, became political and national. In the eyes of some people, and in particular the king and his supporters of strong centralised power, the existence of a Huguenot party was a mortal danger to the kingdom's unity.

The king's attitude towards the Protestants appeared more tolerant than some who organised themselves into the League (Ligue) a close opposing group, comprising opponents of the centralising movement, which had always been the aim of French royalty. The final complicating factor was the underhand or completely overt interference of foreign powers, attempting both to support their co-religionists, Spain for the Catholics and Anglican England for the Protestants, and to encourage all currents opposed to the royal power.

The Italian Wars

From 1492 onwards and for about a half-century French external policy was dominated by the ambitions of the kings, mainly Charles VIII and Francis I, to make what they considered their rights to the Kingdom of Naples prevail. Charles d'Anjou, last representative of his family, had bequeathed to King Louis XI his rights to the crown of Naples which had been taken from him by the Aragon dynasty. Charles VIII, son of Louis XI, wanted to recover this "heritage". Louis XII, husband of Charles VIII's widow, wanted in addition to recover the duchy of Milan, in the hands of the Sforza family, since he was the great-grandson of the Duke Giangaleazzo-Visconti, Lord of Milan. The whole Italian policy failed but the wars enabled the ideas of the Italian Renaissance to spread to France.

The struggle was long and fierce with atrocities committed on both sides, in particular from 1562 to 1593. In 1589 King Henry III, who the League had declared deposed, had to appeal to Protestant troops to bring the situation under control. He died in the effort, assassinated by the monk Jacques Clément after recognising as his successor Henri de Bourbon, who became Henry IV after converting back to Catholicism. To some extent he managed to bring this very serious crisis to an end through his edict of Nantes (1598).

Drive for absolute monarchy: Henry IV, Louis XIII, Louis XIV

There was strong continuity in the action of these three kings, all the more so since there were two features which contributed to the trend: on two occasions it was necessary to institute a regency conducted by the queen-mother owing to the age of the new king (Mary de Médici for Louis XIII and Anne of Austria for Louis XIV: it is noticeable that both of them were foreigners by birth). Secondly, in three cases affairs were directed for a time by a double act: Sully and Henry IV, Richelieu and Louis XIII, Mazarin and Anne of Austria. But the essential point is the continuity of the policy pursued.

The wars of religion might have caused the break-up of national unity but on the rebound they strengthened the centralising policy and the assertion of royal power.

The growth of the merchant economy and its social consequences and birth of the bourgeoisie's power and ambitions, hastened the withering of the feudal system, an obstacle to the exercise of royal authority. The first half of the XVIIth witnessed the last spasm of the nobility opposed to this authority with the *Fronde* movement (1648-1653), which cannot however be reduced to a straight movement of the nobility. Richelieu, who from 1624 onwards was engaged in restricting the power of the nobility, had been sustained by Louis XIII (Day called the "Dupes"). Louis XIV completed the development by domesticating the nobility and preventing the Parlement de Paris, a purely judicial body, from playing a political role issuing remonstrances and refusing to endorse royal decisions.

Royal authoritarianism was strongly present in religious matters. Louis XIII, after a siege, occupied the Protestant fortress of La Rochelle which had wanted to form an alliance with England (1628). Louis XIV intended to settle the Protestant problem by forced conversions; the revocation of the edict of Nantes in 1685 caused both the exile of a large number of Protestants who, welcomed to Brandenbourg made a significant contribution to its development, and the violence visited upon the Protestants of the Cévennes (camisards, 1702-1705). The same forceful attitude applied to the Jansenists with the destruction of the Abbey of Port-Royal in 1709 and the imprisonment of many of them.

Wars of religion

1559: publication of the "Confession of faith" of French Protestants.

1562: start of the wars of religion between Catholics and Protestants.

1572: massacre of Protestants (Saint-Barthélemy).

1598: edict of Nantes of King Henry IV, Protestants converted to Catholicism. Freedom of conscience for Protestants.

1685: Louis XIV revoked the edict of Nantes. Complete suppression of freedom of conscience: conversion or exile for holders of the "religion pretending to be reformed" (RPR).

1702-1710: revolt of the Protestant peasantry of the Cévennes.

1787: Louis XVI's recognition of the civil existence of Protestants.

Colbert introduces members of the Royal Academy of Sciences, founded in 1667, to Louis XIV, by Henri Testelin (1616-1675).
The foundation had a double purpose: first to ensure control over intellectual circles in the most varied fields (Académie Française founded under Louis XIII) and secondly to ensure that scientific discoveries were circulated, calling upon the most varied talents.

Conflict with the papacy (1678-1693) revealed Louis XIV's desire to have the liberties of the Gallic (French) church recognised, in particular over the appointment of bishops, but it was finally Pope Innocent XII who won the argument.

Absolute monarchy and absolutism are not identical terms. Louis XIV's France was still not an integrated state; in regions gradually included in the kingdom states (*états*) still existed i.e. assemblies, which in particular pronounced on the levy of taxes. Certainly the administration's powers had been strengthened, passing into the hands of *intendants* (of police, justice and finance), permanent agents, one for each general district (*généralité*) appointed by the king. They put an authoritarian (Colbertist) economy into practise with inspectors of *manufactures*. The central power was directly in the hands of Louis XIV, without

Racine reading Athalie to Louis XIV and Madame de Maintenon, by Julie Philipaut (1780-1834).

"The century of Louis XIV"

This is the term which is used to describe a period which in fact extends over two reigns (Louis XIII and Louis XIV) and during which France experienced a considerable cultural development: in literature Corneille, Molière, Racine, La Bruyère, La Fontaine, Madame de Sévigné, Pascal, Bossuet, Saint-Simon (famous later), etc.; in painting Le Brun, Mignart, Vouet, Poussin, etc.; in architecture Mansart, Perrault, etc.

Reparation made to Louis XIV by the Doge of Genoa in the Hall of Mirrors at Versailles on 15 May 1685, by Claude Guy Halle (1652-1736). The Doge, under the statutes of the town of Genoa, did not have the right to leave the city, hence the extraordinary nature of this "reparation" which amounted to an humiliating act of submission.

sharing. Ministers were in fact only important clerks: **Colbert** (1619-1683), **Louvois** (1630-1691). The *nobility of the Robe*, arising from the rich bourgeoisie gradually evicted the old *nobility of the Sword* and occupied the main administrative posts.

External policy also featured strong continuity. Under Louis XIII France intervened directly in 1635 in the Thirty Years War (1618-1648) against the Habsburgs of Austria and Spain. France formed an alliance with the Protestant camp led by Sweden and the German princes and also the Dutch Protestants in rebellion against Spain. The Treaty of the Pyrenees (1659) enabled France to acquire Artois and Roussillon. A further war with Spain resulted, with the Treaty of Aix-la-Chapelle – Aachen (1668), in the acquisition of Flanders.

But a new fact, laden with consequences, emerged: worried by the French drive for hegemony England, Sweden and the Netherlands formed a coalition in 1668 which ultimately grouped together almost all Europe: War of Holland starting in 1672. Victory was won by France which, in the Treaty of Nijmegen (1678), obtained Franche-Comté and districts in Flanders (Valenciennes, Cambrai, etc.).

France at the death of Louis XIV

Another war (1688-1697) with the Treaty of Ryswick (1697) marked the end to French hegemony. The end of Louis XIV's reign coincided with a long and difficult war (1701-1714), the War of Spanish Succession; France was allied o Spain where one of Louis XIV's grandsons had become king. France was beaten but kept its territory at the Treaty of Utrecht (1714).

The time of hegemony and even ascendancy had come to an end.

Appearance and spread of new ideas (1715-1789)

Following the deaths of a number of heirs to the throne of Louis XIV the succession of a boy of five years old entailed instituting a regency.

Events, however, did not take place as Louis XIV had foreseen in a will which favoured several of his numerous illegitimate children to the detriment of Philippe of Orléans, his nephew. The latter manoeuvred

Landmarks

1721: "Persian Letters" by Montesquieu (1689-1755)

1722: "Philosophic Letters" by Voltaire (1694-1778)

1723: "Philosophic Thoughts" by Diderot (1713-1784)

1724: "The Spirit of the Laws" by Montesquieu

1725: "Letter on the Blind" by Diderot

1726: "Preliminary Discourse" to the "Encyclopaedia" by D'Alembert (1717-1783)

1755: "Discourse on the Origins of Inequality" by J.-J. Rousseau (1712-1778)

1762: "The Social Contract" by J.-J. Rousseau

1784: "The Marriage of Figaro" by Beaumarchais (1732-1799).

Queen Christine of Sweden surrounded by her court, listening to Descartes give a geometry demonstration, in the presence of the Prince de Condé and Elisabeth of Bavaria, by Louis Michel Dumesnil (1680-1746).
The learned and philosophers of the eighteenth century based their works on scientific and technical discoveries made in the seventeenth century.

very ably with the help of parliament, broke the will and made himself regent.

The regency period (1715-1723) played an important role in the development of ideas and behaviour. Restrictive protocol weighing upon the court was rejected, manners became noticeably more free, Protestants and Jansenists were given recognition and a non-bellicose foreign policy was adopted. All of this revealed a new tone.

The death of Louis XIV brought to light opposing thoughts up to then repressed or self-censured. Fontenelle (1657-1757) and Bayle (1647-1706) were the forerunners in their writing before 1700. The trend, however, broadened and grew from 1720 onwards. The word used to describe it is the "Enlightenment". The "philosophers" of the XVIIIth century wanted the principles that they proclaimed to enlighten the spirit: confidence in reason and its use to submit religious dogma and the trappings of monarchy to criticism. The result was the explicit and direct questioning of principles hitherto considered inviolable.

Interior conflicts increased in intensity, augmented by foreign policy failures and the discredit which to an ever greater extent weighed upon the royal family: Louis XV and his mistresses, Marie-Antoinette and her expenditure.

Two major problems almost permanently disturbed the political, administrative and judicial world. First of all the opposition of the Parliament of Paris which refused to register royal edicts (originally registration, necessary for the edict to have the force of law was a purely formal operation), multiplied remonstrances and went so far as to pretend to be the representative of the nation's interests.

Provincial parliaments did the same.

In its policy of harassment the parliament in particular made use of the second problem, the persecution of priests and the faithful suspected of Jansenism. The discussion culminated in concentrating on the Church's refusal to grant absolution to those who did

Portrait of Charles de Secondat, Baron de Montesquieu (1689-1755), after Jacques-Antoine Dassier.
The main theme of Montesquieu's thought, taken up by the men of the Revolution, was the separation of legislative, executive and judiciary powers, an idea absolutely foreign to the Ancien Régime.

François Marie Arouet, called Voltaire (1694-1778) holding up a copy of "La Henriade", after Maurice Quentin de La Tour (1704-1788).
The name Voltaire came from his action ("Essay on Tolerance", 1763) in the Calas case; he defended a protestant family of Toulouse, wrongly accused of having murdered one of its members who wanted to convert to Catholicism.

not expressly condemn the Jansenist theses. Not content to support the latter, the Parliament and its counterparts in the provinces attacked the Jesuits and ultimately obtained their suppression in 1764.

At the same time the philosophic spirit had to a large extent conquered intellectual life in the increasingly important bourgeois classes of the population and even among the nobility; in this respect its climax was the presentation of the "Marriage of Figaro" at the court of Versailles in 1784.

Denis Diderot, by Louis Michel Van Loo (1707-1771).
Son a cutler from Langres, Diderot's genius shone in many fields. He was the guiding spirit of the "Encyclopaedia".
Musée du Louvre. © RMN, R. G. Ojeda.

Foreign policy of France in the XVIIIth century

The previous continuity was broken in 1756 with a fundamental change in policy.
From 1715-1723 the Regent and Abbot, then Cardinal Dubois, interrupted Louis XIV's aggressive and dominating policy and obtained an agreement with England and the Netherlands.
From 1733 to 1748, Louis XV resumed an interventionist policy: wars of Polish and Austrian succession; in both cases there were military and political failures.
In 1756 Louis XV, at the instigation of Choiseul, overturned the pattern of alliances; henceforth the main enemy was no longer Austria but England owing to colonial rivalry. The Seven Years War (1756-1763) was notable for the crushing French defeat at Rosbach inflicted by Frederic II of Prussia. France lost almost all its colonies. The reversal of alliances was disastrous for France, but Louis XVI seized the opportunity of the revolt of the English-American colonies (1776-1783) to aid the insurgents who as a result of French military, political and financial help acquired their independence in the Treaty of Versailles, which in addition returned some of its colonies to France. Reconciliation with England was cemented in 1786 by a liberal trade treaty (lowering of customs tariffs).

The "Encyclopaedia"

This gigantic work (35 folio volumes including 11 plates), valiantly conducted for 20 years by Diderot and the Chevalier de Jaucourt, stands on its own as the symbol and expression of the spirit of the Enlightenment. A mass of authors contributed to it, of whom only about 150 can now be identified.
Its purpose, as explained by D'Alembert in his "Preliminary Discourse" was to present and glorify the century's knowledge, i.e. at the same time theoretical, scientific and practical, in order to enable the reader to achieve freedom and happiness.
Its influence was considerable, despite the prohibitions and practical difficulties encountered in its publication and circulation. Alone, the "Encyclopaedia" justifies Michelet's words: "The Great Century, I mean the XVIIIth century".

The king and government attempted to react. In 1771 Louis XV's first blow was to impose the judicial reform prepared by Maupéou: suppression of the Parliament of Paris to be replaced by six councils comprising members nominated and appointed by the king (the parliament was made to pay for its behaviour). As soon as he acceded to the throne (1774), Louis XVI annulled this reform but at the same time in a contradictory stand he called upon Turgot, an intendent and friend of the philosophers. The latter's objective was to remove the obstacles to the development of production and trade. Edicts covered the freedom to trade in grain, abolition of the corporations and repeal of the royal labour levy (corvée).

But Turgot wanting to achieve equality for all before tax, encountered the violent opposition of the Parliament, which appointed itself the defender of the privileged, and he had to resign (1776).

Corporations and the labour levy were re-established. Necker revived some of Turgot's projects but had to resign (1781) after having published a statement of budgetary income and expenditure which showed the extent of pensions paid to the privileged and the size of the deficit.

Jean-Jacques Rousseau (1712-1778) by Maurice Quentin de la Tour (1704-1788). Rousseau, born in Geneva, exercised through his "Social Contract", a very strong influence on the men of the Revolution.

Publication of the Peace Treaty of Versailles signed between France and England, in front of the Tuileries Palace on 25 November 1783, by Anton Van Ysendyck (1801-1875). The treaty consolidated the revenge against England.

Birth and beginnings of modern France (1789-1914)

The years which preceded 14 July 1789, the symbolic date for the start of the French Revolution, feature a double tendency; on the one hand reform attempts with the resumption of Turgot and Necker's projects by Calonne (1786) and on the other the rejection of these attempts by the privileged and the Assembly of Notables (1787-1788). Financial difficulties led to bankruptcy and it was necessary to convoke the states general (états généraux) which had not met since 1628.

Tensions then reached their climax. The privileged rejected any attempts upon their privileges. The nobility and clergy retrenched into their place in the feudal system. The parliaments, while opposing the two other orders and pretending to be the representatives of the nation, which they were not, stalled any decision moving in the direction of a reduction in inequalities before the law and taxation. The third estate, particularly the bourgeoisie, which could no longer tolerate feudal burdens, aspired to play its role to the full part.

This popular image shows all the hopes expressed by the young nation in the meeting of the three orders under an egalitarian regime.

Letourny, Orléans, 1791. Collection M. Sclaresky.

Great figures of the Revolution
(The youth of many of them is noticeable)

Brissot (1754-1793): lawyer, deputy of the Gironde to the Convention, hence the name Girondins given to his followers, opponent of Robespierre, guillotined.

Carnot (1752-1823): captain of engineers, deputy to the Convention, "Organiser of Victory".

Condorcet (1743-1794): mathematician, deputy to the Convention, supporter of liberal democracy, opponent of Robespierre, guillotined.

Danton (1759-1794): lawyer, deputy to the Convention, supporter and opponent of Robespierre, guillotined.

Hoche (1768-1797): NCO in1789, General at 25, saved Alsace, pacified the Vendée.

Marat (1744-1793): doctor, deputy to the Convention, assassinated by Charlotte Corday.

Marceau (1769-1796): General at 23 in the Army of the Rhine, killed in battle.

Mirabeau (1749-1791) supported the claims of the Third Estate for which he was a deputy in the States General, died before his role as advisor to Louis XVI was known.

Robespierre (1758-1794): lawyer, deputy to the States General and the Convention, leader of the Committee of Public Safety, guillotined.

Saint-Just (1767-1794): deputy to the Convention, representative for the armies, faithful supporter of Robespierre, guillotined with the latter.

Sieyès (1748-1836): ecclesiastic, author of the famous "What is the Third Estate?" published in January 1789, deputy to the States General and the Convention, specialist in constitutional problems.

Achievements of the Revolution and Empire (1789-1815)

With the perpetration of turbulent and often bloody events, France experienced considerable upheavals. Judging by results, there is strong continuity between the Revolution, the Consulate and the Empire; Napoleon's lawmakers and prefects were often advocates of the Enlightenment (and repented revolutionaries).

The legislation of the Constituent Assembly and the Convention was immense and the Consulate's work often consisted of codifying it, in particular with the Code Napoléon. Over and above these texts the important point is that France became a **nation of citizens** whereas previously it had been a **kingdom of subjects**.

"La Marseillaise", national anthem of 1792.
Editions Aumond, Paris, 1896. Collection M. Sclaresky.

The main work of the Revolution, confirmed by the Empire, was the disappearance of the feudal, seigniorial regime, affecting both persons and goods. The symbolic date was the **night of 4 August 1789**. A whole series of texts have to be taken into account. Accordingly, Article 1 of the Declaration of Rights of Man stated: "Mankind is born free and equal in law; social distinctions can only be based on communal usefulness" and also Article 2 proclaimed: "Natural rights are liberty, property, security and resistance to oppression". The whole economic and social system of the XIXth and XXth centuries is expressed in these statements. The Code Napoléon made these principles explicit and formal.

It is, however, necessary to make distinctions: equality between all was incomplete on the subject of votes and association. From 1789 to 1815 (the 1793 Constitution which prescribed universal suffrage was never applied) the right to vote had been based on the property qualification (censitaire), i.e. reserved for the richest tax-payers. Similarly the right

"La Marseillaise"

The national anthem of France was composed by Rouget de Lisle in Strasbourg in April 1972 as a marching song for the army of the Rhine. The anthem's words and music very soon spread across the country, reaching Paris at the end of July and acquiring particular fame with the arrival at the same moment in the capital of volunteers from Marseilles who gave it their name. "The Marseillaise" only became the national anthem in November 1793, with confirmation in 1795. The Consulate, Empire and the following regimes saw to its official fading but it remained a rallying point for Republicans. It was only on 14 February 1879 that "the Marseillaise" definitely acquired its status as national anthem.

The opening session of the Assembly of the States-General on 5 May 1789, by Louis Charles Auguste Couder (1789-1873).
Castels of Versailles and Trianon. © RMN, G. Blot.

The contrast between the two illustrations (stiffness of the first, enthusiastic movement in the second) mirrors the change in spirit in less than two months. The black clothing of the Third Estate deputies, dictated by royal protocol, it is noticeable.
Our democracy dates from the Tennis Court Oath (The jeu de paume was a kind of barehanded tennis).

The Tennis Court Oath at Versailles at Versailles on 20 June 1789, by Auguste Couder (1789-1873).
Castels of Versailles and Trianon. © RMN, Popovitch.

The three events shown below represent the three vital stages in the process which led to the destruction of the Ancien Regime and the birth of modern France; the fall of the Bastille, symbol of royal oppression, corresponds to the incursion of people's strength onto the political scene; the Mirabeau interlude asserted the incontrovertible transformation of the Third Estate into an assembly wanting to represent France; the return of the royal family after the flight to Varennes, rang the knell on the attempt to install a constitutional monarchy and presaged the proclamation of the republic fifteen months later.

MIRABEAU ET M. DE DREUX-BRÉZÉ : « ALLEZ DIRE A VOTRE MAITRE QUE NOUS SOMMES ICI PAR LA VOLONTÉ DU PEUPLE ET QU'ON NE NOUS EN ARRACHERA QUE PAR LA FORCE DES BAIONNETTES » (23 JUIN 1789).

Scene between Mirabeau and Dreux-Brezé on 23 June 1789.

From *" Cent recits d'histoire de France"*, Hachette, 1904.

The royal family's return to Paris on 25 June 1791.

Water colour, XVIIIth century.

Musée du Louvre, collection Rothschild. © RMN, M. Bellot.

The fall of the Bastille on 14 July 1789 – arrest of the governor.

French School of the XVIIIth century.

Castels of Versailles and Trianon. © RMN.

of association for workers and the strike were considered crimes (law of 1791); every worker had to enter time spent with each employer in a special logbook.

As far as goods were concerned, an immense transfer of property occurred, favourable to the better-placed and the urban bourgeoisie, with the sale of national goods, i.e. all the land and buildings of the clergy and those who had emigrated, its entirety representing about 1/10 of national property wealth. All the peasants, all categories included, received free and absolute ownership of their land, with no charges; this made France a particular case in Europe.

The Code Napoléon (1804) proclaimed the uniformity of law applicable in France (before 1789 a large number of regional customs were applied), liberty and equality and the division of inheritance. It guaranteed transfer after the sale of national goods. The Code, enforced in countries living under French domination (in Italy and Germany), destroyed the systems of feudal society.

The Revolution achieved the true unification of the state.

The Civil Code, soon to be called the Code Napoléon, was one of the "mounds of granite" on which modern France, born in the Revolution, was established; it is the codification of the achievements of the Constituent Assembly and the Convention, a codification carried out by the lawyers, Tronchet, Portails, etc., directed by Bonaparte, before the proclamation of the Empire; imposed on States occupied by the French army, or under its direct influence, it made a powerful contribution to the destruction of the feudal system in these countries.

Castels of Malmaison and Bois-Préau. © RMN, M. André.

It was united by common law, as just noted, but judicial organisation was also affected. In this case a break with the Revolution is noticeable; the latter had decreed the principle of election of judges but the Empire introduced a hierarchical structure dependent upon the central power.

That same contrast applied to local administration: instead of the elective system, Napoleon, with the introduction of prefects, substituted a very strongly centralised and authoritarian system. Local organisation, however, such as we still note with the recent addition of the region, dates from the Constituent Assembly: department and general council, canton and municipal council.

Principal dates of the Revolution

1789: transformation of the third estate deputies (states general) into the National Assembly. Tennis Court Oath (2 June), Storming of the Bastille by the population of Paris (14 July).

1791: flight of the King, arrest at Varennes (June). Inauguration of the Legislative Assembly (October).

1792: suspension, arrest and prosecution of Louis XVI (December) Inauguration of the Convention and Proclamation of the Republic (21 September).

1793: execution of Louis XVI (21 January), victory of the Jacobins (Robespierre) over the Girondins (Brissot).

1794: elimination of Danton (April); overthrow of Robespierre, who was executed with several of his followers (9 Thermidor, 27 July).

1795-1799: Directorate regime (5 people).

1799: Bonaparte's coup d'état (18 Brumaire, 9 November and establishment of the Consulate (three people).

1804: Bonaparte emperor (Napoleon I).

1814: abdication of Napoleon who departed for the Isle of Elba and return of the royalty with Louis XVIII.

1815: return of Napoleon (Hundred Days) and final abdication.

Unification included the school system, where most of the merit lies with the Convention. Certainly under the Legislative Assembly, Condorcet had produced a plan which was used as the basis, as well as another plan proposed by Talleyrand under the Constituent Assembly, for the Lakanal project; some of the measures were enacted but not applied, for example free and compulsory primary state education. To ensure secondary education, central schools (lycées under the empire) were created by department. The Convention re-organised or created a whole series of major schools and scientific institutes: School of Oriental Languages; secondary school (Ecole normale supérieure), Academy of Arts and Careers, National Archives, Polytechnic School, Institute, etc.

In the effort unifying the state, continuity in the substance contrasted with a difference in form between the Revolution and the Empire; the latter's basic characteristic was authoritarian and despotic. The parliamentary system of the revolutionary assemblies was replaced from the Consulate onwards by a system where only the will of the supreme decision-maker, the Emperor, counted; the assemblies (Tribunal, Legislative Body and Senate) were only representational. The right to vote no longer led to elections owing to the procedure based on lists of notabilities.

It was impending bankruptcy, which started the political transformation in 1789. As a remedy, in November 1789 the Constituent Assembly decided "all ecclesiastical goods are at the disposal of the nation" and the sale began, which enabled the issue of notes or 5%interest-bearing bonds (*assignats*) to be guaranteed; holders could use them as a method for paying for the purchase of *national goods*. The volume of bonds issued soon became very large, hence their depreciation. The need to finance the war against the coalition powers under the Convention led to high inflation despite Cambon's strict efforts. In 1797 the consolidated *third* of public debt in fact corresponded to a bankruptcy of two-thirds. Recovery had to await the Consulate: creation of a true financial administration (tax controllers, collectors), the Bank of France

France in 1789 (provinces)

(1800) and the crowning of the whole creation with the Germinal franc.

Religion also provided a good example of the kind of process taking place from 1789 to 1815.

First of all it should be noticed that for both Protestants and Jews the Revolution led to the recognition of their identity: in 1791 Jews became complete French citizens and in 1806 and 1808 they obtained the right to organise themselves both locally and nationally; by the Declaration of Rights Protestants achieved complete equality and a law of 1802 authorised clerical boards (consistoires).

Foreign policy from 1789 to 1815

An article of the 1791 Constitution proclaimed in principle the renunciation of wars of conquest, but the anxiety of foreign sovereigns confronted with the new revolutionary principles, the pressure from French emigrants and revolutionaries' spreading of external propaganda led to a declaration of war on "the King of Bohemia and Hungary" in April 1792. Thereafter a long series of military campaigns started: Valmy (1792), conquest of the left bank of the Rhine (1795), Vendée revolt (1793-1796), campaigns in Italy (1796, 1800), expedition to Egypt (1798-1799), campaigns against Austria, England, Prussia and Russia (Austerlitz 1805, Iéna 1806, Wagram 1809 and the Russian campaign of 1812).
Starting with defence against powers hostile to the new principles, the war soon became one of conquest with the search for natural frontiers (Rhine, Alps) then one of expansion and hegemony pure and simple with a vast empire completed by vassal-kingdoms with members of the imperial family on the throne (Holland, Spain and Naples).
The two Treaties of Paris (1814, 1815) marked the failure of this policy, the abandonment of all conquests and even the loss of a part of the territory by comparison with 1789.

The Catholic Church, deeply faithful to the royal cause and the papacy, suffered the full impact of the turn of events: the transfer to the nation of its immense property holdings (1789), creation of a national church with the civil Constitution of the clergy (1790), repressive measures against ecclesiastics refusing to swear the oath to the Constitution, development of the anti-Christian movement with the cult of the Goddess of Reason and the Supreme Being in 1793 and 1794 and the attempt to create a religion parallel with the belief in God in 1795. The situation stabilised with the Concordat (1801) which remained in force up to 1905: the Catholic religion was recognised as that of "the great majority of French people", the Church accepted the loss of its capital heritage, priests became officials remunerated by the state and bishops were appointed by the Emperor, who was crowned

The painting shows Pope Paus VII's ratification of the Concordat signed in his name in Paris (1801) by Cardinal Consalvi (on the left). The document, in force up to the law separating church and state (1905), made the clergy into paid state officials. Catholicism was no longer, as in 1789, the state religion, but only the religion of the majority of French people.
After Jean-Baptiste Joseph Wicar (1762-1834).
Castels of Versailles and Trianon. © RMN, G. Blot.

Napoleon on the battlefield of Eylau on 9 February 1807, by Jean-Baptiste Mauzaisse (1784-1844), after Antoine Gros Baron. The indecisive battle was fought between the French and the Russians in February 1807 in the north of what is now Poland; it was a veritable "butchery". In front of Napoleon, Murat prances.

The Napoleonic Empire in 1811

The right to vote

The right to vote was acquired by the French Revolution. First of all it was a property suffrage (except for elections to the Convention in 1792), i.e. reserved to the possessors of a given income from 1789 to 1848, date when it became universal but confined to men. It was only in 1945 that the right to vote became truly universal for both men and women of French nationality and entered on electoral rolls. One of the points in the programme of Resistance organisations was thereby achieved. In 1971 the age of majority was lowered from 21 to 18.

by the Pope himself. Desirous to exercise full authority over the clergy like all organs of society, Napoleon clashed with the Pope who he had deported into France.

Alternating regimes (1815-1870)

In fifty-years (as many years as the time since the end of the Second World War) France experienced three regimes: constitutional monarchy (Restoration 1815-1870, July monarchy 1830-1848), Republic (1848-1851) and Empire (1851-1870), but on the whole the period possessed many common features: industrialisation and social transformation, struggles to establish a democratic regime and assertion of France as an international power.

In 1815, after the Waterloo defeat, Napoleon and his regime collapsed under the pressure of the coalition powers (Prussia, Austria, England and Russia), and from the effect of a large number of defections. Its final replacement, after the One Hundred Days interlude, by Louis XVIII took place all the more easily since the Constitutional Charter guaranteed the main achievements of the Revolution: no return to the divine right of kings (even if Catholicism once more became the state religion), confirmation of the sale of national goods and proclamation of equality before the law.

Portraits in the stock exchange, by Edgar Degas (1834-1917). *Emergence of middleclass businessmen.*
Musée d'Orsay. © RMN, H. Lewandowski.

Louis XVIII's position was not accepted by the ultras (Comte d'Artois, Polignac, Villèlle). The White Terror can be attributed to them since elections gave them a very large majority in the "unfindable" Chamber. Purges, condemnation to exile and deaths were frequent. After the 1816 elections, however, a moderate and royalist constitutional party asserted itself. It was the **beginning of the parliamentary regime** with the establishment of a procedure for control over government finances. Laws on the army, electoral system and the press were the reflection of a liberal conception from 1816-1820, in opposition to the ultras. The latter, however, returned to power which they kept, apart from a short period in 1828, up to 1830; this was a real step back with a new electoral law, limitation of freedom of the press, a project (rejected) for the return of the law of primogeniture, heavy penalties for sacrilege, etc.

The insurrection of July 1830 was a success since Charles X had to flee; but the rioters, workers, artisans and students who aimed to establish a republic saw power escape from them to the advantage of the supporters of the Orléans faction. This was exemplified both by the definite emergence of the bourgeois business class and the decline of the great landholding aristocracy. The new regime with opposition between resistance (order) and movement (reform) developed in an increasingly conservative way, while the aspirations of the republican movement continued to grow. Finally the February Days in 1848 put a definite end to the monarchy and its system. Several features and images can summarise this eighteen-year period: Guizot's "enrich yourselves" at the same time as the growth of railways, the steel industry, the birth of a working class without legal protection, the broadening of the electorate, which remained based on the property qualification, the appearance of socialists, the repression of the Lyon silk workers (1831), the massacre in the rue Transnonain (1834) but also the law Guizot (1833) creating primary education.

Lasting from 1848 to 1851, the Second Republic only proved temporary, with the repetition of the overthrow of power in 1830, this time with bloodshed. A double crisis both agricultural (the last famine in French history) and in industry (over-production) combined with the rise in unemployment, the king's refusal to lower the electoral property qualification and the numerous financial scandals all resulted in February 1848 in a Parisian revolt and street-fighting which led to the flight of Louis-Philippe.

From February to May 1848 a provisional government including Lamartine, Arago and Ledru-Rollin took some important decisions:
— introduction of universal manhood suffrage for the election of a Constituent Assembly; the transition was made from 200,000 electors to more than 9 million;
— abolition of slavery in the colonies;

Abolition of slavery in French colonies in 1848, by François Biard (1789-1882)
From 1789 onwards, voices were raised, among them that of the Abbot Grégoire (one of the leading spirits of the Tennis Court Oath), demanding the abolition of slavery. The virulent opposition, however, of plantation owners in the West Indies and those trading with islands (sugar) stopped the movement. It was not until 1848 that the principle of equality of rights for men and women were also applied in the colonies (without going so far as voting rights).

Napoleon III visiting work on the new Louvre, by Nicolas Gosse (1787-1878).

Musée du Louvre. © RMN, G. Blot.

— suppression of the laws restricting freedom of the press and meeting;
— fiintroduction of a 10-hour working day (it had sometimes reached 14 hours);
— setting up of national workshops to give work to the unemployed.

The latter point shook the ***Constituent Assembly*** when it suppressed the workshops, hence the severely repressed revolt of workers in June. The republican party thereupon became divided into supporters and opponents of social reform. The division enabled Napoleon's nephew, Louis-Napoleon Bonaparte, to make himself elected President of the Republic in December 1848. The ***Legislative Assembly***, elected by a restrictive suffrage, had a modest majority in favour of the return of the monarchy. It came into conflict with the President, who, constitutionally unable to bid for a new mandate in 1852, resorted to the coup d'état of 2 December 1851. The coup

Smelting at Creusot around 1864, by François Bonhomme. The industrialisation of France in the nineteenth century was based on coal and steel. Écomusée de la communauté Le Creusot-Montceau-les-Mines.

was confirmed by a plebiscite (7.35 million yes, 640,000 no) after severe repression and reintroduction of universal suffrage. The proclamation of the Empire the following year with a new plebiscite (7.84 million yes and 253,000 no) was only a formality.

The ***Second Empire*** (1852-1870) did not make a break with the previous period insofar as aspirations for a republican and democratic regime remained and economic development revived with great intensity.

Major urban development works particularly in Paris, constructing a large railway network (18,000 kilometres in 1870), foundation of big banking establishments (Crédit Lyonnais, Société Générale), golden age of the stock exchange and growth of the steel industry were the main lines of advance of the Second Empire's economic life. The most successful showcase for this expansion was the organisation of two universal exhibitions in Paris in 1865 and 1867.

Economic activity entailed changes that only later had their full effect on the structure of French society. France remained a profoundly rural country but the needs of the building industry and industry in general attracted people towards the towns, which led to the growth of the nascent working class (in the modern sense of the word). A workers' movement (Tolain, Proudhon), favourable to the ideas of the workers' international association, where Carl Marx was militant, was forming at the same time as strikes except for officials, ceased (1864) to be a crime.

From the political angle, three distinct phases are apparent. From 1852 to 1859 an authoritarian empire was in power with a hounded and muzzled opposition: no freedom

Foreign policy from 1815 to 1870

After the fall of Napoleon and the conclusion of the Holy Alliance between European monarchs against the threat of popular revolt, the French governments concerned, continuing the action of Talleyrand (1754-1838) at the Congress of Vienna, attempted to reinsert the country into the circle of great powers, hence military intervention in Spain (1823) against the liberals and the start of the conquest of Algeria in 1830. Louis-Philippe, first of all allied to England for the independence of Belgium (1832), renounced the idea of natural frontiers but failed in his intervention in favour of the Ottoman sultan (1840) leading to tension with England.
From 1848 onwards, the major problem was the one of nationalities: Italy and Germany sought their unity. Napoleon III supported this idea, hence military intervention in Italy (Magenta and Solférino in 1859) and a position favourable to Prussia against Austria. Despite the slogan "The Empire is peace", France also intervened against Russia in the Crimea (1854) and in Mexico (1862-1866). The rise of Prussian power caused the fall of Napoleon III (1870).

Detail of the Battle of Alma, Crimean War, by Horace Vernet (1789-1863).

of the press, system of official candidature, strict supervision of teaching and only three, then five, republican deputies, including Jules Favre managed to be elected. From 1860 to 1867 the so-called liberal empire was remarkable for an inconsistent mixture of despotism and a few new parliamentary liberties. Paris elected eight republican deputies including Thiers and royalist and republican opposition polled 2 million votes in 1863.

A new phase started in 1867: restoration of freedom of association (with prior authorisation), deputies had the right to interrogate the government and slackening of press restrictions. This produced a division among the republicans, between the "irreconcilables" (Rochefort, Gambetta) and the "rallied" (Emile Ollivier). The 1869 elections revealed intransigent Bonapartists ("mamelouks") in a minority and the appearance of a "third party".

Napoleon III made further concessions in April 1870, which resulted in a parliamentary regime with ministers responsibility before the Chambers. He recovered the political initiative and with the April 1870 plebiscite the regime apparently possessed a large following: 7.5 million yes against 1.57 million no.

Nonetheless, five months later, the regime collapsed. The Second Empire disappeared owing to its adventurous foreign policy: it had caused France to intervene in two wars, against Russia (1854-1856), against Austria (1859). Moreover Napoleon III intervened in all parts of the world: in Algeria (Kabylie and the Algerian South), in Senegal, China and Indo-China, Syria and Mexico. Above all, however, Napoleon had not seen that the rising German power was Prussia, thereby favouring its unifying policy by hostility to Austria. When a diplomatic misunderstanding, heightened by Bismarck's cunning, became a trap through the blindness of the French officials responsible, France on 19 July 1870 declared war on Prussia, presumptuously and without preparations. The end came quickly. On 2 September at Sedan Napoleon III capitulated at the head of a part of the army. It was the greatest military and political disaster in French history. On 4 September the fall of the Empire became final and a **provisional government** was instituted in Paris (Gambetta, J. Favre).

Victory of the Republic (1870-1914)

The Sedan capitulation, followed by Bazaine's surrender at Metz, did not put an end to the war. Quite the contrary, the provisional government organised a true national resistance. But the fall of Paris after a siege marked the end of the war (end of January 1871). The Treaty of Frankfurt in May entailed the cession of Alsace-Lorraine to the new German Empire proclaimed at Versailles.

In the meantime, a **national assembly** distinctly to the right had been elected in February with a royalist majority; it was installed at Versailles until 1880.

The Republicans conducted numerous and intense political battles, as part of a general movement from the right towards the left. The Parisian population, hostile to the armistice and the assembly, in a precarious position after the suspension of payment of rents and debts had ceased with the end of the war, revolted. Thiers and the "Versaillaise" majority very

Proclamation of the Republic on the Place de l'Hôtel-de-Ville. In the foreground, Gambetta.

Popular picture of the period. Collection M. Sclaresky.

severely repressed, with more than 20,000 executions, the "*Commune*" insurrection (March-May 1871) using repatriated of troops made prisoner at Sedan and Metz. Only in 1880 was an amnesty declared.

From 1871 to 1879 political combats centred on the foundation of the republican with several outstanding dates: failure of the attempt to restore the monarchy (1873), republican victory in the municipal elections (1874), vote passing the Wallon amendment, setting the rules for the republican parliamentary regime (constitutional laws of 1875), and lastly the election of a republican (Jules Grévy) as head of State (1879).

The victory was to give political life a new twist with the division of the republican camp into two tendencies: the "opportunists" (Gambetta, Jules Ferry) and the "radicals" (Clemenceau).

Nonetheless opposition to the republic had not disappeared, as shown by the *boulangist* movement (1887-1889), an assortment from all sides around a general, which failed owing to its lack of direction. The republic, on the other hand, was strengthened at the instigation of the Pope Leo XIII (1892)by a party of conservative Catholic forces rallying to it.

Two major affairs showed that the relationship between the forces of the left and right was still fragile. In 1892 and 1893 the shocks of the Panama affair, corruption in political circles caused a rejection of the institutions, going as far an outbreak of violence against the Chamber of Deputies in 1893 and against President Carnot, assassinated in 1894.

Much more important, owing to its causing a rupture in the country, was the *Dreyfus affair* (1898-1899). Those at the head of the General Staff had falsified the so-called proofs to justify the condemnation of an innocent officer, condemned because he was of Jewish origin. It resulted in a veritable political and moral crisis. One side was formed by the majority of officers and clergy, the royalist right and nationalists and the other by the majority of intellectuals and the left.

The desire to restrict the Catholic Church's place in political life twice led to political battle. First in all in 1880 and 1881 there was a passionate debate on the subject of teaching: dissolution of the Jesuits and ban on teaching to unauthorised congregations and the introduction of lay teaching in primary schools. The question recurred with even greater passion with the law separating Church and State (1905); the 1801 Concordat was repealed and the State became neutral.

Général Boulanger (14 July 1886). Painting by Edouard Debat-Ponsan.
Général Boulanger at the 14 July 1886 review, when Minister of War. Without real political prospects, he enjoyed extraordinary popularity for a few years; the republic's opponents wanted to make use of him but he lacked the will at the decisive moment (January 1889); threatened with arrest, he fled to Brussels (April) and committed suicide on his mistress's grave...
Collection M. Sclaresky.

Episode in the 1870 War. Siege of Paris in 1870-1871. Surprise near a bridge defended by the militia, by Gérard Détaille (1848-1912).
Castels of Versailles and Trianon. © RMN, G. Blot.

A Paris street in May 1871, the Commune, by Maximilien Luce (1858-1941).
Musée d'Orsay. © RMN, H. Lewandowski. ADAGP.

Thiers proclaimed "Liberator of the Territory" at the session of the National Assembly held in Versailles on 16 June 1877. After Jules Garnier. Châteaux de Versailles et Trianon. © RMN.

Strike at Creusot, painting by Jules Adler, 1899. Écomusée de la communauté Le Creusot-Montceau-les-Mines.

The moment of truth: the Dreyfuss Affair, around 1898. Paris, musée du Judaïsme. © RMN, J. G Berizzi

On the other hand, on two other questions the division of the left resulted in the right holding the balance: the creation of income tax was rejected, whereas the introduction of three years military service was adopted (1913).

Already noticeable in the previous period, the gap between the economic development of France and that of the two great competitors, Germany and Great Britain, broadened to the point where some foreign observers were already talking of "French decadence".

Intellectual ferment in France

The XIXth was a period of great intellectual activity.

Celebration of scientific progress: Fresnel (1788-1827) and the optician, Sadi Carnot (1796-1832) and driving power, Ampère (1775-1836) and electromagnetism, Gay-Lussac (1778-1850) and chemistry, Niepce (1765-1833) and Daguerre for photography. Mathematical language with Cauchy (1789-1857) and Galois (1811-1832) was increasingly used in science. Claude Bernard (1813-1878) posed the principles of the "experimental method" which Pasteur (1822-1895) put into practice.

Renewal in literature (romanticism, naturalism, symbolism) with Chateaubriand (1768-1848), Lamartine (1790-1869), Hugo (1802-1885), Stendhal (1783-1842), Balzac (1799-1850), George Sand (1804-1876), Flaubert (1821-1880), Baudelaire (1821-1867), Zola (1840-1902), Maupassant (1850-1893), Verlaine (1844-1896), Anatole France (1844-1924).

Renewal also in painting with Delacroix (1798-1863), Courbet (1819-1877), Manet (1832-1883), Monet (1840-1926), Renoir (1841-1919) and sculpture with Rodin (1840-1917), Camille Claudel (1864-1943).

Emergence of socialist doctrines with Saint-Simon (1760-1825), Fourier (1772-1837).

Demographically, France from the start of the Second Empire had experienced a slowdown in growth owing to the fall in the birth-rate (1907 and 1911 more deaths than births). Hence recourse to immigration: in 1913 France contained 1 million foreigners and 250,000 naturalised citizens; it was thanks to them that the slowdown did not become a collapse.

With the Waldeck-Rousseau law in 1884 the trades unions acquired the rights of association. The workers log book was suppressed in 1890, a weekly rest-day became obligatory in 1906 but the legal length of the working day remained at 12 hours (law of 1883): 10 hours for workshops with women and children (1900). Workers' retirement was instituted in 1910. Progress was not achieved without violence: troops' massacre of strikers at Fourmies (1891), railwaymen's strike broken by force by Aristide Briand (1910) and the

Georges Clemenceau making a speech during an electoral meeting held in the Fernando circus in Montmartre in 1883. By Jean-François Raffaelli (1850-1924).
At the time he was head of the extreme radical left. Blistering orator, he was nicknamed "Nemesis of ministeries" before coming to power in 1906; head of government during the First World War ("I make war").

Great figures of the Third Republic

Aristide Briand (1862-1932): lawyer, deputy, head of government or Minister on numerous occasions, specialist in foreign policy after 1918 ("Pilgrim of peace") and supporter of reconciliation with Germany.

Joseph Caillaux (1863-1944): inspector of finance, deputy, senator, head of government, Minister. In 1914 his political career was disturbed by his wife's assassination of the director of "Figaro" and in 1920 he was tried for clandestine negotiations with Austria in 1918.

Georges Clemenceau (1841-1929) doctor, radical, deputy, senator, head of government from 1906 to 1909 and from 1917 to 1920 ("the father of victory").

Jules Ferry (1832-1893): deputy, senator, in power from 1879 to 1885, author of the laws on primary teaching, free, compulsory and lay and the decree dissolving the Order of Jesuits.

Léon Gambetta (1838-1882): deputy, one of the heads of republican opposition under the Empire and one of the leaders of the armed struggle against the Prussian invaders (1870-1871).

Edouard Herriot (1872-1957): teacher, radical, head of government or Minister on numerous occasions after 1918, creator of the expression "average Frenchman".

Jean Jaurès (1859-1914): teacher, socialist, founder of "L'Humanité" assassinated on 31 July 1914.

Jules Méline (1838-1925): deputy, head of government, author of the laws protecting agriculture (1891).

Raymond Poincaré (1860-1934): lawyer, deputy, senator, President of the Republic (1913-1920) previously and subsequently very often Minister and head of government.

Paul Reynaud (1878-1966): lawyer, deputy, Minister on numerous occasions, head of government in 1940.

Pierre Waldeck-Rousseau (1846-1904): lawyer, deputy, holder of the record for ministerial length of office, promoter of the laws on trade union freedom, municipal organisation and freedom of association.

Presidents of the Republic from 1871 to 1913: Adolphe Thiers, Mac Mahon, Jules Grévy, Sadi Carnot, Casimir Périer, Felix Faure, Emile Loubet, Armand Fallières.

Collection M. Sclaresky.

revolt of the Languedoc vineyard workers with the soldier's refusal to intervene (1907) must not be forgotten.

Internationally France was still a world power with a foreign policy with two major preoccupations, relations with Germany and colonial expansion, necessarily linked to each other.

The problem of Alsace-Lorraine remained constant. France therefore sought alliances with the prospect of a conflict with Germany, all the more so since situations arose that could be its cause: in 1886 with the strengthening of nationalist feeling (Boulanger) and in 1905 with Franco-German rivalry in Morocco.

In 1893 France concluded an alliance with Russia, the latter thereby being enabled to procure capital, "Russian funds", necessary for its industrialisation. France formed close relations with Italy in 1896 and established the Entente Cordiale with Great Britain in 1904. Concluding the latter proved possible owing to the settlement of colonial disputes, including Franco-British rivalry in Egypt, which had narrowly escaped degenerating into open conflict in the Fashoda affair in 1898.

After 1870 France in fact became a major colonial power extending its presence in Africa and Asia: protectorates in Tunisia (1881) and Annam (1883), conquest of Tonkin and the Congo (1885), Dahomey (1893), Madagascar (1895), Chad (1901) and the protectorate in Morocco (1912).

Aristide Briand (1862-1932): Deputy from 1902, many times minister or head of government, famous orator ("a cello"), after 1918 he devoted himself to Franco-German relations and the League of Nations (forerunner of UNO).

Collection M. Sclaresky.

"Our soldiers in the colonies"
by Constantin Font (1890-)
Paris, musée des Arts d'Afrique et d'Océanie. © RMN, J. G Berizzi.

Historic political dates

1830, July: fall of Charles X, King of France; Louis-Philippe I, King of the French.

1848, February: proclamation of the Republic.

June: repression of public demonstrations.

1851, December: coup d'état of Louis-Napoleon, President of the Republic.

1852, December: coronation of Napoleon III.

1870, September: proclamation of the Emperor's fall.

1871, March-May: civil war (Paris Commune).

1875: Institution of the Republic by means of the Wallon amendment.

1905: Law separating Church and State.

1919: Treaty of Versailles.

1936: Elections to the legislature giving the majority to the Popular Front (socialists, radicals and communists).

1940, 18 June: General de Gaulle's appeal for resistance from London.

10 July: granting of full powers by the Parliament in Vichy to Marshall Pétain.

From the First to the Second World War (1914-1945)

During the thirty-year period, France experienced ten years in a state of war with, between the two world conflicts, the great 1929 economic crisis.

Consequences of the First World War

Although France had won the war, in 1919 it was in a tragic situation. The consequences of the First World War were extremely grave: certainly there was the re-conquest of Alsace-Lorraine but at the price of 1.4 million dead (mainly the young), 900,000 war-wounded, 600,000 war-widows and 700,000 orphans… without counting material damage. The terrible human haemorrhage accentuated the population decline.

Memories and effects of the war were to influence the internal and external policy of France. Moreover, the great 1929 crisis in the United States was to reach France in 1931.

The war had profoundly changed French society. Thus women came to occupy a large number of jobs previously reserved for men and were integrated into the production process. They were in the majority (1 million war-widows). In 1919, the Chamber of Deputies voted for the extension of the right to vote to women which the Senate rejected. Also the founding of a communist party at the Congress of Tours (1920), seceding from the socialist party, created a new situation.

In a preliminary phase, the government sought to resolve a large part of these difficulties and above all the problem of reconstruction by imposing the payment of reparations on Germany: "Germany will pay". France went as far as to occupy the Ruhr (1923) as collateral. As the years went by, however, up to the Lausanne Agreements (1932) this hope was to fade. The franc, stable with the gold standard since 1801, had to be devalued by Poincaré in 1928.

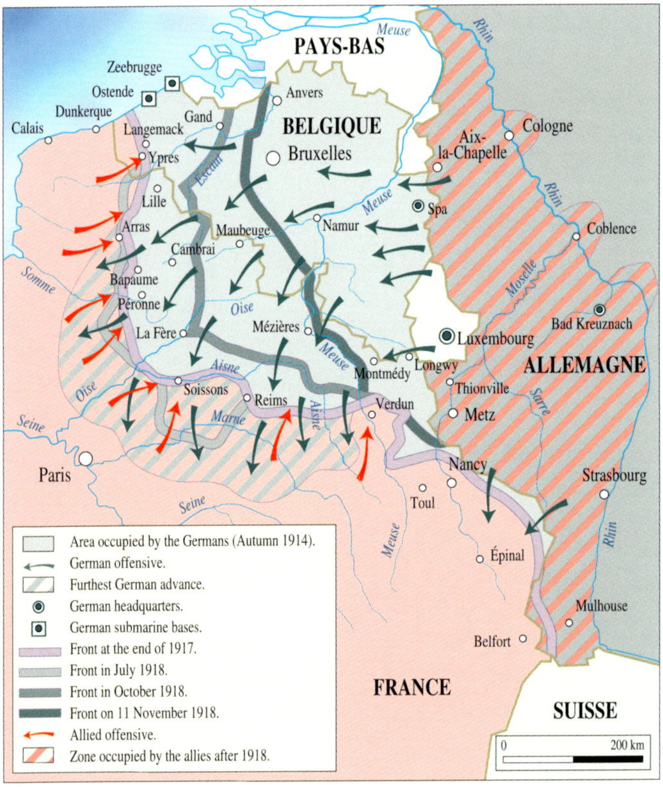

Changes on the front in the First World War from 1914 to 1918.

Jack Photo

L'assassinat de Jaurès provoque d'abord au Conseil des ministres « un prodigieux silence », puis ce commentaire : « Alors quoi ! la guerre étrangère et la guerre civile, tout alors ? » La riposte immédiate des socialistes devait lever toute équivoque : « Ils ont assassiné Jaurès, nous n'assassinons pas la France. » Le 4 août, les funérailles de Jaurès – les « obsèques de la paix » – devaient réunir les personnalités politiques des plus diverses. Ce fut vraiment la première manifestation de l'« Union sacrée », à quelques jours de la première guerre mondiale.

"Jaurès assassinated" shown in "L'Humanité" edition of Saturday 1 August 1914.
Jean Jaurés, prestigious orator, man of broad culture and acknowledged philosopher was elected deputy in 1885. He moved towards the moderate left centre of the Socialist Party; he contributed to involving the latter in defence of Dreyfuss and was opposed to "revenge" policy against Germany led by Poincaré; his assassin, obsessed by the right's violent campaign against Jaurés (German agent), was freed after the war.
Collection M. Sclaresky.

The economic crisis starting in 1931 overtook a country which had not modernised its economy. France, which had remained a country still profoundly rural, thereupon attempted to conduct a policy at the same time both protectionist and deflationary: reduction of government expenditure and rising taxes.

In 1936 France suffered 1 million unemployed.

Internal policy

French internal policy from 1919 to 1939 was somewhat unstable, interspersed with a few strong moments. The 1919 elections gave birth to a Chamber of Deputies described as the "blue horizon" (1920-1924) owing to the large number of ex-servicemen elected and its nationalist complexion. It ratified the Versailles Treaty, attended to the replacement

The Great War, battle of the Aisne, in the trenches. Collection M. Sclaresky.

Victory parade – 14 July 1919 – The flags of the Army of Africa. Collection M. Sclaresky.

of Clemenceau, who had resigned, by Millerand as Head of Government. The latter being elected President of the Republic, several heads of government succeeded one another, the most remarkable was to be Raymond Poincaré from 1922 to 1924.

There was a reversal of direction with the 1924 elections which gave the victory to the Cartel of the left (1924-1927). From 1924 to July 1926, a part of the leftward leaning programme of the Cartel was applied: strengthening of the lay tendency with a new break with the Vatican (relations were interrupted in 1904 and resumed in 1920), the desire to repeal the Concordat in Alsace-Lorraine (the region, then a German Province, had not been affected by the 1905 law) hence agitation in the departments which had become French once more. The flight of capital and the collapse of the franc, however, obliged the Herriot government to resign and give way to Raymond Poincaré. From then on and up to the 1928 elections, the Chamber, elected on a left-wing programme, supported a policy directed towards the right. From 1928 to 1932 the new Chamber with a right-wing majority pursued the same policy in favour of investment and the stability of the new of Poincaré franc. Industrial production for the year 1929 was the highest since 1918. An important measure was taken as part of the struggle against population decline; since the passing of a law in 1893 any child born in France from a foreign man or woman became French and after a law passed in 1927 naturalisation conditions were made easier by decreasing the minimum length of residence in France (3 years instead of 10).

With the Chamber elected in 1932, representing a left-wing majority, there began a period of intense political activity and agitation. "Affairs", in particular the Stavisky affair, caused street demonstrations by ex-servicemen grouped together in rightist associations. On 6 February 1934 Action Française (royalists) and the Camelots du roi (royalists) attempted to take the Palais Bourbon by storm but other participants in the demonstration, the Cross of Fire (ex-servicemen led by Colonel de la Rocque) refused to join them. On the following day there was a further extreme-right demonstration and on 9 February a communist counter demonstration, followed by a general strike on 12 February.

Confronted with the Laval government (June 1935-January 1936), the socialists and communists improvised a programme for a populist grouping (12 January 1936). The

Portrait of Raymond Poincaré (1860-1934),
by Marcel André Baschet (1862-1941).
Lawyer from Metz, very young deputy (for the time) at the age of 27 and Minister at 35, he was elected President of the Republic in 1913; leader in the revenge against Germany, nicknamed "Poincaré the war"; his political career continued after 1918: head of government from 1926-1929, he gave his name to the new franc "Poincaré", given a new parity with gold, signifying France's retreat from the international scene after the demographic and economic bloodbath of the Great War.

Popular Front demonstration, Place de la Nation, 14 July 1936 : Léon Blum, Maurice Thorez, Salenro, Violette, Pierre Cot.

April-May elections in 1936 gave the victory to the Popular Front - communists, socialists and radicals. The Chamber elected on a left-wing programme moved strongly to the right, going as far as to vote full powers to Pétain in 1940.

During the first phase, a left-wing social and political programme was applied, as a result of intense pressure from a general strike and the occupation of the places of work, the whole conducted in an atmosphere of jubilation: creation of paid holidays, 40-hour week, dissolution of the leagues of the extreme-right, rise in wages and nationalisation of key sectors (SNCF, Banque de France etc.). But from the end of 1936 onwards the tendency went into reverse: Léon Blum (1872-1950), socialist, head of government announced a "social pause". The Communist Party, which had refused to take part in the government, withdrew its support. In 1938 Blum resigned and gave way to the Daladier (radical) government assisted by Paul Reynaud (right) at Finance. The official break-up of the Popular Front took place in October 1938 at the time of the Munich Agreements whereby France led by Daladier and Great Britain led by Chamberlain delivered Czechoslovakia to Germany. Socialists and radicals approved these agreements, the communists rejected them.

Foreign policy

In foreign policy during the between-the-wars period two distinct phases are apparent. From 1919 to 1924, there was firmness towards Germany. In the Treaty of Versailles France had only obtained some of the guarantees which it leaders (Clemenceau, Foch) had claimed, i.e. strong commitments from its allies concerning the left bank of the Rhine. Efforts to obtain payment of the prescribed reparations did not result as foreseen despite the numerous international conferences and French troops' occupation of the Ruhr in 1923.

From 1924-1939, a whole series of concessions were made by France. Although in 1924 the Herriot government recognised the existence of the Soviet Union, French diplomacy did not exploit the possibilities of the new counterweight. In 1924 France unconditionally withdrew from the Ruhr, thereby abandoning its Francophile supporters in the Rhineland. It renounced German reparations (the Young Plan in 1929) while maintaining its debt to the United States. Then a whole series of concessions with even graver consequences occurred: acceptance of the 1935 Anglo –German naval agreement enabling Germany, which had become Nazi, to rebuild its battle fleet and acceptance of the English refusal to intervene when Hitler remilitarized the Rhineland in 1936. The word appeasement is the one which best defines French diplomacy, confronted with the plebiscite campaign in the Sarre for its adhesion to Germany (1935), with Germany's annexation of Austria, of Bohemia-Moravia and furthermore when confronted with Germany and Italy's intervention in the Spanish civil war. The list of renunciations and concessions is long and the "Pétite Entente" policy, i.e. alliances with central and east European countries was shown to be illusory when the ultimate crisis, the war with Germany, broke out.

Philippe Pétain (1856-1951) played an important part in the First World War, leading the resistance of Verdun (1916). Given full powers in Vichy (July 1940), he opposed the republican principle and advocated a policy of cooperation with Hitler (Montoire meeting, October 1940). Condemned to death at the Liberation, he finished his days in prison on the île d'Yeu.
Collection M. Sclaresky.

French state

On 10 July 1940, the Chamber of Deputies and the Senate, meeting in Vichy, granted full powers to Philippe Pétain (1856-1951), who had become President of the Council of Ministers from 16 June following Paul Reynaud's resignation; Pétain became "Head of the French State". The government (main members: Laval executed in 1945, Darlan assassinated in Algiers in 1942, Gabolde died a refugee in Madrid in 1977) very soon committed itself to a collaboration policy with the Nazi occupier. From October 1940 onwards it took discriminatory measures against French citizens of Jewish origin, organised their arrest (round up of Vel'd'Hiv' in 1942) and assisted their deportation as well as that of foreigners of Jewish origin to extermination camps. Similarly Vichy in its administration and its police took part in the campaign conducted by the occupier against the Resistance, in particular the communists, (creation of special sections) undertaken by the Milice (created in 1943), its ideological and repressive spearhead against the Resistance as a whole; its head, Darnand was shot at the Liberation. In their retreat in 1945 the German Armies transferred what remained of the Vichy government to Sigmaringen.

Landmarks

1914-1918: Battle of the Marne (1914), Verdun (1916), Chemin des Dames (1917).
1919: the duration of the working day set at 8 hours.
1936: introduction of paid holidays, weekly duration of work set at 40 hours.
1938: Law granting women legal capacity (the possibility of acting without their husband's authorisation). Repeal of the 40 hours law and the re-introduction of 48 hours.
1940: May: German invasion of Belgium and Luxembourg. Breakthrough on the French front in the Ardennes. June: breakthrough on the Aisne and Somme front. General retreat of French forces. End of hostilities.
1941: Leclerc's advance into North Africa from Chad.
1942: violent fighting in Syria between Vichy forces and Free French forces which the latter won with the help of British forces. Participation of Free French forces in the Battle of Bir-Hakeim in Libya against Rommel.
1943: participation of the Army of the future Marshall Juin in the campaign in Italy; liberation of Corsica by Free French troops.
1944: Anglo-American landing in Normandy; march of Leclerc's division on Paris which was liberated (25 August) after an insurrection by Resistance forces (Colonel Rol-Tanguy). Disembarkation in Provence of the French 1st army under the future Marshall de Lattre.
1945 (8 mai): German capitulation.

How can one explain such a series of errors and compromises which led to the Munich Agreements (September 1938) and the abandonment of Czechoslovakia to Germany? Several factors can be quoted, the memory of the massacres of the Great War, the obsession to do nothing without British support, the fear of the expansion of social claims ("Better Hitler than the Popular Front") and the deliberate desire not to use the Soviet card.

On 3 August 1939, France and Great Britain declared war on Germany, which had invaded Poland, their ally. After a period of mutual watchfulness ("the phoney war") military disaster without precedent in the history of France occurred; in a month the army collapsed: 123,000 dead, 1,843,000 prisoners. An armistice was signed at Rethondes on 22 June 1940, cutting the country in two (occupied zone and a so-called free zone).

Two completely contrasting concepts then confronted each other. On one side Marshall Pétain, to whom Parliament on 10 July had given full powers, and on the other a very small minority which had responded to General de Gaulle's appeal launched in London on 18 June. Two powers were thereby constituted: "The French State" in Vichy with Pétain, Laval and erstwhile adversaries of the Republic conducted a collaboration policy with Nazi Germany. The interview between Pétain and Hitler at Montoire in October 1940 gave the signal. Faced with this situation "Free France", with its headquarters in London,

First American troops landed at Utah Beach on 6 June 1944. Mémorial de Caen - US Army/Mémorial.

wanted to continue the war alongside Great Britain in order that France could be present on the day of final victory. For Free France, the Pétain Ministry was a simple de facto authority, dependent upon the enemy.

Little by little forces joined the Free French; individuals coming from the most divergent backgrounds and also entire territories: Chad, the Cameroons, French Congo etc., from 1940 onwards, Syria and the Lebanon in 1941 and Madagascar in 1942. In France itself, the Resistance comprised multiple but not numerically strong separate entities. Networks for the escape of allied airmen shot down, escaped French prisoners who wanted to continue the struggle, for intelligence, sabotage and protection of the Jews etc. formed slowly and with much difficulty. The effectiveness of German police services was strengthened by the help given to them by the French police. Arrests, torture, executions and deportations hindered but did not prevent the growth of Resistance networks. From 1942 onwards and above all in 1943 the introduction of obligatory labour service in Germany helped the formation of an armed "maquis". A decisive stage in the Resistance was the coordination achieved by Jean Moulin in May 1943. After his death under torture, Georges Bidault was elected by the CNR (Committee of National Resistance) to succeed him. The paramilitary groups of the Resistance were formed into French Forces of the Interior (FFI) in February 1944.

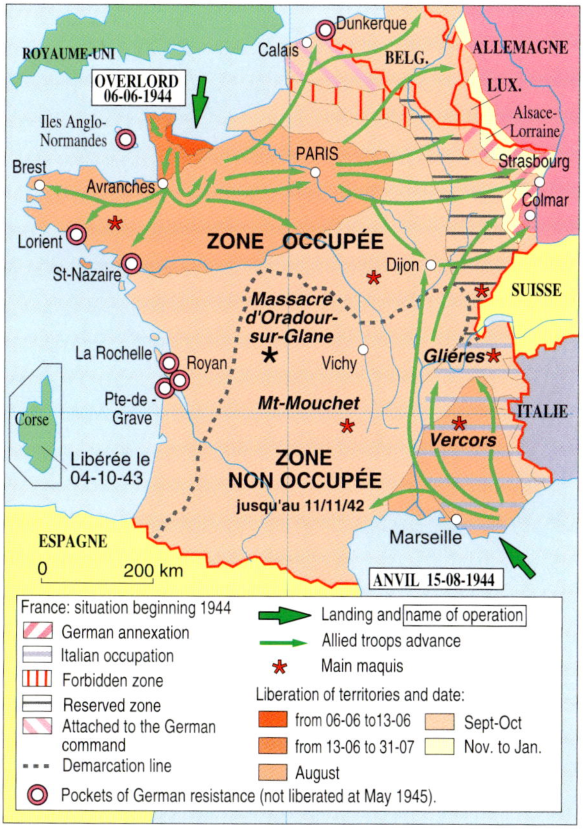

France at the beginning of 1944

Free France

After his appeal for resistance on 18 June 1940, General de Gaulle took the title of "Head of the Free French". A Provisional French National Committee was founded on 7 August and was subsequently transformed into the French National Committee (1941-1943) then the French Committee of National Liberation (1943-1944); a Provisional Advisory Assembly sat in Algiers from 1943 onwards as the Committee became the Provisional Government of the French Republic.

General de Gaulle speaking on the BBC on 30 October 1941.
Radio (television still did not exist) played an essential role for France during the Second World War: it was used for the appeal of 18 June, many speeches by leaders of the free French, led by General de Gaulle, and also for coded messages linking London and the Resistance; radio operators working in France, either resistors or technicians trained in England and parachuted into France, paid a very heavy price for their valiant action.
SIRPA/ECPA.

The Drancy camp where convoys left for the death camps.
Drancy was an antechamber of death for a large number of members of the resistance and Jewish families, in particular the victims of searches made by the French police; also French gendarmes and officials manned the camp.
Bibliothèque du Centre de documentation juive contemporaine.

Arrival of the Americans on 20 June 1944 at Valognes (Manche), town damaged by bombardments from 6 June onward. The resistance of German forces in Normandy resulted in ferocious fighting with allied forces; damage, in particular caused by bombing, was very heavy. The German front was only broken in mid-August 1944.

Mémorial de Caen - US Army/Mémorial.

Generals de Gaulle, Leclerc and Koenig

Charles de Gaulle (1890-1970) was a career soldier; acting Brigadier-General, on 18 June 1940 in London, he launched his famous appeal for resistance; he resigned from his position as president of the provisional government in 1946, founded a political party (the RPF) and after a twelve-year "spell in the wilderness", returned to power in 1958 at the time of the Algerian crisis; for more than ten years he was President of the Republic and resigned in 1969 following failure in the referendum on regionalisation.

Philippe Leclerc de Hautecloque (1902-1947), also career soldier, joined de Gaulle in London in July 1940. Sent to the Cameroon (September 1940), he rallied Gabon to the free French, with his troops he joined the British forces in Tripoli (Libya) after his victories over the Italians at Koufra. At the head of the 2nd Armoured Division, he contributed to the liberation of Paris, liberated Strasbourg and took Berchtesgaden in Bavaria. Head of the military in Indo-China, he was in favour of real negotiations for the independence of Vietnam, but gave in to de Gaulle's opposite opinion. He died in a plane crash in the Sahara.

Pierre Koenig (1898-1970) former seventeen year old volunteer in the First World War, joined de Gaulle in 1940; shone as head of French forces at Bir Hakeim (June 1942); Commander-in-Chief of French forces of the interior (1944) and the French army of occupation in Germany.

Collection M. Sclaresky.

In a half-century, since the end of the Second World War, France experienced considerable change with a noticeable increase in pace since the 1970s. As we shall see no sector escaped this process.

Economic and social upheavals

In the first stage the need was above all to reconstruct an economy ruined by the war and German depredation. This was done first of all within a somewhat authoritarian framework and subsequently from 1950 onwards expansion occurred in a more openly liberal economic system. Inflation was very strong (155% from 1949 to 1968) and only stabilised at a low level after 1982.

"Let us roll up our sleeves, things are going to get better"
Thébaut and Fontséré poster, 1945.
Musée d'Histoire contemporaine. Photo J. L Charmet.

A decisive factor in economic activity was France's opening to the external market, which amounted to a total break with previous protectionist policy. The loss of colonial monopoly, the creation of the European Community arising from the **Treaty of Rome** (1957) and the treaty instituting the European economic area (1982) completely changed the general working conditions of the French economy. It was placed in direct competition with economies with lower production costs owing to the weakness of their social legislation. The globalisation phenomenon has been speeded up by the particularly fast development of the means and techniques of communications, since these have enabled reactions to variations in the financial market to be made in real time.

In the context of frenzied competition, what has been the main transformation in the French economy and society since 1945?

Overall, France has made the transition from being an industrialised country with extensive agriculture to a strongly urbanised state where the service sector occupies a growing place and intensive agriculture ensures an appreciable surplus in the balance of payments.

The following are some figures relating to the division of the working population: in agriculture 10.5% in 1975 and 4.4% in 1998, in industry37.6% and 24.9% and in the service sector system 51.9% and 70.7%. It should be noted that agriculture's share in GDP decreased, 3.7% in 1990 and 2.44% in 1997. The share of the population living in towns (conurbation of more than 2,000 inhabitants) was 56.8% in 1950 and 82.8% in 1990.

The population distinctly increased in the post-war years and then settled at the pace of all other industrialised countries, i.e. a distinct decrease in the birth-rate. But a long-term view must be taken to understand demographic development: France never recovered from the two great "blood-lettings" – the wars of the Revolution and the Empire and the First World War. Immigration had always offset the natural deficit or small surplus. The total population grew from 41.7 million inhabitants in 1950 to 53.7 in 1990 and 58.7 in 1998. Immigration is not a present-day phenomenon and the mass movement was already present from the Second Empire onwards: in 1866 France already accounted for 655,000 foreigners (nearly 1 million in 1901, nearly 3 in 1931).

The economic but also social upheavals were aggravated in their human consequences by the appearance and growth of unemployment from 1975 onwards; it exceeded the 3 million figure in 1993 but has been decreasing slightly but regularly since 1997.

French society has profoundly changed in its behaviour since 1945. 1968 was undoubtedly a crucial date owing to structures stable for decades ceasing to be so. Some data is worth noting:

— life expectancy at birth in 1952 was 65 for men and 71.2 for women, in 1985 71.3 and 79.4 and in 1995 73.9 and 81.9;

— the number of births outside marriage grew from less than 100,000 out of 800,000 in 1975 to 300,000 also out of 800,000; the

Signature of the Treaty of Rome (March 1957): six European ministers signed the Common Market and Euratom Treaties (from left to right: Christian Pineau, Maurice Faure and Adenauer).

marriage institution has lost its habitual character all the more so since the number of divorces had increased (81,200 in 1980, 108,100 in 1992);

— the structure of household expenditure has noticeably changed; 22.3% on food in 1980 and 19.2 in 1995 (declining) and on accommodation 30.2 and 32.4 (growing).

Political transformation

From 1945 until the present time the political regime of France made the transition from parliamentary democracy to the pre-eminence of the executive, but this statement must be treated with caution.

A distinction must be made between two periods, corresponding to two Constitutions.

From ***1946 to 1958,*** it was the turn of the IVth Republic born from the disappearance of the 1875 constitutional provisions and the adoption by referendum of the 1946 Constitution. It was a bicameral system, National Assembly and Council of the Republic subsequently called the Senate, with a President of the Republic elected by the two Assemblies for seven years but with very limited powers. From 1944 to 1946 General de Gaulle presided over a provisional government from which he resigned, being in disagreement with the general direction taken by the Constituent Assembly.

In a first stage, (1946-1947) the government corresponded to a three-party majority: socialists, communists, whose party obtained first place in the legislative elections, and christian democrats (MRP). The communists'

Edgar Faure, President of the National Assembly (1908-1988), reading a message from President Giscard d'Estaing to the assembly. Edgar Faure was a political personality very characteristic of the Fourth Republic; lawyer, successful candidate in Roman Law examinations, armed with agility of mind and exceptional culture, on numerous occasions he undertook ministerial functions from 1949 to 1958 and 1966 and 1973, after having been deputy general prosecutor in the Nuremberg trials; he was President of the National Assembly from 1973 to 1978.

Street demonstrations in May '68, corner of Boulevard Saint-Michel and rue Racine: fight between police and students.
© Keystone.

expulsion from the government in May 1947 gave birth to the era of the "third force", socialists and MRP, confronted by the communists and the party created by General de Gaulle (Rassemblement du peuple français), which governed the country up to 1952. Antoine Pinay then succeeded in dividing the RPF's parliamentary group and including some of its members in the government majority but ministerial crises as in the preceding periods were numerous. External events (to which we will refer later) played an important role; it was the war in Algeria which caused the fall of the regime in May 1958 and the installation of a new constitutional system.

The 1958 Constitution completely changed the political context in France. It strengthened the executive power, giving a predominant role to the President of the Republic (elected by direct universal suffrage from 1965 onwards) and strong decrease in the powers of the National Assembly.

The new period which opened with General de Gaulle's arrival in power and the party which supported him (UNR and RPR) was to change inostensibly but nonetheless distinctly in character after General de Gaulle's resignation in 1969. The **events of May 1968,** first of all a student strike then an enormous movement making social demands supported by a long general strike, profoundly shook the country. The immediate consequence was an election, following the dissolution proclaimed by the President of the Republic, of an Assembly which had become "unfindable" as in 1815.

As a delayed effect of the events of May 1968, a year later General de Gaulle resigned following a referendum rejecting his project for transforming the Senate. A Gaullist, Georges Pompidou, whose announcement of his potential candidature had contributed to de Gaulle's fall, was elected in 1969. On his death, the Gaullist party RPR lost the Presidency of the Republic which it did not recover until 1995.

After having stood against de Gaulle in 1965 and being beaten by Valéry Giscard d'Estaing in 1974, François Mitterrand, Socialist, was elected President of the Republic in 1981. He became, being re-elected in 1988, the only French President to have completed two successive terms of office.

From 1981 to 1983, Pierre Mauroy's government applied Mitterrand's candidature programme but from 1983 onwards, France suffering a financial crisis, reversed its economic policy in a liberal direction in order to remain in the European Monetary System: the march towards the transfer of national prerogatives in currency matters was started.

1995 the cession of power from François Mitterrand to Jacques Chirac.
Ouest-France Archive.

The way the institutions worked was directly influenced by the development of the balance of forces between the left and right with the cohabitation phenomenon, i.e. a situation where the President of the Republic and the Prime Minister belonged to opposing political camps. It occurred three times: from1986 to 1988 François Mitterrand and Jacques Chirac, from 1993 to 1995 François Mitterrand and Edouard Balladur; in 1997 by proceeding with, as far as his own position was concerned, an unexpected and disastrous dissolution of the National Assembly, Jacques Chirac caused a further cohabitation, with Lionel Jospin. It was the third cohabitation which had an impact on the institutions; the position and role of the President of the Republic was lessened whereas the Prime Minister, head of the parliamentary majority, strengthened his authority.

Political life had undergone deeply important changes since 1945. The Communist Party recorded a drastic fall in its influence from 1981 onwards owing both to structural transformations in French society and delay in understanding the nature and consequence of these transformations. Similarly, the 1965 transition to presidential election with universal suffrage and the development of audio-visual techniques changed the behaviour of politicians with an often regrettable replacement of the idea by the image.

All this led to a strong deterioration in public opinion's regard for the political world. The outbreak of numerous "affairs" entailed growing disgust of citizens towards institutions and political personalities and a fall in voting turnout: 18.1% abstentions in the legislative elections in 1946, 18.9% in 1967, 29.6% in 1981 and 31.6% in 1997.

These "affairs" were either purely financial ("insider trading" involving Cabinet Ministers), or human (the losses of Crédit Lyonnais), or political (party finance, illegal behaviour of local bosses).

Political life however in the deeper sense of the term was also influenced by an important effect: in 1995 reversing the position adopted up till then by his predecessors, Jacques Chirac recognised the state's responsibility for its administration's collaboration with the occupying power from 1940 to 1945.

As we have seen above, the Fourth Republic disappeared, owing to its failure to settle a serious question, that of Algeria. Decolonisation problems occupied a very important place in the history of France after 1945 to the extent that it is necessary to grant them priority when reviewing external events.

External problems

In 1945, Algeria was an assembly of French departments (with a population of two unequal rankings), Indochina was a colony like French Equatorial and West Africa and Madagascar, whereas Tunisia and Morocco were protectorates.

France reacted in a different way, according to the case, to the major decolonisation movement which developed after 1945. Its great victory was the independence of India, recognised in 1947 by the imperial power, Great Britain.

The first colony to revolt was Vietnam (Tonkin, Annam, Cochinchina). Cambodia obtained its independence in 1949 whereas Laos only became truly independent in 1954. The war in 1954 lasted nine years (1945-1954); it finished with the defeat at Diên Biên Phu and the Geneva Agreements giving independence to a divided Vietnam.

Several months after these agreements the Algeria uprising occurred (November 1954): the war lasted eight years until the Evian Agreement (1962) which recognised Algeria's independence. The Fourth Republic succumbed to the crisis and General de Gaulle's regime had to confront the advance of the extreme right led by officers taking with them a part of the non-Muslim population.

On the other hand, decolonisation was in general conducted peacefully in the other countries. We should note, however, the violent repression of the Madagascan revolt (1947), and the deposing (1953) and the return of Mohammed V in Morocco, the partial revolt of the Cameroons (1955-1962)

Victory over the French soldier, Vietminh hand-drawn poster, 1945.
B.N.F, Estampes. Photo J.-L. Charmet.

July 1945:ceasefire agreement in Geneva: on the steps from left to right, Phan Van Dong, Mendes France, A. Eden.

© Keystone.

and the troubles in Tunisia with the arrest of Bourguiba (1952) and his return (1955).

The independence of Tunisia (Mendes-France government 1955) and Morocco (Pinay government 1955) was achieved.

Landmarks

Presidents of the Republic
Vincent Auriol 1947-1953
René Coty 1953-1959
Charles de Gaulle 1959-1969
Georges Pompidou 1969-1974
Valéry Giscard d'Estaing 1974-1981
François Mitterrand 1981-1995
Jacques Chirac 1995...

Particularly important laws
1967: contraception made legal (Neuwirth law).
1974: age of majority reduced to 18.
1975: abortion made legal (Simon Veil law).
1981: abolition of the death penalty, retirement at 60.
1982: decentralisation texts.
2000: weekly hours of work reduced to 35.

In black Africa and Madagascar, the process involved two stages: the introduction of local powers (the Defferre framework law in 1956) and subsequently independence in 1958 (Guinea) and 1960 (the other countries).

The case of New Caledonia arose later; the Nouméa Agreements (1992, Jospin Government) opened the way to independence.

In the *international field*, properly speaking, French policy changed considerably, the crucial reference being the position of relations with the United States. From 1945to 1958 France, which was a member of the Atlantic Alliance, did not show any desire to be independent in relations with the Soviet Union, the latter being one of the pillars of the foreign policy conducted by General de Gaulle. Both the political and financial support from the United States, which France needed during the Indochina war, was one of the causes. The same applied to a different degree during the years of the war in Algeria. After 1958 the situation was different: the possession of the nuclear weapon (first test in 1960), withdrawal from NATO, the military organisation of the

Atlantic Alliance (1966) gave definite shape to the desire for an independent policy which, however, must not be overestimated. Thus in 1962 at the time of the Cuban crisis between the Soviet Union and the United States, France placed itself resolutely alongside the United States. But the central idea was, while remaining within the bi-polar world, to positioning itself in a position of power, with the creation of a solid Franco-German connection. Correspondingly, in his Phnom Penh speech (1966) General de Gaulle expressly pronounced his disapproval of American policy in Vietnam.

From the Ecu to the Euro

The first coin named "Ecu" (*sculptum* = buckle supporting armour) dates back to Saint Louis and weighed 4gm of fine gold. The word "franc" was used to describe the fine gold piece (3.8 gm) minted in 1356 to pay the English the ransom for John the Good and thereby making the onus "franc", i.e. free; in 1803 Bonaparte installed the "Germinal franc" (0.29 gm of fine gold) the value of which remained stable until August 1914 (the 20 F piece was the "Napoléon"). Successive devaluations since the "Poincaré franc" (0.059 gm), led to the "new franc" (1959) up to the introduction of the Euro (= 6.56 F).

Funeral of the victims in the Charonne metro (February 1962). The demonstration was the turning point in the process which led to the end of the war in Algeria; the OAS (Secret Army Organisation combining French extremists in Algeria) organised a series of outrages in France; on 7 February 1962, a four-year old girl was disfigured by an explosion in the ground floor of the building in which André Malraux lived. As a protest, a large demonstration was organised on the 8 by supporters of peace in Algeria. Specialised Parisian police units charged the protestors, causing the suffocation of nine demonstrators on the escalator of the Charonne metro. Their funeral was the occasion of a further and impressive demonstration. The Evian Agreements on the independence of Algeria were signed on 18 March 1962.

© Keystone.

A noticeable change in direction in French policy occurred from 1974 onwards and was subsequently to be continued. The collapse of the Soviet system from 1990 onwards completely changed the situation. The world ceased to be bi-polar and the question arose of building a counterweight to United States' influence, which appeared to be without limits. The answer was to be found in the organisation of an autonomous European foreign policy based on the European Union.

In 1957 the Treaty of Rome had been signed, creating a Europe of six powers. But the more important date was 1986 with the Single Act which provided for the creation of a " great single market " on 1 January 1993. The latter's working methods were prescribed in 1992 (Treaty of Maastricht) with in particular the creation of the Euro, the single currency, which amounted, from the political and economic point of view to the abandonment of an essential national prerogative. The treaty was ratified by a referendum with a narrow majority (51.1 %).

In the meantime France became progressively integrated into NATO, took part in the Gulf War led by the United States against Iraq (1991) and attempted in the Kosovo conflict, where the military and political weight of the United States was dominant, to make its voice heard.

Birth of the department

A creation of the French Revolution, the administrative constituency at the end of the century was doubly threatened: from above by the region and below from the locality.

Its birth was not easy owing to several projects being tackled: purely geometric delineation of the territory (80 departments plus Paris, 720 districts and 6,480 cantons), the keeping or not of the boundaries of the old provinces, the more or less high number of departments, the choice of names for departments, the choice of department capitals etc.

The figure of 80 was definitely agreed upon to enable every citizen to reach the department capital from any place in the department in a day's journey.

The Défense district, in the north-west of Paris, was the subject of comprehensive town planning from 1958 onwards; the works, which started in 1965 were completed in 1989. In the exclusively business quarter a huge group of high-rise buildings, in which a large number of national and international companies are installed, extend over 80 hectares.
Photo Hervé Champollion.

Metropolitan France: 96 departments (since 1975),
3,995 cantons (in 1995) and 36,650 municipalities (in 1997)

CONTENTS

Maps : AFDEC (pages 6, 9, 13, 19, 31),
Patrick Mérienne (pages 2, 8, 29, 44, 51, 63).

This work was produced by the printer Imprimerie Pollina s.a. - 85400 Luçon - n° L96942
I.S.B.N. 2.7373.2766.0 - Editor N° 4142.02.1,5.05.05
Legal deposit: March 2001